Studies in J. D. Salinger

REVIEWS, ESSAYS, AND CRITIQUES

of *The Catcher in the Rye*

AND OTHER FICTION

Studies in J. D. Salinger

REVIEWS, ESSAYS, and CRITIQUES

of *The Catcher in the Rye*

AND OTHER FICTION

Edited by

MARVIN LASER *and* NORMAN FRUMAN

LOS ANGELES STATE COLLEGE

THE ODYSSEY PRESS · *New York*

Introduction

The truth of the commonplace charge that ours is an "age of criticism" is perhaps nowhere better illustrated than in the literary career of J. D. Salinger. Though he has published only a single short novel and thirteen short stories (not counting collections of previously published work and some early uncollected stories which the author himself seems willing to forget), Salinger has been subjected to a range and intensity of critical analysis which, before our century, was reserved only for the acknowledged masters of literature.

The complaint of George Steiner and Harvey Swados—in essays reprinted in this book—that Salinger criticism has become an "industry" has in no way abated the steady stream of commentary. Indeed, the appearance of *Franny and Zooey* in 1961, though actually a reprint of two stories published several years before, occasioned not only hundreds of reviews but a flurry of retrospective articles. Nor is interest in Salinger in any sense exclusively an American phenomenon or limited to professional critics as, say, Melville criticism is. *The Catcher in the Rye* has been translated into many languages, and has been received almost everywhere with great popular acclaim. Observers of the American scene know that Salinger is by far the most popular author, living or dead, among college students. So intense is public interest in Salinger's affairs that *Life* felt obliged to publish a long article, the substance of which was an account of their reporter's inability to achieve an interview with the inaccessible author. A cover portrait and feature story on Salinger in *Time* are further testimony of Salinger's extraordinary and in some respects unique hold on the public imagination.

This book originated in our belief that Salinger criticism is of intrinsic interest and importance to students of literature. He has been hailed as a superb artist and dismissed as merely a gifted entertainer. It has been said that Salinger has succeeded in creating a contemporary saint; conversely, Franny and Zooey have been described as "one and a half religious maniacs." If one critic acclaims Salinger for his power to reach a vast youthful audience, another charges that he "flatters the very ignorance and moral shallowness of his younger readers." On the one hand he is celebrated as one of the few genuinely religious writers of our time; on the other he is a provider of "self-help" copy and "positive thinking" for girls' schools and the upper middle class.

Not only have many distinguished critics discussed Salinger (and often, in the process, each other) but their articles reveal a provocative diversity of critical modes: mythological, sociological, psychological, linguistic, and structural, among others. The scope of our editorial purpose broadened when it became apparent that a judicious selection of such articles would reveal much about the contemporary literary scene, particularly if organized chronologically.

Attempts to group the articles by such obvious and attractive schemes as major critical modes proved futile and misleading. Few articles are "pure" in this sense, and we have not wished to impose arbitrary descriptive labels. Arrangement by order of publication, however, not only reveals a great deal about the general function and quality of book reviewing in the United States but highlights the initial impact of *The Catcher in the Rye* and enables a reader to trace the development of Salinger's reputation, the character of the original interest in Salinger among critics, and the broadening circle of critical attention. For example, after the reviews of *Nine Stories* in 1953 there was a nearly total silence among critics for fully three years. The first articles not specifically tied to the publication of a Salinger book began appearing in 1956—slowly at first, and then in a sudden storm. With the exception of John Aldridge's brief, and hostile, discussion of Salinger in *In Search of Heresy* (1956), it was not until Maxwell Geismar devoted a full chapter to Salinger in *American Moderns* (1958) that Salinger criticism ceased to be the exclusive domain of the college teacher. One can speculate, moreover, that the publication of so many articles by college teachers, primarily in professional journals, was the result of continuing student interest in *The Catcher in the Rye* and of the introduction of the book into the classroom. The early articles are also quite suggestive in what they imply about the fundamental interests of the academic critic.

The articles reprinted in this book consequently appear—with a few exceptions—in their original order of publication. We have thought it useful to place Gutwillig's article first because it supplies a printing history of *The Catcher in the Rye* and other background material helpful to a reading of the critical pieces which follow it. We have also disregarded strict chronology in grouping the three pieces that deal with the censorship controversy over *The Catcher in the Rye* and in grouping the four pieces (Kermode, Bungert, Chugunov, and Way) that represent views of European critics.

The primary focus of the book is on *The Catcher in the Rye*, but exclusive concern with the novel would have proved repetitious and unnecessarily restrictive. From the beginning Salinger has been used by some critics merely as a springboard for discussion of American youth, Zen, politics, madness, suicide, or alienation. This has been particularly true since the publication in book form of *Franny and Zooey*. Inasmuch as we have wished to avoid diffuseness and at the same time to provide as wide a range as possible of first-rate criticism, a substantial number of articles has been included which begin with comment on the later short stories but are not solely confined to them. An exception appears in "Appendix A." The "close reading" of a text, in which the importance of detail in relation to the writer's controlling purpose is stressed, is one of the most widely practised and influential modes of modern literary criticism. But it is a technique more easily practised on a poem or short story than on even so brief a novel as *The Catcher in the Rye*. Since examples devoted to the latter are scarce, we have included a group of four articles on "For Esmé—with Love and Squalor," Salinger's most popular and, technically, perhaps most complex story.

A Note on the Text

Wherever possible, articles have been reprinted intact. Passages have, however, been excerpted from discussions where Salinger appears only in a subordinate connection. Repetitive plot summaries have been excised. Cuts of more than one page have been identified and, where necessary, explanatory bridges have been provided within brackets.

Bibliographical apparatus has been supplied for the convenience of teachers and students. It is hoped that the book will prove especially useful in courses where practice in the formal documentation of papers is hampered by insufficient time or overtaxed libraries. Only the slash marks which identify the end of each page of the original source (e.g., /21/) may disturb the otherwise normal appearance of the text. If the instructor so desires, papers may be documented by referring to the page of the original work. All sources are identified in a full bibliographical reference at the foot of the first page of each selection. Obvious misprints in the original have been silently corrected. Since consistency is the soul of bibliographical notation, the student should know that the variety of forms in which acknowledgments are given derives from specific directives issued by some publishers.

To all authors of selections included in this book and to their publishers who have graciously accorded reprinting rights, the editors extend their thanks. We also wish to thank Mr. William R. Eshelman, Librarian of Los Angeles State College, for bibliographical assistance.

M. L.
N. F.

Los Angeles, California

CONTENTS

ix

CONTENTS

Studies in J. D. Salinger

REVIEWS, ESSAYS, AND CRITIQUES
of *The Catcher in the Rye*
AND OTHER FICTION

I

Everybody's Caught *The Catcher in the Rye*

ROBERT GUTWILLIG

Many an observer of the manners and mores of American youth contends that a first novel published ten years ago occupies much the same place in the affection of today's college generation as F. Scott Fitzgerald's "This Side of Paradise" did for their parents in the Nineteen Twenties.

The novel is "The Catcher in the Rye," by J. D. Salinger, which since its publication on July 16, 1951, has sold a total of 1,500,000 copies in the United States alone—1,250,000 of them, significantly enough, in paperbound form. This year, for the second successive year, so many bookstores, especially those in college communities, reported it among their most-wanted paperbacks that it has won a place on this Review's paperback best seller list.

Of the 250,000 paperback copies sold this year, a goodly number went to students of Yale, Northern Baptist Theological Seminary and 275 other colleges and universities across the country who have adopted the book for required or supplementary reading in English, psychology and other courses. The appeal of "The Catcher in the Rye" extends also to the younger brothers and sisters of the college crowd. Thousands of secondary school students find themselves academically involved with Holden Caulfield and the week-end of his flight from Pencey Prep, although Holden's actions, thoughts and language have occasioned moral tremors in the past among parents and school officials in Tulsa, Miami and Louisville. There is currently a similar convulsion in Marin County, Calif.

From *The New York Times Book Review Paperback Section*, January 15, 1961. Copyright 1961 by the New York Times. Reprinted by permission of the New York Times and the author.

"The Catcher in the Rye" is available in four editions, three in hard cover and the best-selling paperback. Little, Brown, Holden's original publisher, reports that its edition sold better last year than in the preceding several years. Grosset and Dunlap reprinted the book in 1952. New American Library, which offers the novel in its paperback Signet series at 50 cents, reports it as one of its steadiest sellers since it became available in March, 1953. Modern Library issued the novel in 1958 and has had a most satisfactory sale, again largely to college and university bookstores.

One of the more obvious tests of a book's quality, appeal and endurance, is the sale of translation rights for publication in foreign countries. There never has been a more "American" novel than "The Catcher in the Rye"; that is, a novel that in the publishing trade's opinion is so colloquial it will not translate easily or well and whose surface, values, interpretations and meanings are so right, unique and hidden that foreigners will find the book ultimately inscrutable. Imagine, for instance, what would happen to the rhythms of Holden's opening salvo if translated into Finnish.

"If you really want to hear about it, the first thing you'll probably want to know is where I was born, and what my lousy childhood was like, and how my parents were occupied and all before they had me, and all that David Copperfield kind of crap, but I don't feel like going into it, if you want to know the truth."

And yet the novel has been published with great commercial and critical success in about a dozen countries, including Finland, Germany, France, Italy, Poland, Israel and Great Britain. In 1959, everywhere I went, England, France, Germany, Poland, Czechoslovakia, I was asked if I knew Salinger and did I know what his new book was about and when it was coming out. "The Catcher in the Rye" will shortly be published in Russia, and perhaps a mark of even greater distinction is that it was banned on moral grounds for short periods in Australia and South Africa.

Critically, ten years after publication, Salinger, his novel, and his previous and subsequent work are not only the subjects of numerous articles in Time, Newsweek, Harper's Magazine, Saturday Review, The Nation, New Republic and The Common-weal, but also are soberly and not so soberly evaluated in master theses, "little" magazines and literary quarterlies such as the Chicago Review, the Western Humanities Review, College English and American Quarterly. Currently, a mild critical reversal is in progress. Mr. Salinger, we are told, is a minor writer, a *brilliant* minor writer, to be sure, but still one who has published just one short (277-page) novel and a dozen or so serious short stories. But Salinger and Caulfield continue to move and amuse the current school and college generation, and the quarterly critics, most of whom are college teachers, know it. One of them wrote recently in some exasperation: "Mr. Jerome David Salinger is neither Molière nor Chekhov. He is not yet Mark Twain (and by a long shot)."

Clearly, "The Catcher in the Rye," its critical and commercial success past and present, are literary phenomena of the first order and, therefore, it might prove illuminating to look back and see how and why it all happened. On July 16, 1951, J. D. Salinger was 32 years old, but he was not an unknown young writer. He had been publishing short stories for ten years in the Saturday Evening Post, Collier's and elsewhere but most importantly, of course, in the New Yorker. In fact, seven of his 1953 collection, "Nine Stories" appeared between 1948 and 1951. Curiously, almost no one remembered that two chapters of "The Catcher" had already appeared in somewhat different form as short stories: "I'm Crazy," in Collier's in 1945, and "Slight Rebellion off Madison" in the New Yorker in 1946.

There's nothing quite like the Book-of-the-Month Club to give a publisher confidence, and when the club made the novel its midsummer selection there must have been joy as well as shock at Little, Brown in Boston. Clifton Fadiman wrote the board's report, concluding: "That rare miracle of fiction has again come to pass: a human being has been created out of ink, paper and the imagination." William Maxwell of the New Yorker wrote a brief profile of Salinger for the club news. It has been quoted and plagiarized for ten years now, chiefly, one suspects, because more literary and personal information about the author has not been forthcoming.

The book was reprinted five times that July, three times in August and twice in September. Two weeks after publication it was fourteenth on The New York Times best-seller list; three weeks later it was fourth. And that was the summer "The Caine Mutiny" and "From Here to Eternity" shared the top two spots. Looking back over the contemporary reviews of "The Catcher in the Rye" one is immediately struck by two things: how many of them there were and how poor they were, too. Almost two hundred newspapers and magazines reviewed or commented upon the book; no more than twenty (if that many) were perceptive, let alone intelligent. A good many were inaccurate: Holden was misnamed Homer, his age was variously given as 15, 16 and 17 (he is 16), and the novel's action was said to have taken place over three, four or five days (three is correct). Mr. Salinger may have been pleased, bored or annoyed by these pieces; he could not have learned very much, nor could the readers.

Most of the reviews were wildly or mildly favorable. Time, Newsweek, Saturday Review liked it very much. Charles Poore wrote in Harper's: "* * * Probably the most distinguished first novel, the most truly new novel in style and accent of the year." The reviewers for both the daily and Sunday Times /38/ thought the book good. The critique in this review was written entirely in Holdenese, something to which a number of other reviewers partially succumbed (and it's still happening. John Wain gave it a go in his review of the Penguin edition of the novel in the Observer in 1959). William Poster in The Commonweal remarked unhappily and accurately that Salinger's idiom and style were "a tour de force the American fiction writer will probably find himself increasingly doomed to attempt * * *." Not only American, it's turned out.

"The Catcher in the Rye" was favorably compared to "The Adventures of Huckleberry Finn," "Seventeen" and "The Lost Weekend" (of all books), and Salinger also reminded people of Ring Lardner. But not everyone was so taken. Some reviewers, like The New York Herald Tribune's, simply did not like the novel: "* * * an irritated and irritating bore * * * the book just about killed me, it really did." Some felt the novel, which originally had been a ninety-page novelette, was attenuated, thin and merely a character sketch. Finally, a small but vocal minority felt "The Catcher in the Rye" was a dirty book. "* * * not fit for children * * * Many adults as well will not wish to condition themselves to Holden's language. Indeed, one finds it hard to believe that a true lover of children could father this tale," said the Christian Science Monitor.

What was it about the novel that struck Americans so squarely ten years ago and continues to hit the mark still? Primarily it was, I think, the shock and thrill of recognition. Many of my friends and this writer himself identified completely with Holden. I went to a school much like Pencey Prep. One of my friends had a younger brother like Allie, who had died, another an older brother like D. B., still another a younger sister like Phoebe. After reading the novel, several of us went out and bought ourselves red caps with earflaps, and we all took to calling each other "Ace" and "Prince."

Salinger has, to quote Arthur Mizener, "his own special insight into the meaning of experience," an insight and a method of expressing it that set him apart from other contemporary writers and seem to push him closer than anyone else to his characters and his readers. "The Catcher in the Rye" has become a crucial American novel without the help or hindrance of television, movies, or dramatization, for Salinger has always refused to permit any kind of adaptation of the book, possibly as the result of a film, "My Foolish Heart," starring Susan Hayward and Dana Andrews, based, as the saying goes, on "Uncle Wiggily in Connecticut."

The book has not only been bought, it has been read. I believe that, despite its flaws, it will continue to be read. As others have noted, toward the end of the book Holden fulfills his ambition to become a catcher in the rye when he refuses to let Phoebe run away with him. "What I have to do," Holden says, "I have to catch everybody if they start to go over the cliff." So there is hope and, more important, there is moving, communicated urgency. Holden takes Phoebe to the carrousel. He stands in the rain, watching her "going around and around in her blue coat and all." "God," he says, I wish you could have been there." We are there.

/39/

Salinger: The Early Reviews

THE EDITORS

The Catcher in the Rye was published in 1951—in July, usually a doldrum month in American publishing. With millions of readers away on vacation or responding to the local call of the outdoors, publishers tend to cut their summer advertising budgets drastically. Externally considered, the whole industry seems to be marking time, waiting for the big push that comes in the Fall, when the nation is back on the job and the great metropolitan centers hum at full speed again. After Labor Day, book review sections revive from their summer lethargy and the publishing industry moves into high gear.

Successive delays, resulting in part from the long consideration given Salinger's manuscript by the officers of the powerful Book-of-the-Month Club, prevented earlier publication. The author, always strong willed in such matters and understandably impatient, finally insisted on publication forthwith, despite the inauspicious season. He and his publishers, Little, Brown and Company of Boston, were well aware that *The Catcher in the Rye,* though a first novel, was eagerly anticipated. In retrospect it is easy to exaggerate, for Salinger had achieved a small reputation as a short story writer among readers of the *New Yorker*'s fiction, but his reputation was local and the commercial power of his name among readers at large was slight.

Whatever Little, Brown and Company's original publicity plans, adoption of the novel by the Book-of-the-Month Club automatically destined it for vast sales and widespread attention. An extremely favorable review by Clifton Fadiman, circulated to the club's huge membership, made it certain that formal publication of *The Catcher* would fall into the category of a newsworthy event. Fadiman, one of the nation's best-known literary personalities, hailed it as a book one reads "hardly knowing whether to chuckle or cry . . . that rare miracle of fiction has again come to pass: a human being has been created out of ink, paper and the imagination."

In the middle of July, reviews began appearing in all the major newspapers and general-circulation magazines. Review space was adequate, by American standards, and location prominent. Both the New York *Times* and *Herald Tribune* carried substantial notices toward the front of their Sunday book sections. The reviewers were, on the whole, fairly well known, an unusual though not extraordinary circumstance.

Practically the first periodicals to comment on *The Catcher* were two professional journals, chiefly of interest to librarians, publishers, and bookstore owners. They dealt with the novel in customarily succinct fashion. Harold L. Roth, in a single paragraph in the *Library Journal* (July 1951), described it as

a successful attempt . . . to picture a boy's analysis of himself, developing his likes and dislikes and pointing out the problems of a highly developed imagination that has as yet not been trained to work in other than the most egoistic way. This may be a shock to many parents who wonder about a young man's thoughts and actions, but its effect can be a salutary one. An *adult* book (very frank) and highly recommended. (pp. 1125-26)

A one-paragraph unsigned review in the July 15 *Booklist* (p. 401) called it "an unusual book on a pertinent theme" and noted "imaginative, repetitious and often coarse language. . . ." The writer thought the work would "not appeal to everyone but is certainly worth attention for its sensitive insight into a currently important topic, as well as for the quality of the writing." No suggestion that the book might possibly have enduring value was given. Curiously, the reviewer thought that the narrative was being told by Holden to a psychologist.

The first important discussion appeared in the *Saturday Review* on July 14, 1951 (p. 13). Harrison Smith wrote: "[It is] a remarkable and absorbing novel . . . a profoundly moving and dis-

turbing book, but it is pathetic rather than tragic." Holden's
problem was asserted to lie in "his moral revulsion against anything that was ugly, evil, cruel, or what he called 'phoney'. . . ."
Smith located the "magic" of the novel in the "authenticity of
the language," and concluded: "this is a book to be read thought-
fully and more than once. It is about an unusually sensitive and
intelligent boy. . . ." The quoted excerpts, however, give no impression of how restrained even so apparently glowing an appraisal reads in retrospect. One has no sense of the complexities,
depths, and literary values to be explored by later critics.

On Sunday, July 15, the two major New York newspaper book
reviews carried prominent notices. Virgilia Peterson in the *Herald Tribune* (p. 3) noted that Salinger's first novel had been
eagerly awaited. She found in the book "the implication that our
youth today has no moorings, no criterion beyond instinct, no
railing to grasp along the steep ascent to maturity. This is the
importance of 'The Catcher in the Rye,' and it is upon the integrity of his portrait of a so-called privileged American youth
that Mr. Salinger's novel stands or falls." After summarizing the
plot, Miss Peterson turned her attention to Holden:

> Like most of his literary predecessors—that host of sad twigs being
> arbitrarily bent to make twisted trees—Holden Caulfield is on the side
> of the angels. Contaminated he is, of course, by vulgarity, lust, lies,
> temptations, recklessness, and cynicism. But these are merely the devils
> that try him externally; inside, his spirit is intact. Unlike so many of his
> literary predecessors, however, he does not oversimplify his troubles.
> He is not tilting against the whole adult world (there are some decent
> adults); nor does he altogether loathe his worst contemporaries (he
> hates to leave them). He sees the mixtures, the inextricably mingled
> good and bad, as it is, but the very knowledge of reality is what almost
> breaks his heart. For Holden Caulfield, despite all the realism with
> which he is supposedly depicted, is nevertheless a skinless perfectionist.

From the very beginning, the language of the novel aroused
some pained comment, such as Miss Peterson's:

> Had Ring Lardner and Ernest Hemingway never existed, Mr. Salinger
> might have had to invent the manner of his tale, if not the matter. "The
> Catcher in the Rye" repeats and repeats, like an incantation, the pseudo-

natural cadences of a flat, colloquial prose which at best, banked down and understated, has a truly moving impact and at worst is casually obscene. Recent war novels have accustomed us all to ugly words and images, but from the mouths of the very young and protected they sound peculiarly offensive. There is probably not one phrase in the whole book that Holden Caulfield would not have used upon occasion, but when they are piled upon each other in cumulative monotony, the ear refuses to believe.

Having argued that the value of the novel depends on the integrity of the portrait of Holden, Miss Peterson offered to teen-age readers the responsibility of evaluating him:

... before it is possible to nominate Mr. Salinger as the top-flight catcher in the rye for the year or the day, it would be interesting and enlightening to know what Holden Caulfield's contemporaries, male and female, think of him. Their opinion would constitute the real test of Mr. Salinger's validity. The question of authenticity is one to which no parent can really guess the reply.

Holden's contemporaries have long since spoken, and if the critic is indeed content to accept their collective judgment, the novel must be ranked as one of the small number of American books which not only had great immediate impact but have steadily grown in stature.

James Stern's review in the Sunday New York *Times* (July '15, p. 5) wears a shabby appearance when disinterred from newspaper files. Under the title "Aw, the World's a Crumby Place," Stern attempted to use Holden's vernacular to assess the book, e.g., "This Salinger, he's a short story guy. And he knows how to write about kids. This book though, it's too long. Gets kind of monotonous. And he should've cut out a lot about those jerks and all at that crumby school." Although the final scene was found to be "terrific," one reads the review with the impression that the book's importance to Stern was the occasion it offered to be clever, presumably at the expense of the book's style. This gambit, it may be noted, was popular with critics across the country.

In the very same newspaper the next day, one of the *Times*'s daily reviewers, Nash K. Burger, came to a radically different assessment (p. 19): "Holden's story is told in Holden's own strange, wonderful language . . . in an unusually brilliant first novel. . . ." Although the narrator was adjudged "bewildered, lonely, ludicrous and pitiful," Burger found that "his troubles, his failings are not of his own making but of a world that is out of joint. There is nothing wrong with him that a little understanding and affection, preferably from his parents, couldn't have set right. . . . His delinquencies seem minor indeed when contrasted with the adult delinquencies with which he is confronted."

Like many other reviewers, Burger found Phoebe a "wonderful creation," and speculated about Holden's future: "we still think he's going to turn out all right. We wouldn't even be surprised if he grew up to write a few books . . . books like 'Of Human Bondage,' 'Look Homeward, Angel,' or 'The Catcher in the Rye'—nothing so childish as 'Seventeen' though."

Neither of the nation's two major weekly newsmagazines was especially perceptive. *Newsweek* (July 16, 1951) provided an inept summary of the plot, the effect of which was to make the book seem ridiculous, e.g., "in the end Holden thought he would bum his way out West, build a cabin, and pretend to be a deaf mute to avoid stupid, useless conversation with people" (p. 90). Apart from noting the presence of "humor," no indication was given of any other literary values. *Time*'s lead paragraph enthusiastically declared that the book "deals out some of the most acidly humorous deadpan satire since the late great Ring Lardner" (July 16, 1951, p. 96). In the remainder of the review, however, "Timestyle" was more in evidence than criticism. Holden, for example, "is sure that all the world is out of step but him. His code is the survival of the flippest. . . ." The scene with the prostitute Sunny was duly noted, but Holden's refusal to sleep with her was seen only as resulting from "hopeless embarrassment as soon as the tart snakes out of her dress" (p. 97). *Time*'s judgment was that for "U.S. readers, the prize catch in The Catcher in the Rye may well be Novelist Salinger himself. He can understand the adolescent mind without displaying one" (p. 97). The reference to "acidly humorous deadpan satire" suggests a radical misreading of the book's tone and the character of Holden Caulfield. Indeed,

the reviewer seems to approve of Salinger on the assumption
that Salinger disapproves of Holden.

Anne L. Goodman in the *New Republic* (July 16, 1951, p. 21)
began by praising Salinger's early short stories, and relating the
themes of "A Perfect Day for Bananafish" and "For Esmé—with
Love and Squalor" to *The Catcher in the Rye:*

> In all three cases the children and the boy-men are exceedingly well
> done. In each case, despite the similarity of situation, they are quite
> different and distinct individuals. The final scene in *The Catcher in
> the Rye* is as good as anything that Salinger has written, which means
> very good indeed. But the book as a whole is disappointing, and not
> merely because it is a reworking of a theme that one begins to suspect
> must obsess the author. Holden Caulfield, the main character who tells
> his own story, is an extraordinary portrait, but there is too much of him.
> He describes himself early on and, with the sureness of a wire recording,
> he remains strictly in character throughout:
>
> > I shook my head. I shake my head quite a lot. "Boy!" I said. I
> > also say "Boy!" quite a lot. Partly because I have a lousy vocabulary
> > and partly because I act quite young for my age sometimes. I was
> > sixteen then, and I'm seventeen now, and sometimes I act like I'm
> > about thirteen. It's really ironical because I'm six foot two and I
> > have gray hair. I really do. The one side of my head, the right side—
> > is full of millions of gray hairs. I've had them ever since I was a kid.
> > And yet I still act sometimes like I was only about twelve.
>
> In the course of 277 pages the reader wearies of this kind of explicit-
> ness, repetition and adolescence, exactly as one would weary of Holden
> himself. And this reader at least suffered from an irritated feeling that
> Holden was not quite so sensitive and perceptive as he, and his creator,
> thought he was. In any case he is so completely self-centered that the
> other characters who wander through the book—with the notable excep-
> tion of his sister Phoebe—have nothing like his authenticity. *The Catcher
> in the Rye* is a brilliant tour-de-force, but in a writer of Salinger's un-
> deniable talent one expects something more.

T. Morris Longstreth, writing in the *Christian Science Monitor*
three days later (July 19, p. 5), was still harsher. The newspaper
unexpectedly provided a box in the center of the review to answer the question, "Why do you give precious space to books you

cannot recommend?" The editors replied, "We endeavor to cover books that are 'news' for any legitimate reason," and stressed that Salinger's book had been recommended by a well-known publication as "one every parent should read."

Longstreth argued that the work was "not fit for children to read. . . . Indeed, one finds it hard to believe that a true lover of children could father this tale." Longstreth further found that

[Holden's] conduct is a nightmarish medley of loneliness, bravado, and supineness. . . . [His] dead-pan narrative is quick-moving, absurd, and wholly repellent in its mingled vulgarity, naïveté, and sly perversion.

"The Catcher in the Rye" purports to be the "Seventeen" of our times, though it is as remote in conception from the Tarkington masterpiece, still much alive,[1] as the television age from Indiana in 1916. . . . [Holden] suffers from loneliness because he has shut himself away from the normal activities of boyhood, games, the outdoors, friendship. . . . He is alive, human, preposterous, profane and pathetic beyond belief.

Fortunately, there cannot be many of him yet. But one fears that a book like this given wide circulation may multiply his kind—as too easily happens when immorality and perversion are recounted by writers

[1] Since Nash K. Burger called *Seventeen* "childish," and Mr. Longstreth has just hailed it as a masterpiece, both in relation to *The Catcher in the Rye*, it may be of interest to quote the opening sentences of both novels. Much, obviously, has happened to the mind of America and to literary technique in the 35 years which passed between the publication of both books.

Seventeen: "William Sylvanus Baxter paused for a moment of thought in front of the drug-store at the corner of Washington Street and Central Avenue. He had an internal question to settle before he entered the store: he wished to allow the young man at the soda-fountain no excuse for saying, "Well, make up your mind what it's goin' to be, can't you?" Rudeness of this kind, especially in the presence of girls and women, was hard to bear, and though William Sylvanus Baxter had borne it upon occasion, he had reached an age when he found it intolerable. . . ."

The Catcher in the Rye: "If you really want to hear about it, the first thing you probably want to know is where I was born, and what my lousy childhood was like, and how my parents were occupied and all before they had me, and all that David Copperfield kind of crap, but I don't feel like going into it, if you want to know the truth. In the first place, that stuff bores me, and in the second place, my parents would have about two hemorrhages apiece if I told anything personal about them. They're quite touchy about anything like that, especially my father. They're *nice* and all—I'm not saying that—but they're also touchy as hell. Besides, I'm not going to tell you my whole goddam autobiography or anything. I'll just tell you about this madman stuff that happened to me around last Christmas just before I got pretty run-down and had to come out here and take it easy. . . ."

of talent whose work is countenanced in the name of art or good intention.

On August 11, S. N. Behrman published in the *New Yorker* by far the longest review *The Catcher in the Rye* received. The bulk of it was given to a detailed account of the story, with very liberal quotation. Behrman "loved" the book, as he says in his penultimate sentence (p. 76), but this seems essentially a reflection of his attitude toward Holden and Phoebe, considered as living people. The review is far too long to quote in any detail, but the following excerpts will suggest Behrman's reading: "Phoebe is one of the most exquisitely created and engaging children in any novel" (p. 73). "The dialogue and descriptions are economical and lean [when Holden is not communicating with himself]" (p. 75). "The literalness and innocence of Holden's point of view in the face of the tremendously complicated and often depraved facts of life make for the humor of this novel" (p. 75). ". . . one of the funniest expeditions, surely, in the history of juvenilia" (pp. 75-76). Behrman concludes:

Holden's contacts with the outside world are generally extremely funny. It is his self-communings that are tragic and touching—a dark whirlpool churning fiercely below the unflagging hilarity of the surface activities. Holden's difficulties affect his nervous system but never his vision. It is the vision of the innocent. . . .[T]here is an exhilaration, an immense relief in the final scene of this novel, at the Central Park carrousel with Phoebe. ("I felt so damn happy all of a sudden, the way old Phoebe kept going around and around.") Holden will be all right. One day, he will probably find himself in the mood to call up Jane. He will even become more tolerant of phonies—it is part of the mechanics of living. . . . He may even, someday, write a novel. I would like to read it. I loved *this* one. I mean it—I really did. (p. 76)

Harvey Breit in the August *Atlantic* (p. 82) prefaced his discussion of *The Catcher* with some general observations about "summer novels": "the danger of reading 'summer' novels in the summertime is that we relax our innermost demands on the literature in hand. . . . What is wrong with that? My reply is simply that pleasure derived from the suppression of the intelligence is diluted pleasure very much akin to dissipation." "The two summer novels I have just read . . . are nearly good enough of their kind for the reader to be immensely grateful—and to let it go at that. What is more interesting, and necessary, is to attempt to find out why Salinger's novel is a near miss. . . ." From a vantage point more than a decade later, it seems odd that anyone should ever have identified, praised, or attacked *The Catcher in the Rye* as a "summer" novel.

After noting that the book "For all its surface guilelessness, is a critique of the contemporary, grown-up world," Breit proceeded to compare it with *The Adventures of Huckleberry Finn,* and so became perhaps the first critic in print to relate the two novels. (Two enormously developed and detailed comparisons will be found elsewhere in this book.) Breit observes:

Holden Caulfield struck me as an urban, a transplanted Huck Finn. He has a colloquialism as marked as Huck's. . . . Like Huck, Holden is neither comical nor misanthropic. He is an observer. Unlike Huck, he makes judgments by the dozen, but these are not to be taken seriously; they are conceits. There is a drollery, too, that is common to both, and a quality of seeing that creates farce.

What is crucial is where Huck and Holden part company. T. S. Eliot once pointed out that we see the world through Huck's eyes. Well, we do not see it through Holden's. We see Holden as a smiling adult sees a boy, and we smile at his spectral, incredible world. I think that is the decisive failure: whatever is serious and implicit in the novel is overwhelmed by the more powerful comic element. What remains is a brilliant *tour de force,* one that has sufficient power and cleverness to make the reader chuckle and—rare indeed—even laugh aloud.

Because late reviews of books which have achieved great popular or critical acclaim appear in a radically altered public context, they almost invariably differ in character from early reviews. The critic knows that he will be read with particular attention, and that his remarks are likely to be measured against the reader's knowledge of other opinions, perhaps his own. As a consequence, late reviews are frequently unusually decisive in tone and judgments are rendered with more than characteristic vigor.

Since the nearly crippling burden of the newspaper or weekly magazine critic is not present, i.e., the necessity of reading and evaluating a book under severe time pressure, the late reviewer may be held more accountable for his judgments. It is, therefore, of particular interest to examine two of the last American reviews, and to glance at the reception of *The Catcher in the Rye* in England, where critics read and wrote with the knowledge of the book's extraordinary American success.

Writing in *The Nation* (September 1, 1951, p. 176), Ernest Jones[2] took for granted in his audience a knowledge both of the book's general contents and the wide interest it had aroused. The review is interesting in several ways, not least in that it indicates how intense, some seven weeks after publication of the book, was the discussion centering upon Holden's personality:

. . . Holden Caulfield is friendly, "democratic," well-bred, and snobbish in ways peculiar to adolescence. He has the beginnings of taste; "corny" is a term frequent in his speech. A virgin, he never knows exactly what any girl may be expecting of him and is afraid to make love to the prostitute supplied by an obliging bellhop. He mistakes whatever is spontaneous in his behavior for madness: "But I'm crazy. I swear to God I am"; if he acts on impulse he feels guilty, though also boastful: "I'm the most terrific liar you ever saw in your life." Bravado and buffoonery imperfectly disguise his conviction of madness and guilt. . . . With his alienation go assorted hatreds—of the movies, of night clubs, of social and intellectual pretension, and so on. And physical disgust: pimples, sex, an old man picking his nose are all equally cause for nausea. . . . After every other human being has failed him, Caulfield still has his loving ten-year-old sister to love; she embodies the innocence we all hope we have preserved and the wisdom we all hope we have acquired.

The skill with which all this has been worked into 277 pages is most ingenious. But as it proceeds on its insights, which are not really insights since they are so general, "The Catcher in the Rye" becomes more and more a case history of all of us. Radically this writing depends on the reader's recollection of merely similar difficulties; the unique crisis and

[2] An English teacher at Queens College, New York, and not to be confused with the renowned British psychoanalyst and biographer of Freud, as he sometimes has been in Salinger criticism.

the unique anguish are not re-created. These emotional ups and downs become increasingly factitious—so much must be included to elicit memories of so many callow heartbreaks—and though always lively in its parts, the book as a whole is predictable and boring.

Jones's review, though damning, indicated by its length alone that Salinger's novel posed a substantial problem in evaluation. The *Catholic World,* however, in its November issue (p. 154) dismissed the book in two paragraphs, concluding with:

It's a mad mélange of ice-skating at Radio City, interviewing a prostitute in his [Holden's] hotel room, escaping from a homosexual, and so on. Not only do some of the events stretch probability, but Holden's character as iconoclast, a kind of latter-day Tom Sawyer or Huck Finn, is made monotonous and phony by the formidably excessive use of amateur swearing and coarse language.

The initial critical reception of *The Catcher in the Rye* in England reveals that British reviewers were intimidated neither by the book's reputation nor the approval, however qualified, of many American colleagues. Judgments of the book were in general less sympathetic and more summary. R. D. Charques, for example, writing in the widely circulated magazine *The Spectator* (August 17, 1951, p. 224), considered four books in a one-column review, with a single paragraph devoted to *The Catcher.* He found it

a somewhat inconclusive story of a New York schoolboy of lively and honest mind who for one reason or another, perhaps as much through excess of adolescent sensibility as anything else, looks like turning into a neurotic or delinquent. The tale is presented in the sixteen-year-old's first person recital of events, which superimposes upon a crude and undifferentiated American vernacular a restricted schoolboy idiom. Altogether, though a little showy in effect, the style of the book is quite a performance.

After summarizing the plot in two sentences, Charques concluded: "In the event, we are asked to believe, he [Holden] discovers how mean the world is and falls straight on the psychi-

atrist's sofa. Intelligent, humorous, acute and sympathetic in observation, the tale is rather too formless to do quite the sort of
thing it was evidently intended to do."

The most respected and august of all literary periodicals in
England, the *Times Literary Supplement* (London), gave one
paragraph to *The Catcher* in a discussion of three new novels
(September 7, 1951, p. 561). Following another two-sentence summary of the story, the anonymous critic observed:

Actually the boy appears to be a very normal specimen of his age and
most of his troubles, certainly his dislike for his studies, are obviously
due to the fact that he has outgrown his strength. Mr. Salinger . . . has
not achieved sufficient variety in this book for a full-length novel. The
boy is really very touching; but the endless stream of blasphemy and
obscenity in which he thinks, credible as it is, palls after the first chapter.
One would like to hear more of what his parents and teachers have to
say about him.

At least 200 reviews of *The Catcher in the Rye* appeared in
the months immediately following its publication. The overwhelming majority—brief, ephemeral notices in local newspapers—are without critical interest of any kind. In an essay published in 1958 (reprinted in this book), Maxwell Geismar sharply
dissented from what he considered to be a too high respect for
Salinger's talents among critics. In so doing he repeated the common belief that *The Catcher in the Rye* had been *initially* hailed
on all sides as a brilliant achievement. The preceding pages make
it quite clear that this was not so. Many reviewers were indifferent and some notably hostile. Perhaps no critic deserves to be
severely chastised for failing to predict the extraordinary staying
power of *The Catcher in the Rye,* but there is singularly little in
any of the early reviews to indicate that the book either would
or deserved to survive beyond the immediate season.

Almost two years passed before the appearance of Salinger's
next book, *Nine Stories,* which was made up almost entirely of
stories previously published. Collections of short stories very
rarely receive the critical attention accorded novels. *Nine Stories,*

while not nearly so widely reviewed as *The Catcher,* nevertheless received a quite unusual amount of attention. The reviews disclose that Salinger's reputation was gathering momentum, though slowly. Reviewers often took the opportunity to look back upon *The Catcher,* still selling widely, and reprinted in paperback just a month before *Nine Stories* appeared.

One of the earliest reviews came from the pen of Eudora Welty, a short story writer, novelist and critic of renown. In the New York *Times Book Review* (April 5, 1953, p. 4), Miss Welty described Salinger's writing as "original, first rate, serious and beautiful." The stories were accorded very high praise, and Salinger himself hailed as a "born writer" with a "sensitive eye . . . incredibly great ear, and something I can think of no word for but grace." Miss Welty noted a characteristic of Salinger's art that was to be much discussed years later: ". . . Mr. Salinger has never, here [in *Nine Stories*], *directly* touched upon what he has the most to say about: love. Love averts itself in pity, laughter, or a gesture or vision of finality possibly too easy or simple in stories that are neither easy nor simple in any degree." Near the close of her generally glowing tribute, Miss Welty observed:

> Mr. Salinger is a very serious artist, and it is likely that what he has to say will find many forms as time goes by—interesting forms, too. His novel, "The Catcher in the Rye," was good and extremely moving, although—for this reader—all its virtues can be had in a short story by the same author, where they are somehow more at home.

On one point—of the utmost importance with respect to Salinger's growth as an artist—Miss Welty was quite wrong. Salinger has not found many forms ("interesting forms, too") for what he wished to say. Since the appearance of *Nine Stories,* he has published only four stories: "Franny," "Raise High the Roof Beam, Carpenters," "Zooey," and "Seymour: An Introduction." These are in no way a decisive departure, either in technique or form, from what he had published by 1953.

William Peden, in the *Saturday Review* (April 11, 1953, p. 44), had high praise for Salinger in particular and three of the short stories: "For Esmé—with Love and Squalor," "A Perfect Day for

Bananafish," and "Uncle Wiggily in Connecticut." In the same article, however, Peden acclaimed with equal enthusiasm a book of short stories by John Cheever, and offered the observation that Cheever's stories "improve with re-reading, which is not usually true of a Salinger piece."

The Nation (April 18, 1953, p. 332) called the stories "accomplished and effective," and presented the odd opinion that the child prodigy in "Teddy" pushed his sister into the empty swimming pool. "Mr. Salinger is a fiction writer of great brilliance," the writer continued; "the danger is that he will become one of definite and ultimately disappointing limitations. Just as Saroyan has succumbed to the glamour of a happy childhood, it is possible to be infatuated by the charms of juvenile diseases at the expense of a larger and more complex area of human suffering. This is sickness of mind in a very small world for a writer of large gifts."

The Commonweal (April 24, 1953, p. 78) gave its reviewer, Seymour Krim, a full page for a discussion of *Nine Stories*. Although holding that the stories read together were "not quite as impressive as they seemed when read individually," Krim argued that the stories reveal "a unique talent, and more, a born writer. . . ." Very high praise of some of the stories followed, approval for "the author's feeling for textures, and situations, and the freshness of his irony." "They [the stories] are all imaginative, felt (for the most part) , and strikingly fresh. They have that invaluable quality, in Johnson's words, of making the familiar new and the new familiar."

A brief discussion of Salinger's limitations followed:

> To reduce it to fundamentals, I believe that Salinger is not quite clear about the meaning of his material; he is extremely deft, sometimes over-sophisticated in his surface technique, and for the most part it is a pure pleasure to follow his artistic strokes. But underneath, where it is a question of values and finally of the iron moral grasp of meaning, one suspects a dodging of issues.

Writing one month later in the *New Republic* (April 25) , Arthur Mizener noted that "for all the prejudices against short

stories, his [Salinger's] *Nine Stories* has made the best-seller lists."
Mizener continued:

> This is—as things seldom are—as it ought to be for Mr. Salinger is a
> talented writer. Even if this success is a mere by-product of *The Catcher
> in the Rye,* it is rough justice; for all its brilliance, *The Catcher in the
> Rye* does not quite come off as a whole; the best of these stories do. They
> have, as the novel did not, a controlling intention which is at once
> complex enough for Mr. Salinger's awareness and firm enough to give
> it a purpose. . . . "A Perfect Day for Bananafish," "De Daumier-Smith's
> Blue Period," and large units of several other stories are better than
> anything in *The Catcher in the Rye.* (p. 26)

The Summer issue of the *Yale Review* (1953, p. XII) gave one
highly concentrated paragraph of critical observation to the collection. "For Esmé—with Love and Squalor" was hailed as "certainly one of the great stories of the last decade, and technically
one of the most dazzling I know. The other eight stories are very
nearly as remarkable." The thematic content, however, was seen
as extremely limited: "one may feel that for the health of his
writing, if nothing more, Mr. Salinger should become interested
in something else—beekeeping or Peruvian pottery or anything—
so that his characters can stop picking at the scab of their own
suffering to see if the blood still flows beneath. . . ."

In the Autumn number of the *Hudson Review* (1953, p. 467),
Sidney Monas gave an account of some of the stories and concluded:

> Although the stories in this book are none of them quite as good as
> *The Catcher in the Rye,* some are very good indeed. Salinger has a quick
> ear and a fine talent . . . but to a certain extent he lacks detachment and
> disinterestedness. One has sometimes an oppressive and uncomfortable
> awareness of the author's nervous involvement in the hurt of his sen-
> sitive, witty, suicidal heroes. One also senses in these stories, as in the
> novel, a peculiar conceptual separation of the child from the adult, as
> though they were of different species, not merely different ages. For
> the child, anything is possible; for the adult, conformity or death.

Martin Hansford, in the Winter issue of the *Western Review*
(1954), dealt with the Salinger book together with recently pub-

lished collections of short stories by Jean Stafford, Ray Bradbury, and Budd Schulberg. The harshness of the single paragraph Hansford devoted to Salinger still provides a shock:

> Even before J. D. Salinger's first novel appeared, such stories of his as "For Esmé—with Love and Squalor" had been exciting considerable admiration among the *New Yorker* kind of enthusiast. At that time I was unable to see anything more to his work than the end product of a competent hand, with more craft than art, but containing soothing portions of both skills. The compilation of nine stories reinforces the sense of desperate slyness, warily disguised by the simulation of surface honesty. Almost all these stories are "trick" stories, with snappers in place of endings; the method of O. Henry overlaid by a manner the late Condé Nast would have envied. Even the superficial verisimilitude is not so convincing in bulk; it is somehow a little too good, too careful; like one of Hollywood's carefully documented historical epics, TV, or John O'Hara, the result of such an excess of actuality is a sense of un-reality. (p. 172)

Of the four authors Hansford dealt with, Jean Stafford was seen as "undoubtedly the only serious writer. . . ." (p. 173)

Hansford's extreme disapproval was exceptional. On the whole, *Nine Stories* appears to have received more favorable critical judgment than *The Catcher in the Rye*. The collection was noticed in an unusually large number of publications and, moreover, was discussed in such journals as the *Yale Review, Western Review,* and *Hudson Review,* periodicals of limited circulation and largely addressed to an intellectual or learned audience. Such publications had almost entirely ignored *The Catcher in the Rye.*

It is to be noted also that references to Salinger's only novel were frequent and were presented in such a way as to reveal that *The Catcher* was still a much discussed book. Above all, even the negative criticism had a quality reserved only for writers of literary substance or public importance. Seymour Krim put it well, commenting on his own strictures:

> . . . when you come right down to it, the chivvying of a genuine writer is a form of complimenting him. In the majority of cases the "magic" simply isn't there, and one makes criticism a form of duty; in Salinger's instance, where the gem of his talent shines, there is real concern that

the author make the very best use of it. Such freshness isn't given freely, and its ownership implies a responsibility which transcends self. (*loc. cit.*)

Clearly, by 1953, J. D. Salinger was a writer the literary world was watching with alert attention—waiting, above all, for the stream of stories and novels so widely expected from so gifted a pen. It was to prove a vexing and inconclusive wait, for in the decade following *Nine Stories* Salinger was to publish only four short stories. Since "Seymour: An Introduction" (1959), there has been nothing new. Two of the stories appeared in book form as *Franny and Zooey;* the remaining two, dealing with Seymour, have been similarly republished. But of fresh creative work, there has been only Salinger's statement on the dust jackets of these two books that he is engaged in writing "a narrative series . . . about a family of settlers in twentieth-century New York, the Glasses. It is a long-term project, patently an ambitious one. . . ."

The essays which follow in this book not only offer an opportunity to study the development of Salinger's reputation, but provide a startling contrast in quality of literary criticism. An examination of the initial reception of Salinger's early work raises fundamental questions about the specific function and ultimate value of book reviewing in the United States. It is obvious that the overwhelming majority of all the reviews of *The Catcher in the Rye* were written on editorial assignment, with the reviewer required to meet early and inflexible press schedules. Despite a few careful and perceptive reviews, the overwhelming impression they provide is of work swiftly and mechanically done. And it should also be remembered that the few glowing tributes to *The Catcher in the Rye* could easily be matched by equally enthusiastic reviews by equally experienced critics for books which have long since vanished into literary limbo.

J. D. Salinger: Some Crazy Cliff

ARTHUR HEISERMAN AND JAMES E. MILLER, JR.

It is clear that J. D. Salinger's *The Catcher in the Rye* belongs to an ancient and honorable narrative tradition, perhaps the most profound in western fiction. The tradition is the central pattern of the epic and has been enriched by every tongue; for not only is it in itself exciting but also it provides the artist a framework upon which he may hang almost any fabric of events and characters.

It is, of course, the tradition of the Quest. We use the medieval term because it signifies a seeking after what is tremendous, greater than the love of a woman. The love of woman may be part of the seeking, part even of the object sought, for we have been told that the Grail has gender and Penelope did wait in Ithaca. But if the love of woman is essential to the seeking or to the object sought, we must call the search a romance. These two terms (quest and romance) distinguish thematic patterns, and have nothing to do with tragic or comic effects. Furthermore, the same plots, characters, and idioms might be employed inside either pattern. But somewhere upon the arc of the Quest, the love of woman must be eschewed or absorbed: the hero must bind himself to the mast, or must seek his Ducalinda because she is Virtue, not because she is Female.

There are at least two sorts of quests, depending upon the object sought. Stephen Dedalus sought a reality uncontaminated by home, country, church; for like Eugene Gant and Natty Bumppo he knew that social institutions tend to force what is ingenious in a man into their own channels. He sought the opposite of se-

From *Western Humanities Review*, X (Spring 1956), 129-137. Copyright 1956 by the University of Utah. Reprinted by permission.

curity, for security was a cataract of the eye. Bloom, on the other hand, was already an outcast and sought acceptance by an Ithaca and a Penelope which despised him. And, tragically enough, he also /129/ sought an Icarian son who had fled the very maze which he, Bloom, desired to enter. So the two kinds of quests, the one seeking acceptance and stability, the other precisely the opposite, differ significantly, and can cross only briefly to the drunken wonder of both heroes. Bloom, the protagonist of *The Waste Land,* the Joads, Alyosha Karamazov, Aeneas, Ulysses, Gatsby—these heroes seek acceptance, stability, a life embosomed upon what is known and can be trusted. Dedalus, Huck Finn, Ishmael, Hans Castorp, Huxley's heroes, Dostoevski's Idiot—these protagonists place themselves outside the bounds of what is known and seek not stability but a Truth which is unwarped by stability.

American literature seems fascinated with the outcast, the person who defies traditions in order to arrive at some pristine knowledge, some personal integrity. Natty Bumppo maintains his integrity out-of-doors only, for upon the frontier a man must be a man or perish. For Huck Finn both sides of the Mississippi are lined with fraud and hatred; and because the great brown river acts as a kind of sewer, you're liable to find murderers and thieves afloat on it—even the father whom you fled might turn up dead in it, as though the river were a dream. But in the middle of the great natural river, when you're naked of civilization and in company with an outcast more untarnished and childlike than yourself—*there* is peace. And in northern Mississippi, in the ante-Snopes era, frontiersmen conquer the wilderness using only their courage and their fury; and they behave, even when civilization has almost extinguished them, with the kind of insane honor that drives Quentin Compson outside of society and into suicide. And the hunter, as he tracks the great mythic bear or the incredible whale, must leave behind whatever is unnatural or convenient. Similarly, when the bull charges, you are faced with the same compulsion for integrity as is required by the wilderness, the whale, the bear, the river; and very often, the world so botches things that you must "make a separate peace" in order to maintain your moral entity intact.

All the virtues of these American heroes are personal ones:

they most often, as a matter of fact, are in conflict with home, family, church. The typical American hero must flee these institutions, become a tramp in the earth, cut himself off from Chicago, Winesburg, Hannibal, Cooperstown, New York, Asheville, Minneapolis. For only by flight can he find knowledge of what is real. And if he does not flee, he at least defies.

The protagonist of *The Catcher in the Rye,* Holden Caulfield, is one of these American heroes, but with a significant difference. He seems to be engaged in both sorts of quests at once; he needs to go home and he needs /130/ to leave it. Unlike the other American knight errants, Holden seeks Virtue second to Love. He wants to be good. When the little children are playing in the rye-field on the clifftop, Holden wants to be the one who catches them before they fall off the cliff. He is not driven toward honor or courage. He is not driven toward love of woman. Holden is driven toward love of his fellow-man, charity—virtues which were perhaps not quite virile enough for Natty Bumppo, Ishmael, Huck Finn, or Nick Adams. Holden is actually frightened by a frontier code of masculinity—a code which sometimes requires its adherents to behave in sentimental and bumptious fashions. But like these American heroes, Holden is a wanderer, for in order to be good he has to be more of a bad boy than the puritanical Huck could have imagined. Holden has had enough of both Hannibal, Missouri, *and* the Mississippi; and his tragedy is that when he starts back up the river, he has no place to go—save, of course, a California psychiatrist's couch.

So Salinger translates the old tradition into contemporary terms. The phoniness of society forces Holden Caulfield to leave it, but he is seeking nothing less than stability and love. He would like nothing better than a home, a life embosomed upon what is known and can be trusted; he is a very wise sheep forced into lone wolf's clothing; he is Stephen Dedalus and Leopold Bloom rolled into one crazy kid. And here is the point; for poor Holden, there is no Ithaca. Ithaca has not merely been defiled by a horde of suitors: it has sunk beneath waves of phoniness. He does, of course, have a Penelope who is still intact. She is his little sister Phoebe whom he must protect at all costs from the phantoms of lust, hypocrisy, conceit and fear—all of the attributes which Holden sees in society and which Huck Finn saw on the banks of the Mississippi and Dedalus saw in Dublin. So at the end, like the hero of *Antic Hay*, Holden delights in circles— a comforting, bounded figure which yet connotes hopelessness. He breaks down as he watches his beloved little Phoebe going round and round on a carousel; she is so *damned* happy. From that lunatic delight in a circle, he is shipped off to the psychiatrist. For Holden loves the world more than the world can bear.

Holden's Quest takes him outside society; yet the grail he seeks is the world and the grail is full of love. To be a catcher in the rye in this world is possible only at the price of leaving it. To be good is to be a "case," a "bad boy" who confounds the society of men. So Holden seeks the one role which would allow him to be a catcher, and that role is the role of the child. As a child, he would be condoned, for a child is a sort of savage and a pariah because he is innocent and good. But it is Holden's tragedy that /131/ he is sixteen, and like Wordsworth he can never be less. In childhood he had what he is now seeking—non-phoniness, truth, innocence. He can find it now only in Phoebe and in his dead brother Allie's baseball mitt, in a red hunting cap and the tender little nuns. Still, unlike all of us, Holden refuses to compromise with adulthood and its necessary adulteries; and his heroism drives him berserk. Huck Finn had the Mississippi and at the end of the Mississippi he had the wild west beyond Arkansas. The hero of *The Waste Land* had Shantih, the peace which passes human understanding. Bloom had Molly and his own ignorance; Dedalus had Paris and Zurich. But for Holden, there is no place to go. . . . /132/

The flight out of the world, out of the ordinary, and into an Eden of innocence or childhood is a common flight indeed, and it is one which Salinger's heroes are constantly attempting. But Salinger's childism is consubstantial with his concern for love and neurosis. Adultism is precisely "the suffering of being unable to love," and it is that which produces neurosis. Everyone able to love in Salinger's stories is either a child or a man influenced by a child. All the adults not informed by love and innocence are by definition phonies and prostitutes. "You take adults, they always look lousy when they're asleep with their mouths open, but kids don't . . . They look all right." Kids like Phoebe shut up when they haven't anything to say. They even say "thank you" when you tighten their skates, and they don't go behind a post to button their pants. The nuns expect no swanky lunches after standing on a corner to collect money. Young James Castle would not go back on his word even though he had to jump from a window to keep it.

Holden is the kind of person who feels sorry for the teachers who have to flunk him. He fears for the ducks when the lagoon freezes over, for he is a duck himself with no place to go. He must enter his own home like a crook, lying to elevator boys and tiptoeing past bedrooms. His dad "will kill" him and his mother will weep for his incorrigible "laziness." He wants only to pretend he is a deaf-mute and live as a hermit filling-station operator in Colorado, but he winds up where the frontier ends, California, in an institution for sick rich kids. And we can see, on the final note of irony in the book, that that frontier west which represented escape from "sivilization" for Huck Finn has ended by becoming the symbol for depravity and phoniness in our national shrine at Hollywood. . . . /133/

It is . . . poignance which characterizes all of Salinger's humor, this catch in the throat that accompanies all of the laughs. Holden Caulfield is no clown nor is he a tragic hero; he is a sixteen-year-old lad whose vivid encounter with everyday life is tragically humorous—or humorously tragic. At the end of the novel, as we leave Holden in the psychiatric ward of the California hospital, we come to the realization that the abundant and richly varied humor of the novel has reenforced the serious intensity of Holden's frantic flight from Adultism and his frenzied search for the genuine in a terrifying phony world.

Holden Caulfield, like Huckleberry Finn, tells his own story and it is in the language of the telling in both books that a great part of the humor lies. In the nineteenth century, Huck began, "You don't know about me without you have read a book by the name of *The Adventures of Tom Sawyer:* but that ain't no matter." The English of Huck's twentieth century counterpart, Holden Caulfield, is perhaps more correct but none-the-less distinctive: "If you really want to hear about it, the first thing you'll probably want to know is where I was born, and what my lousy childhood was like, and how my parents were occupied and all before they had me, and all that David Copperfield kind of crap, but I don't feel like going into it, if you want to know the truth."

The skepticism inherent in that casual phrase, "if you want to know the truth," suggesting that as a matter of fact in the world of Holden Caulfield very few people do, characterizes this sixteen-year-old "crazy mixed up kid" more sharply and vividly than pages of character "analysis" possibly could. In a similar manner Huck's "that ain't no matter" speaks volumes for his relationship to the alien adult world in which he finds himself a sojourner. But if these two boys lay their souls bare by their own voices, in doing so they provoke smiles at their mishandling and sometimes downright mangling of the English language.

Huck's spelling of *sivilization* gives the word a look which makes what it stands for understandably distasteful. Holden's incorrectness frequently appears to be a straining after correctness ("She'd give Allie or I a push. . . .") which suggests a subconscious will to non-conformity. But the similarities of language of Huck and Holden are balanced by marked differences. Both boys are fugitives from education, but Holden has suffered more of the evil than Huck. Holden's best subject in the several schools he has tolerated briefly is English. And, too, Holden is a child of the twentieth century. Mark Twain himself would probably be startled not at the frankness of Holden's language but at the daring of J. D. Salinger in copying it so faithfully.

But of course neither J. D. Salinger nor Mark Twain really "copied" anything. Their books would be unreadable had they merely recorded intact the language of a real-life Huck and a real-life Holden. Their genius lies in their mastery of the technique of first person narration which /135/ through meticulous selection, creates vividly the illusion of life: gradually and subtly their narrators emerge and stand revealed, stripped to their innermost beings. It is a mark of their creators' mastery that Huck and Holden appear to reveal themselves.

It is not the least surprising aspect of *The Catcher in the Rye* that trite expressions and metaphors with which we are all familiar and even bored turn out, when emerging from the mouth of a sixteen-year-old, to be funny. The unimaginative repetition of identical expressions in countless situations intensifies the humor. The things in Holden's world are always jumping up and down or bouncing or scattering "like madmen." Holden always lets us know when he has insight into the absurdity of the endless absurd situations which make up the life of a sixteen-year-old by exclaiming, "It killed me." In a phony world Holden feels compelled to reenforce his sincerity and truthfulness constantly with, "It really is" or "It really did." Incongruously the adjective "old" serves as a term of endearment, from "old" Thomas Hardy to "old" Phoebe. And many of the things Holden does, he does, ambiguously, "like a bastard."

Holden is a master of the ludicrous irrelevancy. Indeed, a large part of *The Catcher in the Rye* consists of the relevantly irrelevant. On the opening page, Holden says, "I'm not going to tell you my whole goddam autobiography or anything. I'll just tell you about this madman stuff that happened to me around last Christmas. . . ." By the time we have finished *Catcher* we feel that we know Holden as thoroughly as any biography could reveal him, and one of the reasons is that he has not hesitated to follow in his tale wherever whim and fancy lead him. For example, in the early part of the novel, Holden goes at some length into the history of the Ossenburger Memorial Wing of the new dorms, his place of residence. Ossenburger, we are told, was the Pencey alumnus who made a "pot of dough" in the undertaking business, and who, after giving money to Pencey, gave a speech in chapel "that lasted about ten hours." "He told us we should always pray to God—talk to Him and all—wherever we were. He told us we ought to think of Jesus as our buddy and all. He said *he* talked to Jesus all of the time. Even when he was driving his car. That killed me. I can just see the big phony bastard shifting into first gear and asking Jesus to send him a few more stiffs." Ossenburger, of course, has nothing to do, directly, with the "madman stuff" that happened to Holden around Christmas; but Holden's value judgment of the phony Ossenburger is certainly relevant to Salinger's purpose, the revelation of Holden's character. /136/

When Holden refuses to express aggressive dislike of the repulsive Ackley, the pimply boy whose teeth "looked mossy and awful," he is not being facetious nor is he lying. He is simply expressing an innocence incapable of genuine hatred. Holden does not suffer from the inability to love, but he does despair of finding a place to bestow his love. The depth of Holden's capacity for love is revealed in his final words, as he sits in the psychiatric ward musing over his nightmarish adventures: "If you want to know the truth, I don't *know* what I think about it. I'm sorry I told so many people about it. About all I know is, I sort of miss everybody I told about. Even old Stradlater and Ackley, for instance. I think I even miss that goddam Maurice. It's funny. Don't ever tell anybody anything. If you do, you start missing everybody." We agree with Holden that it is funny, but it is funny in a pathetic kind of way. As we leave Holden alone in his room in the psychiatric ward, we are aware of the book's last ironic incongruity. It is not Holden who should be examined for a sickness of the mind, but the world in which he has sojourned and found himself an alien. To "cure" Holden, he must be given the contagious, almost universal disease of phony adultism; he must be pushed over that "crazy cliff." /137/

Holden and Huck: The Odysseys of Youth

CHARLES KAPLAN

Henry Thoreau, himself an interior traveler of some note, says in *A Week on the Concord and Merrimac Rivers:* "The traveller must be born again on the road, and earn a passport from the elements, the principal powers that be for him." In Mark Twain's *Adventures of Huckleberry Finn* (1884) and in J. D. Salinger's *The Catcher in the Rye* (1951) we meet two young travelers— travelers in their native land and also in the geography of their souls. Their narratives are separated in time by almost seventy years, but the psychic connection between them eliminates mere temporal distance: Huck Finn and Holden Caulfield are true blood-brothers, speaking to us in terms that lift their /76/ wanderings from the level of the merely picaresque to that of a sensitive and insightful criticism of American life.

Each work, to begin with, is a fine comic novel. Each is rich in incident, varied in characterization, and meaningful in its entirety. In each the story is narrated by the central figure, an adolescent whose remarkable language is both a reflection and a criticism of his education, his environment, and his times. Each is fundamentally a story of a quest—an adventure story in the age-old pattern of a young lad making his way in a not particularly friendly adult world. An outcast, to all intents without family and friends, the protagonist flees the restraints of the civilization which would make him its victim, and journeys through the world in search of what he thinks is freedom—but which we, his adult readers, recognize to be primarily understanding. Society regards him as a rogue, a ne'er-do-well whose career consists of

From *College English*, XVIII (November 1956), 76-80. Reprinted by permission of the author and the National Council of Teachers of English.

one scrape after another; but the extent to which he is constantly
embroiled with authority is exactly the index of his independence, his sometimes pathetic self-reliance, and his freedom of
spirit. He is a total realist, with an acute and instinctive register
of mind which enables him to penetrate sham and pretense—
qualities which, the more he travels through the adult world, the
more he sees as most frequently recurring. He has somehow acquired a code of ethics and a standard of value against which he
measures mankind—including, mercilessly, himself. There are
[some] people and things—not many, however—that are (in
Holden's term) "nice"; there are many more that are "phony."
He does not understand the world, but he knows how one should
behave in it. The comic irony that gives each novel its characteristic intellectual slant is provided by the judgments of these
young realists on the false ideals and romanticized versions of life
which they encounter on their travels.

The slangy, idiomatic, frequently vulgar language which
Twain and Salinger put in the mouths of their heroes is remarkable for the clarity of the self-portraits that emerge, as well as for
the effortless accuracy of the talk itself. F. R. Leavis describes
Huck's colloquial language as a literary medium that is "Shake-
spearian in its range and subtlety." Likewise, Holden's twentieth-
century prep-school vernacular, despite its automatic and somehow innocent obscenities and its hackneyed coinages, also manages to communicate ideas and feelings of a quite complex sort
within its sharply delimited boundaries. The language, in each
case, is personal, distinctive, and descriptive of character. Holden
and Huck are moralists as well as realists: each has a deep concern with ethical valuation, and each responds fully to the experiences which life offers him. It is the tension between their
apparently inadequate idiom and their instinctively full and humane ethics that both Twain and Salinger exploit for comic purposes.

"The traveller must be born again," said Thoreau; and Huck's
voyage down the Mississippi is a series of constant rebirths, a
search for identity. Beginning with the elaborately staged mock
murder which sets him free from the clutches of Pap, Huck assumes a series of varied roles, playing each one like the brilliant

improviser that he is. Twain counterpoints Huck's hoaxes against the villainous or merely mercenary pretenses of the Duke and the Dauphin; the boy's sometimes desperate shifts are necessary for his survival and to both his moral and physical progress. The series reaches a climax in the sequence at the Phelps farm, when Huck is forced to assume the identity of Tom Sawyer—when, for the first time, he cannot choose his own role.

This, it seems to me, is a significant variation, pointing to the world which begins to close in upon Huck toward the end of the novel. Not only is an identity /77/ forced upon him, but with the appearance of the real Tom Sawyer upon the scene, Huck surrenders the initiative in planning and, in effect, loses control of his own fate. This is the tragedy of Huckleberry Finn: that he has gone so far only to surrender at the end to the forces which have been seeking to capture him. For despite the apparent similarities, there is a vital difference between Huck and Tom: Tom behaves "by the book"; Tom relies on historical precedent; Tom operates within the conventions of the civilized world, accepting its values and standards, and merely play-acting at rebellion— Tom, in short, is no rebel at all, but a romanticizer of reality. Huck's term to describe Tom's method of doing things is that it has "style." Style it may have, but it lacks design. Huck's willingness to let Tom take over Jim's rescue indicates Twain's final acquiescence to the world which has been criticized throughout. True, Huck is going to light out again, he tells us in the last lines: "Aunt Sally she's going to adopt me and sivilize me, and I can't stand it. I been there before." But, despite the expression of sentiments pointing to another future escape—and the fact that the limiting article is not part of Twain's title—Huck, by the end of the novel, has been trapped. I should like to add my bit to the perennial debate concerning the artistic validity of the final sequence, and suggest that it is both ironical and true to life. Tom's play-acting before Huck sets off down the river—his ambuscade of the "A-rabs," for example—seems innocent and amusing; but the rescue of Jim seems, as I think it is meant to seem, tedious and irrelevant. After all, something has happened to Huck—and to us—between chapters 3 and 43.

Huck is trapped by a society whose shortcomings he sees, and he says, "I can't stand it." Holden's terminology is "It depresses me" and "It kills me." Ironically, he is revealed as telling us his narrative from an institution of some kind—psychiatric, we are led to suspect—having also been trapped by the people who want to "sivilize" him.

Holden's instinctive nonconformity asserts itself early in the novel. He has been told by one of the masters at Pencey Prep, from which he is about to be dismissed, that life is a game. "Some game," Holden comments. "If you get on the side where all the hot-shots are, then it's a game, all right—I'll admit that. But if you get on the *other* side, where there aren't any hot-shots, then what's a game about it. Nothing. No game." At the age of seventeen he has learned to suspect the glib philosophies of his elders, and to test the coin of experience by determining whether it rings true or false for him, personally.

Like Huck, Holden is also a refugee. He flees the campus of Pencey Prep before he is formally expelled, and returns to New York City to have three days of freedom before rejoining his family. Pencey Prep is merely the most recent in a series of unsatisfactory academic experiences for him. "One of the biggest reasons I left Elkton Hills was because I was surrounded by phonies. That's all. They were coming in the goddam window. I can't stand that stuff. It drives me crazy. It makes me so depressed I go crazy."

Also like Huck, Holden assumes a series of guises during his lone wanderings. "I'm the most terrific liar you ever saw in your life. It's awful. If I'm on the way to the store to buy a magazine, even, and somebody asks me where I'm going. I'm liable to say I'm going to the opera. It's terrible." In a sequence which reminds one forcibly of Huck Finn, Holden finds himself in conversation with the mother of one of his classmates, Ernie Morrow, whom he describes as "doubtless the biggest bastard that ever went to Pencey, in the whole crumby history of the school." But Holden, adopting the name of "Rudolf Schmidt" (the janitor), tells her what she wants to hear about her /78/ son, to her wonder and delight. Holden's comment is: "Mothers are all slightly insane. The thing is, though, I liked old Morrow's mother. She was all right." His imagination rampant, Holden tells her a cock-and-bull story which includes an impending brain operation and a trip to South America to visit his grandmother, but he stops just short of revealing himself completely. It is a wonderfully funny scene, showing Holden in several aspects: his instinctive evaluation of the mother's "rightness" overcoming his profound distaste for her son, his adolescent imagination in a frenzy of wild invention, and his own awareness of the limits to which he can act his suddenly-adopted role of Rudolf Schmidt.

Huck's tortured decision not to "turn in" Jim is made on the basis of his own feelings, which he automatically assumes to be sinful since they have so often put him at odds with society. His personal moral code seems always to run counter to his duty to society, a conflict which serves to confirm him in the belief that wickedness is in his line, "being brung up to it." In the crucial moral act of the novel, Huck must "decide, forever, betwixt two things, and I knowed it. I studied a minute, sort of holding my breath, and then says to myself, 'All right, then I'll *go* to hell.' " Huck's humanity overcomes the so-called duty to society. Holden, also, is "depressed" by the notion that he is somehow a misfit, that he does strange, irrational things, that he is fighting a constant war with society—but his awareness of his own weaknesses (his compulsive lying, for example) is the result of his searching honesty.

The yardstick which Holden applies to the world is a simple one—too simple, perhaps, too rigorous, too uncompromising, for anyone but an adolescent (or, as the popular phrase has it, "a crazy mixed-up kid") to attempt to apply to a complex world: it is the test of truth. The world is full of phonies—so Holden dreams of running away and building his own cabin, where people would come and visit him. "I'd have this rule that nobody could do anything phony when they visited me. If anybody tried to do anything phony, they couldn't stay."

Huck's world, realistically depicted as mid-America in the middle of the nineteenth century, is also the world where the established codes are penetrated as being either hypocritical or superficial; Huck finds peace and reassurance away from the

haunts of man, out on the river. After the waste and folly of the
Grangerford-Shepherdson sequence, for example, Huck retreats
to the river:

Sometimes we'd have that whole river all to ourselves for the longest
time. Yonder was the banks and the islands, across the water; and maybe
a spark—which was a candle in a cabin window; and sometimes on the
water you could see a spark or two—on a raft or a scow, you know;
and maybe you could hear a fiddle or a song coming over from one of
them crafts. It's lovely to live on a raft.

But the idyll is interrupted shortly thereafter with "a couple of
men tearing up the path as tight as they could foot it"—the Duke
and the Dauphin imposing their unsavory world upon Huck's.

Holden's world is post-war New York City, from the Metropolitan Museum to Greenwich Village, during Christmas week,
where, in successive incidents, he encounters pompous hypocrisy,
ignorance, indifference, moral corruption, sexual perversion, and
—pervading all—"phoniness." Holden's older brother, a once
promising writer, is now a Hollywood scenarist; the corruption
of his talent is symptomatic to Holden of the general influence
of the movies: "They can ruin you. I'm not kidding." They represent the world at its "phoniest" in their falsification of reality;
in addition, they corrupt their audiences, converting them into
people like the three pathetic girls from Seattle who spend all
evening in a second-rate night club looking for movie stars, or
like the woman Holden observes at the /79/ Radio City Music
Hall. She cries through the entire picture, and "the phonier it
got, the more she cried. . . . She had this little kid with her that
was bored as hell and had to go to the bathroom, but she wouldn't
take him. . . . She was about as kind-hearted as a goddam wolf."

Holden's awareness of sham sensitizes him to its manifestations wherever it appears: in the pseudo-religious Christmas spec-
tacle at Radio City ("I can't see anything religious or pretty, for
God's sake, about a bunch of actors carrying crucifixes all over
the stage"); in ministers with "Holy Joe" voices; in magazine
fiction, with its "lean-jawed guys named David" and "phony girls
named Linda or Marcia"; and in the performance of a gifted

night-club pianist as well as that of the Lunts. His reaction to the performances of all three is a comment on the relationship between virtuosity and integrity: "If you do something *too* good, then, after a while, if you don't watch it, you start showing off. And then you're not as good any more." Both mock humility and casual bravura are dangerous to the integrity of the individual: Holden finds no "naturalness" in the finished and most artistic performers in his world. His world, he comes to feel, is full of obscenities, both figurative and actual; even a million years would be inadequate to erase all the obscenities scribbled on all the walls. His week-end in New York reminds him of the time an alumnus of Pencey visited the school and inspected the doors in the men's toilet to see if his initials were still carved there. While he searched for this memento of his past, he solemnly gave platitudinous advice to the boys. The glaring disparity between what even "good guys" say and what they do is enough to make Holden despair of finding anyone, except his sister Phoebe, with whom he can communicate honestly.

A few things Holden encounters on his voyage through the metropolis make him "feel better." Like Huck, who has to retreat regularly to the river, to reestablish his contacts with his sources of value, Holden several times meets perfectly "natural" things which delight him: the kettle-drummer in the orchestra, who never looks bored, but who bangs his drums "so nice and sweet, with this nervous expression on his face"; a Dixieland song recorded by a Negro girl who doesn't make it sound "mushy" or "cute"; and the sight of a family coming out of church. But these incidents merely serve to reveal in sharper contrast the phoniness and the tinsel of the adult world which seeks to victimize Holden, and which, in the end, finally does. Like Huck, he finds himself at the mercy of the kindly enemy. The realist's sharp perceptions of the world about him are treated either as the uncivilized remarks of an ignorant waif or—supreme irony!—as lunacy.

In addition to being comic masterpieces and superb portrayals of perplexed, sensitive adolescence, these two novels thus deal obliquely and poetically with a major theme in American life, past and present—the right of the nonconformist to assert his nonconformity, even to the point of being "handled with a chain." In them, 1884 and 1951 speak to us in the idiom and accent of two youthful travelers who have earned their passports to literary immortality.

————

Note: An article by Arthur Heiserman and James E. Miller, Jr., entitled "J. D. Salinger: Some Crazy Cliff," *WHR,* X (Spring 1956), 129-137, which relates the adventures of Holden and Huck to the traditional theme of the Quest, places them in the company of Stephen Dedalus, Ishmael, Hans Castorp, and Dostoievski's Idiot, and contains many illuminating comparisons. My article having been accepted by *CE* before the appearance of the Heiserman-Miller article, the numerous parallels between the two can be attributed only to coincidental simultaneous generation. /80/

V

Mark Twain and J. D. Salinger: A Study in Literary Continuity

EDGAR BRANCH

In J. D. Salinger's *The Catcher in the Rye* Holden Caulfield reflects on Mr. Antolini, his former teacher, from whose homosexual pettings he has just fled in panic: "I started thinking that even if he was a flit he certainly'd been very nice to me. I thought how he hadn't minded it when I'd called him up so late, and how he'd told me to come right over . . . And how he went to all that trouble giving me that advice about finding out the size of your mind and all . . ." Huckleberry Finn, in his "close place" a century earlier, muses on his best teacher, Jim: "I . . . got to thinking over our trip down the river; and I see Jim . . . standing my watch on top of his'n, . . . so I could go on sleeping; and see him how glad he was when I come back out of the fog . . . and such-like times; and would always call me honey, and pet me and do everything he could think of for me . . ." Huck can always depend on Jim; their physical relationship is consciously innocent. But Mr. Antolini is Holden's last adult refuge in his disintegrating world. Huck, resolving his inner conflict by a free moral decision, takes immediate bold steps to help Jim. But Holden becomes "more depressed and screwed up" than ever after fleeing Mr. Antolini. Ominously, as he walks down Fifth Avenue, he feels he is disappearing. He retreats to the Museum of Natural History, the "place where the mummies were" and a favorite childhood haunt that he remembers as "so nice and peaceful"—like Huck's raft. But even there life-obscenity in-

From *American Quarterly*, IX (Summer 1957), 144-158. Copyright by American Studies Association. Reprinted by permission of the author and *American Quarterly*.

trudes—Huck's raft has its Duke and Dauphin too—and he learns that "You can't ever find a place that's nice and peaceful, because there isn't any." Each of these experienced boys knows all about fraud /144/ and violence but retains the charity of an innocent heart. Each is a measure of the need and possibility for human love in his society.

Holden's society differs as dramatically from Huck's as does a Broadway traffic jam from a raft drifting down the Mississippi a long century ago. Yet a flight down the river and a flight through New York streets turn out to be not so different after all. The pattern of Holden's experience is essentially Huck's. Salinger's writing carries familiar rhythms and attitudes. The creative imaginations of these two authors who fuse given fact and boyish consciousness into expressive, dramatized narrative are strikingly similar. *The Catcher in the Rye*, in fact, is a kind of *Huckleberry Finn* in modern dress. This paper does not propose to reveal any direct, "real" or conscious "influences"—if these exist at all—that *Huckleberry Finn* had upon Salinger's novel. Nor is its purpose to compare the "then" and "now" of American society through the illustrative use of these books. Rather, it attempts to bare one nerve of cultural continuity in America by dissecting some literary relationships between the two novels.

II

Consider first the narrative patterns and styles.

Huck initially flees conventionalities, constraint and terror. On the river he meets murderous thieves, a treacherous fog, Negro-hunters and a steamboat that rips through the raft and thrusts him among feuding country gentility. He lives with professional crooks who fatten on "greenhorns" and "flatheads." He sees a harmless drunk shot dead and a Southern Colonel almost lynched, observes some theatrical obscenities and at great personal risk saves the inheritance of three innocent girls. Experience teaches Huck that truth is usually weak, trouble best avoided and evil often inevitable. It confirms his love of beauty and peaceful security. But notably in his greatest struggle, over Jim, he acts spontaneously and defiantly for goodness. Huck eventually comes to the Phelps plantation, the homelike place where Jim finds freedom and where Huck will take leave of "sivilization" by going West.

Holden Caulfield, intensely troubled, escapes initially from the stupid constraints and violence of his prep school life. Like Huck, he enters a jungle world, New York City, where he knows his way around but from which he is alienated. There for two hectic days and nights he steers his course through battering adventures with fearsome "dopes," "fakers," "morons" and sluggers. On this journey Holden's Jim is primarily the recurring image of Jane Gallagher, an old friend who needs love and whom he loves with strange unawareness. Holden's Jim is also all little children, whom he would save from adult sexuality. Like Huck, Holden has a conflict. His adolescent sexual urges are somehow entangled with /145/ what is predatory in the "mean guys" he hates. They befoul his sense of the fine and good. Although not as self-sufficient as Huck, Holden is usually as realistic, and he too loves beauty and peace. Yet he values goodness above know-how, sophistication, style, success. After a secret visit home, he plans to lead a hermit's life in the West, but is reconciled to the city by the love of his little sister Phoebe. Physically weakened and psychically wounded, he is last seen recuperating in a sanitarium. Clearly Mark Twain and Salinger present parallel myths of American youth confronting his world—Huck Finn over many months, when time was expendable; Holden over two days when, Salinger seems to imply, time is rapidly running out.

Each novel employs an appropriate first person vernacular. Holden has the more "educated" vocabulary, he speaks with a modern schoolboy's idiom and slang and he can spell. Also he can swear. Both boys observe accurately and swiftly. Both are artists of deadpan, yet can subtly convey the interplay of feeling and scene. Huck arrives at the Phelps farm: "When I got there it was all still and Sunday-like, and hot and sunshiny—the hands was gone to the fields; and there was them kind of faint dronings of bugs and flies in the air that makes it seem so lonesome and like everybody's dead and gone; and if a breeze fans along and quivers the leaves, it makes you feel mournful, because you feel like it's spirits whispering—spirits that's been dead ever so many years—and you always think they're talking about *you*. As a gen-

eral thing it makes a body wish *he* was dead, too, and done with
it all." Holden observes New York's streets from a taxicab:
"What made it worse, it was so quiet and lonesome out, even
though it was Saturday night. I didn't see hardly anybody on the
street. Now and then you just saw a man and a girl crossing a
street, with their arms around each other's waists and all, or a
bunch of hoodlumy-looking guys and their dates, all of them
laughing like hyenas at something you could just bet wasn't
funny. New York's terrible when somebody laughs on the street
very late at night. You can hear it for miles. It makes you feel so
lonesome and depressed. I kept wishing I could go home."

Huck's speech, usually dispassionate and matter-of-fact, is re-
laxed and flexibly rhythmical. Holden, frequently conscious of
the smothering omnipresence of sex, draws most things taut. Nervous, jerky reiteration often points up his emotional tensions. His
speech is sometimes raucous and jarring. He tends to rail and
condemn. Huck's direct apprehension gives us an objective recording rich in implication. His vision etches an open world,
clear, solid, real, with living characters moving autonomously
in it. Holden's tense outpouring is a convincing expression of
his psychological unrest and of the release he is finding in psychiatric treatment. His speech carries hints of the frantic over-
tones of a Poe character speaking from a mad-/146/house (hu-
manized by delightful comedy), and his world and its people,
though violently alive, revolve in the whirlpool of his egocentric-
ity. Both styles are effectively ironic and humorous.

Perhaps Huck's profoundest relation to life is an animal faith,
an acceptance of reality that assimilates the irrational and cruel
even while it condemns them through exposure. That acceptance
promotes a classic simplicity of style, the more dignified for the
dark undertones present. But Holden's rejection and disgust create a feverish modern dissonance. Alienation is expressed by obsessive revelation, sometimes more suggestive of Theodor Fischer
in Mark Twain's *The Mysterious Stranger* than of Huck Finn.
Holden's speech is indeed suited to his neurotic experience of
the all-engulfing modern city. Huck's speech is equally well suited
to his personality and to what Mark Twain had to say about a
vanished era, a time permitting Huck's hard won victory over self
and circumstance. Salinger's adaptation of the language to his

hero's speech habits, character and times points up the stylistic continuity between the two books. . . . /147/

[Sections III and IV are omitted here. In Section III Mr. Branch provides—in answer to the question, "What experience brings Holden to the sanitarium?"—a detailed consideration of the events of the novel. Section IV is an extended discussion of the characterization of the hero in both Twain's and Salinger's novels.]

V

Huckleberry Finn and *The Catcher in the Rye* are akin also in ethical-social import. Each book is a devastating criticism of American society and voices a morality of love and humanity.

In many important matters, as we have just seen, Huck and Holden—not to speak of others like Jim and Phoebe—affirm goodness, honesty and loyalty. Huck does so almost unconsciously, backhandedly, often against his conventional conscience, and Holden does so with an agonizing self-consciousness and a bitter spirit. In each the perception of innocence is radical: from their mouths come pessimistic judgments damning the social forms that help make men less than fully human. "Human beings *can* be awful cruel to one another," observes Huck after seeing the Duke and Dauphin tarred and feathered. And Huck assumes his share of the guilt. Holden, with searingly honest insight that gets to the root of sadistic practices and class jealousies, remarks: "I can even get to hate somebody, just *looking* at them, if they have cheap suitcases with them. . . . it's really hard to be roommates with people if your suitcases are much better than theirs . . . You think if they're intelligent . . . they don't give a damn whose suitcases are better, but they do. They really do." To Aunt Sally's question whether anybody was hurt in the steamboat accident, Huck replies, "No'm. Killed a nigger," and the blindness of a civilization is bared with terrible casualness. The same ironic exposure comes in Holden's apology for having to like a girl before he can get sexy—"I mean *really* sexy"—with her. So he remarks, "My sex life stinks." And Carl Luce, the modern expert on love, answers: "Naturally it does, for God's sake."

Such examples might easily be multiplied: the vision is often identical. Yet we must grant that the reliability and quality of

Holden's vision are complicated, far beyond Huck's straightfor-
ward objectivity, by the loss he has sustained. As Holden recognizes, he is mentally ill. "I don't get hardly anything out of anything. I'm in bad shape. I'm in *lousy* shape." Bad as the modern
world is, his view of it adds a distortion not found in Huck's picture. Almost everyone in Holden's world is "phony"—headmasters, students, alumni, bar-tenders, movie actors, movie goers,
people who say "Glad to've met you" or "Good luck!" or
"Grand!," virile handshakers, /153/ Holy Joe ministers, even partially bald men who hopefully comb their hair over the bald spot.
The book reeks with Holden's revulsion and nausea. He experiences things in an aura of disgusting physical details. The park
is "lousy" with "dog crap, globs of spit and cigar butts." A chair
is "vomity" looking. A cab smells as though someone had "tossed
his cookies in it." Moreover, although Holden keeps his innocent
heart, his adolescence has riddled the innocence of mind, that
naiveté, which Huck in good measure still possesses. What Holden's heart seeks and responds to, his mind sees is violated every
where by the mere fact of human maturity. Adult activities become expressive masks for adult sexuality. The four-letter word
he reads with horror—and erases—on the wall of Phoebe's school,
follows him wherever he goes. In the quiet tomb of Pharaoh in
the Museum, he feels at peace for the first time—until suddenly
he sees the same word in red crayon on the wall. Despairingly,
hysterically, he thinks that even in death he will not escape that
word which someone surely will write on his tombstone. A great
difference between the two boys is measured by Huck's sensitive
but reserved opinion of the obscene words on the wall of the
abandoned house floating down the June rise: "the ignorantest
kind of words . . ."

Certainly if Huck's vision reveals both the limitations and
promises of democracy—the hope and despair—Holden's, in direct descent from Huck's, focuses upon the despair. In the predatory wasteland of the city, Holden can foresee no future refuge
or good. (Is it by accident that some lines of weary futility from
"The Love Song of J. Alfred Prufrock" are echoed in Holden's
words to Sally Hayes: "It wouldn't be the same at all. You don't
see what I mean at all"?) If he and Sally were married, Holden
knows he would be an office worker "making a lot of dough, and

riding to work in . . . Madison Avenue buses, and reading newspapers, and playing bridge all the time, and going to the movies and seeing a lot of stupid shorts and coming attractions and newsreels." He accurately describes the commercialized Christmas spirit as something over which "old Jesus probably would've puked if He could see it." He damns the competitive drive for status. Even the cab drivers, primitives of the city, are suspicious, raw-nerved. And nowhere is there peace. Holden's view of modern war concludes: "I'm sort of glad they've got the atomic bomb invented. If there's ever another war, I'm going to sit right the hell on top of it. I'll volunteer for it . . ." Neurotic or not, Holden's criticism often hits home.

Like Holden, Huck knows the meaning of respectable routine, competition and violence, but the difference is that what is organized nightmare in Holden's world is merely nascent in Huck's. Everyone can remember /154/ the brutal and degenerate persons Huck encounters and some of the dozen or more corpses that bloody up his story. Holden's society holds far more possibilities for horror and depravity, and on a massive scale. Feverishly, obsessively on the move, it has more irritants and fewer profound satisfactions than does Huck's. Holden's cherished memory of one little duck pond in Central Park replaces Huck's Jackson's Island and lazy days on the Mississippi. The three or four lights Huck sees, "twinkling where there were sick folks, maybe," are not so much, compared to the health, the beauty, the freedom of the river. The sparkling metropolis Holden sees looming over the forlorn duck pond is inescapable, portentous. The life Huck explores, despite its evil and treachery, is still daring and redemptive, not just sodden, mean and self-destructive.

Given such contrasting conditions, what moral destiny confronts the individual in the worlds Salinger and Mark Twain create? Like the Central Park ducks in winter, Holden is essentially homeless, frozen out. But Huck, although an outcast, is a true home-maker wherever he is. Allie's baseball mitt is all that is left to Holden of Allie's love, and unlike Huck, he seems unable to break through the ring of hostility to find new sources of affection. Deprived of real opportunity for the sort of soul-shaking sacrifice Huck makes for Jim, Holden expresses his love for Phoebe by the gift of a phonograph record—which breaks. Of greater significance, Huck has Jim; but Holden, so desperately in need of love, is one of the loneliest characters in fiction. Obviously Huck is not as critically wounded as Holden. He has far more resilience, a stronger power of renewal. Necessity shows him the wisdom of prudence, and his natural environment provides therapeutic primal sanities. Both boys are rebels—with a difference. Huck can often go naked, but Holden can defy convention only by wearing his "corny" red hunting cap. Capable of making a free choice, Huck outwits his enemies and rises above the compulsions within. He is a practical rebel like Thoreau. He runs away to confront and modify reality, and thereby he proves, for his day, the explosive force of individual ethical action. Holden runs off too, but his actions are usually ineffective, and the path of escape leads him deeper into the mire of his personal difficulties.

Huckleberry Finn, in short, recognizes both necessity and freedom, the restrictions limiting moral accomplishment and its possibility. *The Catcher in the Rye* leaves us doubtful that the individual, even assisted by the analyst's best efforts, can ever truly escape the double trap of society and self. How well the two concluding scenes contrast these moral outlooks! Throughout *The Catcher in the Rye* Holden makes, and is, a telling criticism of our civilization: his "madness" in itself is a damning fact of our times; yet, doubly damning, what the "madman" says is often true, /155/ what he feels often unimpeachable. Supremely ironical, then, is our last glimpse of Holden making recovery and adjustment in the sanitarium—a prelude to compromise in the outside world—as Father Peter in Mark Twain's *The Mysterious Stranger* can not do. Holden says: "I sort of *miss* everybody I told about. Even old Stradlater and Ackley, for instance. I think I even miss that goddam Maurice. It's funny. Don't ever tell anybody anything. If you do, you start missing everybody." Modern therapy takes over, Holden will return. For Holden's sake we wouldn't have it otherwise, even though it's a return to the big money and dopey newsreels. But we remember Huck with admiration and with confidence in his personal future as, Jim freed and the Duke and Dauphin in limbo, he says: "I reckon I got to light out for the Territory ahead of the rest, because Aunt Sally she's going to adopt me and sivilize me and I can't stand it. I been there before."

No wonder Holden wants to remain forever the catcher in the rye—*his* free Territory—oblivious to the trap that maturity finally springs. His recessive traits suggest that the logical, perhaps desirable, end for him and his civilization is the pure silence of death, the final release from imperfect life. *Huckleberry Finn,* as Philip Young has recently realized, appeals to rescuing death in the series of escapes—gliding, still and dark—made by Huck and Jim as the raft slips into the flowing, mythic river.[1] Huck, too, has guilt-feelings that, if sufficiently intensified, could conceivably lead to self-destruction. But such suggestions are muted in Huck's story, for Huck is committed to life. In Salinger's book death symbols are more pronounced, and death openly fascinates Holden not only for its horror but for the peaceful refuge it offers from the consciousness of life. Beneath the appealing and often hilarious humor, comparable to some of the best of Mark Twain's, life is felt in this book fundamentally as a ceaseless, pushing round of activity that one would be well rid of. Holden carries with him a dim sense of the eternal and transcendental. He is something like a soul unknowingly striving to rise from the muck of this world to the peace of nirvana. Jane Gallagher is always beyond his reach; he must settle for Sally Hayes, the "queen of the Phonies." Like Teddy McArdle in Salinger's story "Teddy," Holden might have called his contemporaries a "bunch of apple-eaters." Like Jean in Salinger's "De Daumier—Smith's Blue Period," Holden might have felt that in this life he "would always at best be a visitor in a garden of enamel urinals and bedpans, with a sightless, wooden dummy-deity standing by . . ." But for Jean, "the sun came up." Sudden spiritual insight transforms that garden into a "shimmering field of /156/ exquisite, twice-blessed, enamel flowers." Nirvana is here and now. Holden, of course, has hardly begun to find the peace and illumination inherent in a full understanding of the Zen koan inscribed in Salinger's second book, *Nine Stories:*

[1] Philip Young, *Ernest Hemingway* (New York: Rinehart and Company, 1952), p. 181 ff. /156/

We know the sound of two hands clapping.
But what is the sound of one hand clapping?

but the urge to find them works deeply within him. Salinger's social criticism, it would seem, has a mystical base, a support more profound than mere belief in Holden's Christian virtues, though that belief is present too. It constantly implies a religious feeling, possibly a conviction, that dimly hints a way out of the life-trap. Mark Twain's social criticism in *Huckleberry Finn* is more simply that of the rational democrat and humanitarian who has not lost faith in the practical effectiveness of the good heart on this earth.

We have seen that *Huckleberry Finn* and *The Catcher in the Rye* share certain ethical and social attitudes. Yet Salinger's critical view assumes a cultural determinism that in *Huckleberry Finn,* although always present, permits freedom through self-guidance. Salinger's viewpoint also draws upon a mystical sense merely inchoate in Mark Twain's imagination. We have seen too that Holden's neuroticism is both literary cause and social effect. It is Salinger's means of etching the modern picture the more deeply, and a product of the culture it so sweepingly condemns on moral grounds. But Mark Twain's moral vision is projected through the prevailing normality of Huck's temperament. It is eminently central; fundamentally there is nothing rigged about Huck's experience or eccentric in his responses. So Huck on a raft, as profoundly symbolic today as Thoreau in his cabin, is ever more meaningful as our national experience hurtles us along routes more menacing than the Mississippi. *The Catcher in the Rye,* always cautionary, often horrifying in moral tone, creates an overwhelming sense of that hurtling. The point is not that Salinger's moral vision is therefore defective. Rather, because his vision is lit by the sick lamps of civilization, *The Catcher in the Rye* is as appropriate to our age as *Huckleberry Finn* is to an earlier America. Salinger's novel, in fact, suggests great truths about our times, as Whitman's *Democratic Vistas* did, in polemic form, about an earlier age that was cankered, crude, materialistic, depraved. *The Catcher in the Rye* has the same awesome relevance to our collective civilized fate that more subtly pervades Mark Twain's masterpiece. Nowhere is its literary descent from

Huckleberry Finn more clearly seen than in its critical modern dramatization of moral and social themes. /157/

VI

To conclude, the two novels are clearly related in narrative pattern and style, characterization of the hero and critical import—the three areas discussed in this paper. The relationship argues the continuing vitality of Huck's archetypal story, absorbed by generations and still creatively at work in contemporary thought and art. *The Catcher in the Rye* takes its place in that literary tradition—spreading beyond Anderson, Lardner, Hemingway, Faulkner—that has one of its great sources in *Huckleberry Finn*.[2] But the literary kinship of these two novels presupposes a type of cultural continuity more basic than the dynamics of literary tradition or than the persistence of Huck's story in the popular imagination. We have seen that each author responds sensitively to the times he depicts, appropriately choosing his facts and shaping his language and meaning to portray the social and moral realities clustered in and about his hero. Yet the resulting differences do not obscure the similarity in the conformations of character and social relationships that emerge. Fundamentally these books are brothers under the skin because they reflect a slowly developing but always recognizable pattern of moral and social meaning that is part of the active experience of young Americans let loose in the world, in this century and the last. Independently and in his own right, each author has probed beneath surface facts—so dramatically contrasted in Huck's and Holden's environments—to the experiential continuity of American life. /158/

[2] See, for example: Horace Gregory (ed.), *The Portable Sherwood Anderson* (New York: The Viking Press, 1949), pp. 8-9; Irving Howe, *Sherwood Anderson* (New York: William Sloane Associates, 1951), pp. 94, 124-27; Gilbert Seldes (ed.), *The Portable Ring Lardner* (New York: The Viking Press, 1946), pp. 1-2, 13-15; Carlos Baker, *Hemingway the Writer as Artist* (Princeton, N.J.: Princeton University Press, 1952), pp. 180-81; Philip Young, *Ernest Hemingway* (New York: Rinehart and Company, 1952), pp. 159-61, 181-212; Malcolm Cowley (ed.), *The Portable Faulkner* (New York: The Viking Press, 1946), p. 22; Randall Stewart and Dorothy Bethurum (eds.), *Modern American Narration, Mark Twain, Ernest Hemingway, William Faulkner* (Chicago: Scott Foresman and Company, 1954), "Foreword." /158/

Cynical, Defiant, and Blind*

JOHN W. ALDRIDGE

Mr. Salinger's *The Catcher in the Rye*, like *The Adventures of Huckleberry Finn*, is a study in the spiritual picaresque, the journey that for the young is all one way, from holy innocence to such knowledge as the world offers, from the reality which illusion demands and thinks it sees to the illusion which reality insists, at the point of madness, we settle for. But the great difference between the two novels is the measure not merely of the change in time and history of a cultural situation, but of the changed moral circumstances in which innocence typically finds itself in crisis and lends itself to drama. The innocence of *Huckleberry Finn* is a compound of frontier ignorance, juvenile delinquency, and penny-dreadful heroism. It begs for the challenge of thugs, thieves, swindlers, and feuds, and that is what it gets and delights in, takes such delight in, in fact, that even when the dangers become real and the escapes increasingly narrow, we know it is all in fun, that this is innocence living out its concocted daydream of glory in which no one really gets hurt, and even the corpses climb to their feet and dust themselves off at dinnertime. Still, in the suspension of our disbelief, in the planned illusion of the novel itself, the innocence and the world of violence appear to be seriously and effectively opposed. The innocence is the raft to which Huck and Jim, in flight from the dangers of the shore, make their narrow escapes. It is the river itself, time, faith, /129/ continuity, moving endlessly and dependably beside and be-

* Title supplied by the editors.
From *In Search of Heresy: American Literature in An Age of Conformity.*
Copyright 1956 by John W. Aldridge. Published by McGraw-Hill Book Company, Inc. Reprinted by permission of Mr. Aldridge.

tween the temporary and futile altercations of men. And it is the raft and the river together which give the innocence of *Huckleberry Finn* its focus and breadth of implication, so that it exists at once on the level of naivete at which it responds to adventure and on the level of maturity at which it lends itself to allegory.

The innocence of Mr. Salinger's Holden Caulfield, on the other hand, is a compound of urban intelligence, juvenile contempt, and *New Yorker* sentimentalism, and the only challenge it begs for, the only challenge it has left to beg for, is the challenge of the genuine, the truly human, in a world which has lost both the means of adventure and the means of love. But it is in the nature of Holden's dilemma, his spiritual confinement in this world, that he lacks a concrete basis, can find no concrete embodiment, for the ideal against which he judges, and finds wanting, the life around him. He has objects for his contempt but no objects other than his sister for his love—no raft, no river, no Jim, and no Tom. He is forced, consequently, simply to register his contempt, his developing disillusionment; and it is inevitable that he should seem after a time to be registering it in a vacuum, for just as he can find no concrete equivalent in life for the ideal which he wishes life to embody, so the persons on whom he registers his contempt seem inadequate to it and unjustly accused by it. The boorish prep school roommate, the hypocritical teacher, the stupid women in the Lavender Room, the resentful prostitute, the conventional girl friend, the bewildered cab driver, the affected young man at the theater, the old friend who reveals that his interest in Holden is homosexual—these people are all /130/ truly objectionable and deserve the places Holden assigns them in his secret hierarchy of class with its categories of phonies, bores, deceivers, and perverts. But they are nonetheless human, albeit dehumanized, and constitute a fair average of what the culture affords. They are part of the truth which Holden does not see and, as it turns out, is never able to see—that this is what one part of humanity *is;* the lies, the phoniness, the hypocrisy are the compromises which innocence is forced by the world to make. This is the reality on which Holden's illusion is finally broken, but no recognition follows, and no conversion. He remains at the end what he was at the beginning—

cynical, defiant, and blind. And as for ourselves, there is identification but no insight, a sense of pathos but not of tragedy. It may be Mr. Salinger made the most of his subject, but his subject was not adequate to his intention, just as Holden's world is not adequate to his contempt, and that is probably because it does not possess sufficient humanity to make the search for humanity dramatically feasible. . . . /131/

VII

Incommunicability in Salinger's
The Catcher in the Rye

CHARLES H. KEGEL

Admirers of J. D. Salinger's *The Catcher in the Rye* ought to have welcomed the exciting analysis of that novel in the Spring, 1956 issue of *WHR*. One may not agree in every particular with Heiserman and Miller's "J. D. Salinger: Some Crazy Cliff," yet the article serves as a very convincing notice to students of recent American fiction that *The Catcher in the Rye* deserves careful, critical attention. Notwithstanding the rather insensitive and highhanded action of puritanical censorship groups like the Detroit Police Department, which removed the work from Detroit book stalls as "pornographic trash," many once-through-quickly readers have sensed in Salinger's novel a dignity which transcends the apprehension of prudish minds. Heiserman and Miller have gone still further and have shown that that dignity governs both the theme and the structure of the novel. By doing so, they have sent us back for a fresh and more serious look.

The Catcher in the Rye can certainly be read, as Heiserman and Miller suggest, as a double-barreled quest: first, for "acceptance, stability, a life embosomed upon what is known and can be trusted," second, for "a Truth which is unwarped by stability." Without contradicting this interpretation, however, the novel can also be read as Holden Caulfield's quest for communicability with his fellow man, and the hero's first person after-the-fact narration indicates, of course, that he has been successful in his quest.

Like Stephen Dedalus of *A Portrait of the Artist as a Young*

From *Western Humanities Review*, XI (Spring 1957), 188-190. Reprinted by permission.

Man, Caulfield is in search of the Word. His problem is one of communication: as a teen-ager, he simply cannot get through to the adult world which surrounds him; as a *sensitive* teen-ager, he cannot even get through to others of his own age. The same impulse which caused Dedalus to contemplate subtle and slight differences in the meaning of words—"Canker is a disease of plants,/Cancer one of animals"—activates a comparable sensitivity in Caulfield, especially with word formulas. After his interview, for example, with Mr. Spencer, his history teacher at Pencey, Caulfield says, "He yelled something at me, but I couldn't exactly hear him. I'm pretty sure he yelled 'Good luck!' at me. I hope not. I hope to hell not. I'd never yell 'Good luck!' at anybody. It sounds terrible, when you think about it."

Caulfield places most of his attention, however, on the sympathetic rapport which must exist between communicators. He asks but one thing of those he talks with, sincerity; he asks only that they *mean* what they say. If they tell him, as does Maurice, the elevator operator, that the price of goods is "Five bucks a throw," Caulfield expects to pay only five dollars. If they ask, as did Mrs. Antolini, about the health of his mother, Caulfield expects sincere concern about his mother's health; he expects that the questioner /188/ *actually* wants an answer to her question and will not interrupt him half way through it. Throughout the novel, he is troubled with people who are not listening to what he says, who are talking only to be polite, not because they want to communicate ideas. Like Hamlet, a "sad, screwed-up type guy" like himself, Caulfield is bothered by words and word formulas which only "seem," which are "phony." The honesty and sincerity which he cannot find in others, he attempts to maintain in himself. His repeated assertions that something he has said is *"really"* so demonstrate his attempt to keep faith with the Word. He is particularly distressed by the occasional realization that he too must be phony to exist in the adult world. With regard to the insincere "Glad to've met you" formula, he laments that "if you want to stay alive, you have to say that stuff, though."

As I have indicated, the main reason for Caulfield's communicative difficulty lies in his absolute hatred of phoniness. And he finds that phoniness, that hypocrisy, not only in the world of his personal contacts, but in the world of art as well. He detests phony books, phony music, phony movies and plays. He sees Hamlet as a "sad, screwed-up type guy" and wants him played that way instead of "like a goddam general." Likewise he is bothered by the way people "clap for the wrong things" and hence corrupt the promising artist. Very poignantly he understands the plight of Ernie, the piano player, or of brother D. B., once a sincere writer, but now "out in Hollywood . . . being a prostitute." He wants more Thomas Hardys—"old Thomas Hardy" Caulfield calls him endearingly—because he knows that the creator of "old Eustacia Vye" refused to prostitute himself, refused to be phony.

Holden Caulfield's inability to communicate satisfactorily with others represents itself symbolically in the uncompleted telephone calls and undelivered messages which permeate the novel. Seeing a phone booth is almost more than he can stand, for he almost constantly feels like "giving somebody a buzz." On fifteen separate occasions he gets the urge to communicate by phone, yet only four calls are completed, and those with unfortunate results. Usually the urge dies without his having even attempted to place the call; he seems fearful of what the results will be and rationalizes, "I wasn't in the mood." Likewise, none of the several verbal messages he asks others to deliver for him gets through to the intended receiver; he simply cannot succeed in making contact.

Growing logically out of this prolonged incommunicability is Caulfield's intention to become a deaf-mute. So repulsed is he by the phoniness around him that he despairs of communicating with anybody, and in a passage fraught with import, he contemplates a retreat within himself.

I figured I could get a job at a filling station somewhere, putting gas and oil in people's cars. I didn't care what kind of a job it was, though. Just so people didn't know me /189/ and I didn't know anybody. I thought what I'd do was, I'd pretend I was one of those deaf-mutes. That way I wouldn't have to have any goddam stupid useless conversations with anybody. If anybody wanted to tell me something, they'd have to write it on a piece of paper and shove it over to me. They'd get bored as hell doing that after a while, and then I'd be through with having conversations for the rest of my life. Everybody'd think I was

just a poor deaf-mute bastard and they'd leave me alone. . . . I'd cook
all my own food, and later on, if I wanted to get married or something,
I'd meet this beautiful girl that was also a deaf-mute and we'd get married. She'd come and live in my cabin with me, and if she wanted to say
anything to me, she'd have to write it on a goddam piece of paper, like
everybody else.

Significantly, the fact that a message does get through to
Phoebe—the only successful communication in the entire novel—
leads toward the abandonment of the deaf-mute retreat. The
Rousseauistic-Wordsworthian theme of childhood innocence and
sincerity which Salinger had played upon so effectively in "For
Esmé—with Love and Squalor" works its magic again. It is
Phoebe who furnishes the clue to the solution of his problem,
and when he refuses to ride the carrousel with her and thus gives
up his idealistic attempts "to grab for the gold ring," he has initiated his transition from adolescence to adulthood. He does not,
of course, capitulate to the phoniness of life, but he attains an
attitude of tolerance, understanding, and love which will make it
endurable. There can be no doubt but that when he returns to
New York—for he, unlike Dedalus, will return home—he will be
in the mood to give "old Jane a buzz." /190/

VIII

J. D. Salinger: Rare Quixotic Gesture

IHAB HASSAN

> Through our own recovered innocence we
> discern the innocence of our neighbors.
>
> THOREAU
>
> We know the sound of two hands clapping.
> But what is the sound of one hand clapping?
>
> A ZEN KOAN

I

The worried hush with which each Salinger story is now anticipated in the pages of the *New Yorker* has become almost audible.
Rumors seek the author in his stern retirement from the public
glare and dwell on his silences with the insistence criticism re-
serves to his speech. The satiric author of American adolescence
in revolt already commands the authority of a prophet, the sanctity of a guru, and the teasing charm of a Zen Master. And yet it
was only in 1951 that the apotheosis of *The Catcher in the Rye*
as a Book-of-the-Month selection took place. Since then American
youth has learned to speak of Salinger and Dostoyevsky in the
same breath, and to read them in the same measure, as a recent
survey in *The Nation* claimed. This is all very well. James Dean
and Elvis Presley have also had their moments. But we do Salinger ill-service to base his reputation on anything less enduring
than his art.

Salinger, of course, has written some of the best fiction of our

From *Radical Innocence: Studies in the Contemporary American Novel* by
Ihab Hassan. Copyright © 1961 by Princeton University Press. Reprinted by
permission. Originally published in slightly different form in *Western Review*,
XXI (Summer 1957), 261-280.

time. His voice is genuine, new, and startingly uneven. In his work we find no showy or covert gesture in the direction of Symbolism or Naturalism, Gothic design or Freudian chiaroscuro; and indeed there was a time when we were unsure whether /259/ his intentions came closer to those of Fielding or Firbank, Twain or Chekov. If close to anything, Salinger's intentions are probably more in keeping with Fitzgerald's idea of self-created innocence and Lardner's biting renderings of corruption, with the spiritual assumptions of Martin Buber, and, more recently, with those of primitive Christianity and Zen. Yet to speak of his uniqueness in these terms is simply to indulge in the small talk of criticism. We are more anxious, nowadays, to discover the opportunities of literary significance, the conditions of heresy, and protocols of formal excellence. We question *Kitch* and middle-brow art to the extent that we consume it in prodigious quantities, and are adversely disposed to any serious work that carries the aura of either. It is in response to this line of criticism that the work of Salinger proves itself to be seriously engaged by a current and a traditional aspect of reality in America.

The traditional aspect wears no elaborate disguise. It is the new look of the American Dream, specifically dramatized by the encounter between a vision of innocence and the reality of guilt, between the forms love and power have tended to assume in America. The natural locus of that conflict in the work of Salinger is childhood and adolescence. In them the counterplay of hope and despair, truth and mendacity, participation and withdrawal, commands a full range of comic, that is ambivalent, reference: it is the old story of the self against the world in outlines blurred by a mass society. To say as Fiedler does that the "images of childhood and adolescence haunt our greatest works as an unintended symbolic confession of the inadequacy we sense but cannot remedy" is to view a profound truth in a partial perspective.[1] Nostalgia . . . is the result of our compulsion to reenact the story of the American fall. We do not always resist it well. But nostalgia, when it is known to itself, has its ironic and artistic uses. The retreat to childhood is not simply an escape; it is also criticism, an affirmation of values which, for better or worse, we still cher-

---

[1] Leslie Fiedler, *An End to Innocence* (Boston, 1955), p. 209. /260/

ish; /260/ and the need for adolescent disaffiliation, the refusal of
initiation, expresses the need to reconceive American reality.

Yet it is hard for some critics to recognize that no act of denial
in Salinger's work is without some dramatic and social correlative, which is more than we can generally say of equally serious
novelists writing today. The urban, suburban, and exurban society which circumscribes Salinger's child and adolescent characters—the white dinner, not black leather, jacket circle—is usually
well specified. About that society we have recently learned a good
deal. We know that it exhibits a sad decay of genuine sensibility
and even of simple truth. There are, no doubt, many opportunities of significant action still left in it, and we are justified in re-
questing our best writers to discover them. But the nature of action is such that its results are seldom commensurate with its mo-
tives. And the reverse is no less true. The anger of a child confronted for the first time with the force of anti-Semitism, the spirit
of an adolescent who dons a red hunting cap in New York City,
the tender cruelty of a woman, who is bereaved of her lover, toward her child, even the suicide of a misfit genius, can suggest
possibilities of action which we hastily reject in favor of a mechanical gesture at the polling booth. Social realities are no
doubt repressed in the work of Salinger—note how gingerly he
handles his Jews—and this puts a limit on the total significance
we can accord to it. Yet it is by what an author manages to *drama-
tize* that we must finally judge him.

The dramatic conflict which so many of Salinger's stories present obviously does not lend itself to sociological classification. It
is more loving and particular, and it partakes of situations that
have been traditionally available to literature. The conflict,
however, suggests a certain polarity between what might be
called, with all due exaggeration, the Assertive Vulgarian and
the Responsive Outsider. Both types recur with sufficient frequency to warrant the distinction, and their interplay defines
much that is most central to Salinger's fiction. The /261/ Vulgarian, who carries the burden of squalor, stands for all that is crude,
venal, self-absorbed, and sequacious in our culture. He has no
access to knowledge or feeling or beauty, which makes him all
the more invulnerable, and his relationship to the world is largely

predicated by Buber's I-It dyad. He or she can be rich or poor: Evelyn Cooney in "Elaine," Mrs. Ford and the Croftses in "The Inverted Forest," Sandra and Mrs. Snell in "Down at the Dinghy," Joanie in "Pretty Mouth and Green My Eyes," The Matron of Honor in "Raise High the Roof Beam, Carpenters," Maurice, Stradlater, or any number of others in *The Catcher in the Rye*. These, in a sense, are Spiritual Tramps, as Seymour called his wife in "A Perfect Day for Banana Fish," though he might have better said it of her mother. The Outsider, on the other hand, carries the burden of love. The burden makes of him sometimes a victim, and sometimes a scapegoat saint. His life is like "a great inverted forest/with all foliage underground."[2] It is a quick, generous, and responsive life, somehow preserved against hardness and corruption, and always attempting to reach out from its isolation in accordance with Buber's I-Thou dyad. Often there is something in the situation of the Outsider to isolate him, to set him off, however slightly, from the rest of mankind. He might be a child or an adolescent, might wear glasses or appear disfigured, might be Jewish, though seldom is he as crippled or exotic as the characters of Capote and McCullers often are. His ultimate defense, as Rilke, to whom Salinger refers, put it, is defenselessness. Raymond Ford, Boo Boo Tannenbaum (Glass) and her son, Lionel, Seymour and other members of the Glass family, Holden and Phoebe, in the previous stories, are examples of that type.

The response of these outsiders and victims to the dull or angry world about them is not simply one of withdrawal: it often takes the form of a strange, quixotic gesture. The gesture, one feels sure, is the bright metaphor of Salinger's sensibility, /262/ the center from which meaning drives, and ultimately the reach of his commitment to past innocence and current guilt. It is a gesture at once of pure expression and of expectation, of protest and prayer, of aesthetic form and spiritual content—as Blackmur would say, it is behavior that sings. There is often something prodigal and spontaneous about it, something humorous or whimsical, something that disrupts our habits of gray acquiescence and revives our faith in the willingness of the human spirit.

[2] See J. D. Salinger, "The Inverted Forest," *Cosmopolitan*, December 1947, pp. 73-109. /262/

But above all, it gives of itself as only a *religious* gesture can. In another age, Cervantes endowed Don Quixote with the capacity to perform it, and so did Twain and Fitzgerald endow their best creations. For the gesture, after all, has an unmistakably American flourish. The quest of American adolescents, as we saw, has always been for an idea of truth. It is this very idea of truth that the quixotic gesture is constantly seeking to embody. The embodiment is style in action: the twist and tang, the stammering and improvisations, the glint and humor of Salinger's language. Hence the examples of the deserted husband who memorizes his wife's farewell note backwards, the woman who, out of pity, starts smacking her husband at the sight of any dead animal, the man about to commit suicide who makes up a story about banana fish for a little girl, the lover who calls the sprained ankle of his sweetheart Uncle Wiggily, the young man who insists on giving half a chicken sandwich to a stranger, the college girl who trains herself to pray incessantly and does so in the toilet of a restaurant, and the bridegroom who is too happy to appear at his wedding. Out of context these may well sound trite or crazy; in their proper place they are nodes of dramatic significance.

But gesture is language too. The quixotic gesture, the central dramatic metaphor, to which Salinger has committed himself defines the limits of his language and the forms his fiction takes. When the gesture aspires to pure religious expression—this is one pole—language reaches into silence. To a writer of /263/ fiction, this is a holy dead end, much as the experiments of Mallarmé, say, impose a profane—that is, aesthetic—limit on the language of poetry. (One of "The Four Statements" of Zen, we recall, is: "No dependence upon words and letters.") When, on the other hand, the gesture reveals its purely satiric content—this is the other pole—language begins to lapse into sentimentality. This is the most persistent charge leveled against Salinger. Salinger's "sentimentality," however, is not obedient to the *New Yorker* doctrine of sardonic tenderness, which is really a way of grudging life emotions that the writer feigns to indulge. But if sentimentality means a response more generous than the situation seems objectively to warrant, then Salinger may choose to plead guilty. And he would be right to do so, for the spiritual facts of our situation invite us to reconceive our notions of dramatic objectivity, and the right kind of emotional excess, nowadays, can be as effective as the sharpest irony.

Between the poles of silence and sentiment, language reels and totters. Salinger's cumbersome experiments with character, tense, and point of view in his most recent stories betray his efforts to discover a language which can reconcile the worldless impulse of love to the discursive irony of squalor. In the past, while the quixotic gesture could still convey the force of his vision, reconciliation took the shape of the short story, that genre so richly exploited by the single lyric impulse seeking embodiment in dramatic form. But the quixotic motif seems no longer commensurate with the complex spiritual states by which Salinger has lately been possessed. Language must be refracted into its components —speech, letters, diaries, etc.—and the form of the short story itself must be broken and expanded into something that is neither a short story proper nor yet a novelette. In this development, the risks Salinger has taken with his art are contained in the risks he must take with his religious view of things. /264/

II

In the two decades which constitute Salinger's professional career, he has published one novel, three novelettes, and some thirty short stories. This fair-sized body of work—fair-sized by contemporary standards but slim in comparison with the output of many earlier writers—may be classified into four "periods": the early tentative efforts, up to "The Inverted Forest," 1947; the fine stories which appeared in the *New Yorker* and were later included in the collection *Nine Stories*, 1953; *The Catcher in the Rye*, 1951; and finally the more recent narratives, beginning with "De Daumier-Smith's Blue Period," 1953, which express a new religious bent. Since the focus of our inquiry is the American novel, it is natural that the longer works of Salinger must receive our greatest attention. Salinger, however, is the kind of writer who returns to favored themes and characters with some consistency. *The Catcher in the Rye* was in fact developed from six earlier stories in which the two Caulfield brothers, Vincent and

Holden, appear; and the central sibling relation between Holden
and Phoebe is prefigured by the relation of Babe Gladwaller to
his sister, Mattie. There is also the hope some critics entertain
that the Glass family stories—all seven of them and perhaps more
to come—will be some day transmuted by a miracle of chance or
art into a novel. Finally, one must defer to the opinion Salinger
expressed of himself, even though it was expressed in 1945: "I've
been writing short stories since I was fifteen. I have trouble writing simply and naturally. . . . I am a dash man and not a miler,
and it is probable that I will never write a novel."[3] It seems
therefore an act of necessity rather than piety to consider Salinger's longer works in the light of his shorter pieces. . . . /265/

[The rest of Section II deals with Salinger's early short stories,
including some which have not been collected.]

III

The Catcher in the Rye inevitably stands out as Salinger's only
novel to date. As a "neo-picaresque," the book shows itself to be
concerned far less with the education or initiation of an adolescent than with a dramatic exposure of the manner in which
ideals are denied access to our lives and of the modes which
mendacity assumes in our urban culture. The moving, even stab-
bing, qualities of the novel derive, to some extent, from Salinger's
refusal to adopt a satirical stance. The work, instead, confirms
the saving grace of vulnerability; its protest, debunking, and
indictments presuppose a willing responsiveness on the part of
its hero.

On the surface, Holden Caulfield is Salinger's typical quixotic
hero in search, once again, of the simple truth. Actually, Holden
is in flight from mendacity rather than in search of truth, and his
sensitivity to the failures of the world is compounded with his
self-disgust. In comparison with his dear, dead brother, Allie, a
kind of redheaded saint who united intelligence and compassion
as no other member of the family could, setting for all a standard of performance which they try to recapture, Holden seems

[3] J. D. Salinger, "Backstage With Esquire," *Esquire,* October 1945, p. 34. /265/

intolerant, perhaps even harsh. The controlling mood of the novel—and it is so consistent as to be a principle of unity—is one of acute depression always on the point of breaking loose. But despair and depression are kept, throughout, in check by Holden's remarkable lack of self-interest, a quality of self-heedlessness which is nearly saintly, and by his capacity to invoke his adolescent imagination, to "horse around," when he is most likely to go to pot. These contrary pressures keep the actions of the novel in tension and keep the theme of sentimental disenchantment on the stretch; and they are sustained by a style of versatile humor. /272/

The action begins at a prep school from which Holden has flunked out, and continues in various parts of Manhattan; it covers some three days of the Christmas season. The big city, decked out in holiday splendor and gaudiness, is nevertheless unprepared for Holden's naked vision, and it seldom yields any occasions of peace, charity, or even genuine merriment. From the moment Holden leaves Pencey behind, leaves its Stradlaters and Ackleys, its oafs, creeps, and hypocrites, and dons his red hunting cap— why not, it's a mad world, isn't it?—we know that we are on to an adventure of pure self-expression, if not self-discovery.

In New York, it is once again the same story of creeps and hypocrites revealed in larger perspective. We hardly need to recapitulate the crowded incidents of the novel to see that Holden is motivated by a compelling desire to commune and communicate, a desire constantly thwarted by the phoniness, indifference, and vulgarity that surround him. He resents the conditions which force upon him the burden of rejection. In protest against these conditions, he has devised a curious game of play-acting, of harmless and gratuitous lying, which is his way of coming to terms with a blistered sensibility, and of affirming his values of truth and imagination. But above all, he is continually performing the quixotic gesture. Thus he socks Stradlater, who is twice his weight, because he suspects the latter of having seduced Jean [sic] Gallagher, without any consideration of the fact that she is the kind of girl to keep all her kings, at checkers, in the back row. He gives money away to nuns. He can read a child's notebook all day and night. He furiously rubs out obscenities from the walls of schools. And when Phoebe asks him very seriously what he would like to be, he muses on Robert Burns's song, "If a body meet a body coming through the rye," which he had heard a kid hum in the street, and answers back: ". . . I keep picturing all these kids playing some game in this big field of rye and all. Thousands of little kids, and nobody's around—nobody big, I mean /273/ —except me. And I'm standing on the edge of some crazy cliff. . . . That's all I'd do all day. I'd just be the catcher in the rye and all. I know it's crazy. . . ."[9]

A closer look at *The Catcher in the Rye* might allow us to separate its real from imaginary failings. Mr. Aldridge, for instance, taking his cue perhaps from Phoebe's comment to her brother, "You don't like *anything* that's happening," has recently observed—Maxwell Geismar makes exactly the same point—that Holden "has objects for his contempt but no objects other than his sister for his love."[10] It is true that Holden has *more* objects for his contempt than his love—this is the expense of his idealism and the price of his rebellion. But it is impossible to overlook his various degrees of affection for Allie, his dead brother, for James Castle, the boy who was killed because he wouldn't retract a statement he thought true, for the kettle drummer at Radio City, the nuns at the lunch counter, the kid humming the title song, or even the ducks in the park, without missing something of Holden's principal commitments. And his answer to Phoebe, "People never think anything is anything *really*. I'm getting goddam sick of it," may do for those who find these commitments rather slim.[11] Nor can we disallow the feeling of pity which often modifies Holden's scorn, his pity for Ackley and the girls in the Lavender Room, or his confession to Antolini that he can hate people only part of the time, and that he quickly misses those whom he may have once hated. Holden, of course, is not in the least cynical; nor is he blind except to part of the truth which he can otherwise entertain so steadily. Still, there are those who feel that the novel accords no recognition to its hero, and that it fails to enlist our sense of tragedy. The lack of recognition, the avoid-

[9] J. D. Salinger, *The Catcher in the Rye* (New York, 1953), p. 130.
[10] John W. Aldridge, *In Search of Heresy* (New York, 1956), p. 130.
[11] *The Catcher in the Rye*, p. 129. /274/

ance of conversion and initiation, is almost as inherent in the structure of the novel as it is consonant with the bias of the American novel of adolescence. The action of the book is recollected by Holden who is out West recuperating from his illness, and Holden only chooses to tell us "about this /274/ madman stuff that happened to me around last Christmas"—nothing more.[12] He refuses to relate incidents to his past or to his character, and he refuses to draw any conclusions from his experience: "If you want to know the truth, I don't *know* what I think about it. . . . About all I know is, I sort of *miss* everybody I told about. Even old Stradlater and Ackley, for instance. . . . Don't ever tell anybody anything. If you do, you start missing everybody."[13] This is an embarrassed testament of love, full of unresolved ambiguities, the only lyrical and undramatic recognition the novel can afford. The partial blindness of Holden, which has been correctly attributed to Holden's juvenile impatience with the reality of compromise, is made more serious by Salinger's failure to modify Holden's point of view by any other. In *Joseph Andrews,* for instance, the innocence of Adams is constantly criticized by the tone of the book and the nature of its comic incidents. There is also some danger that we may be too easily disarmed by the confessional candor of Salinger's novel. When Holden says time and time again, "I swear to God I'm crazy," the danger is equally great in taking Holden at his word as in totally discounting his claim. Holden does succeed in making us perceive that the world is crazy, but his vision is also a function of his own adolescent instability, and the vision, we must admit, is more narrow and biased than that of Huck Finn, Parson Adams, or Don Quixote. It is this narrowness that limits the comic effects of the work. Funny it is without any doubt, and in a fashion that has been long absent from American fiction. But we must recall that true comedy is informed by the spirit of compromise, not intransigence. Huck Finn and Augie March are both, in this sense, closer to the assumptions of comedy than Holden Caulfield. This once understood, we can see how *The Catcher in the Rye* is *both* a funny and terrifying work—traditional distinctions of modes have

[12] *Ibid.,* p. 7.
[13] *Ibid.,* p. 159. /275/

broken down in our time—a work full of pathos in the original sense of the word. But suffering is a subjective thing, and the novel's sly insistence on suffering makes it a /275/ more subjective work than the two novels which relate the adventures of Huck Finn and Augie March. Adventure is precisely what Holden does not endure; his sallies into the world are feigned; his sacrificial burden, carried with whimsey and sardonic defiance, determines his fate. The fate is that of the American rebel-victim. . . . /276/

[Section IV, omitted here, deals with Salinger's fiction published after *The Catcher in the Rye,* particularly with the stories about the Glass family. From Section V we have excerpted the conclusion.]

V

. . . In retrospect, the artistic identity of Salinger, which also may be called his limitation, appears clear enough. Despite his striking gifts for dialogue—Salinger had once expressed the hope of becoming a playwright—the broad sense of dramatic participation is lacking in his fiction. The lack is not occasioned by the refusal of Salinger's characters to engage reality; rather is it occasioned by their insistence to engage no more of reality than they can ultimately criticize. Their access to social facts remains limited. And their very identity, their recurrent types and their intransigence toward experience, often admits to their vision— and to ours, since no other vision qualifies theirs—such extremes of corruption and innocence as make the complex entanglements of life beyond their reach. Then, too, the cult they make of vulnerability, of amateurism in life, which is the very opposite of Hemingway's cult of professionalism, diffuses the pressure of Salinger's insight onto a rather thin surface. The quixotic gesture— Seymour searching for God by poking his finger into ashtrays—is made to carry a heavier burden of meaning than it can sustain. Love averts itself easily in whimsey or laughter. The highest candor requires us to praise things by adjectives no more complex than the word "nice." /288/

But from the early search for innocence to the later testament of love, from the slick adequacy of his earlier style to the tense lyrical form of his later, if not latest, stories, Salinger has kept faith with the redeeming powers of outrage and compassion. His faith in these has not always allowed him to reconcile their shifting focus or to create the forms of dramatic permanence. When reconciliation is granted, when the rare, quixotic gesture, striking through, becomes the form of fiction, incarnate and ineluctable, we see Salinger at last for what he is: an American poet, his thin and intelligent face all but lost among the countless faces of the modern city, his vision, forever lonely and responsive, troubled by the dream of innocence and riddled by the presence both of love and of squalor. What saves Salinger's vision from sentimentality is the knowledge that no man can give an object more tenderness than God accords to it. His heroes, children, adolescents, or adult victims to the affluence of their own spirit, play upon our nostalgia for a mythic American past. They also manage to raise nostalgia to the condition of hope. /289/

The Adolescent in American Fiction

FREDERIC I. CARPENTER

Like *Huck Finn, The Catcher in the Rye* is narrated in the first person, and in the vernacular, by a boy who is badly "mixed up." But both Huck and Holden are intellectually honest, and both succeed in communicating their confusion and in suggesting some of the reasons for it. Both are ambivalent, and even flaunt their confusion—Huck by praising Tom Sawyer's plans as "mixed up and splendid," and Holden by defiantly wearing his red hunting cap backwards through New York City. In the end Huck plans to "light out for the territory," and Holden thinks of fleeing West, but is dissuaded by his attachment to his family, and is sent to a psychiatrist instead.

Of course the two novels differ as much as they resemble each other, and I do not mean to suggest that *The Catcher . . .* is a rival of *Huck Finn*. Where Huck was the typical American democrat, Holden is a snob who criticizes his friends for the shabby suitcases they carry. Where Huck lived in the rich heartland of America, Holden is the product of an exclusive New York City. Salinger himself seems almost the typical New Yorker, and his short stories emphasize the emotional starvation and brittleness of the city life, which his novel only suggests. Yet his New York and its problems are perhaps as central to modern America as Mark Twain's Mississippi River was to the pioneer nineteenth century.

The quality which makes Huck Finn and Holden Caulfield

From *The English Journal,* XLVI (September 1957), 313-319. Reprinted by permission of the author and the National Council of Teachers of English. [The original article also discusses thematically related fiction by Carson McCullers and Jessamyn West.]

brothers under the skin—and which runs through all the best of these novels—is a common hatred of hypocrisy and a search for integrity. And this emerges in spite of—or perhaps as a reaction against—the love of play-acting which is a natural and inevitable aspect of all adolescence. Just as Huck plays along with Tom's mixed up schemes, and observes the deceptions of the Duke and the Dauphin with reluctant admiration, so Holden ironically admires the amatory techniques of his roommate Stradlater who speaks in "this sincere voice," and himself makes up absurd phantasies for the mother of a classmate whom he meets on the train. Yet Holden's chief contempt is for "all those phonies," and his admiration goes out to the genuine sincerity of the two nuns he meets, and of his sister Phoebe.

Perhaps the central theme of these novels of adolescence is the individual's search for genuine values. At the end Phoebe typically corrects her brother's misquotation of the poem:

—"If a body catch a body comin' through the rye"
—"It's 'if a body *meet* a body . . .' "

In the confused rye fields of life the worldly characters seek to "catch" people, and in revulsion Holden imagines "catching" all innocent children to protect them from destruction. "I know it's crazy," admits Holden, who suffers a nervous breakdown at the end. And similarly Huck Finn ended by exclaiming: "I can't stand it. I been there before." In their confusion, these heroes desperately seek truth.

But the ambivalence of adolescence, which runs after experience yet fears /315/ it, and admires the mixed up and splendid world while still idealizing innocence, merely reflects the similar ambivalence of American society. And here *The Catcher . . .* goes beyond *Huck Finn*—partly in that it describes an older boy who confronts the larger problems of sex which Huck Finn never faced, and partly in that it describes an America which also has reached "an end to innocence." Where Huck had been able to escape "civilization and its discontents" by "lighting out for the territory," now Holden must consult a psychiatrist and face those problems of growing up which our maturing society must also face.

From another perspective these same problems are described with even greater clarity and poignancy in Salinger's short story, "For Esmé—with Love and Squalor." This time the narrator is a mature American soldier, who meets an adolescent English Esmé during World War II. The clear-eyed British girl, whose father has been killed in the war, asks the American if he writes stories about "squalor" as well as "love," because she recognizes that her genteel upbringing has shielded her from experience of the dark side of life. The second half of the story then describes the chaos of the invasion of Europe, from which the narrator is saved, psychologically, by remembering the "love" of the young English Esmé. Where *The Catcher* . . . described only the confusions of innocence facing the evils of experience, "Esmé" now suggests the possible resolution of his conflict, through a recognition and acceptance of apparently "evil" experiences. The mature individual must experience and accept "squalor" as well as "love," and not try to "catch" those innocents who rush confusedly towards the experience of what may seem evil. /316/

J. D. Salinger: The Wise Child and the *New Yorker* School of Fiction

MAXWELL GEISMAR

He worked on *The Catcher in the Rye* for about ten years, J. D. Salinger told us, and when it appeared in 1951, it evoked both critical and popular acclaim. Here was a fresh voice, said Clifton Fadiman in the Book-of-the-Month Club *News*. "One can actually hear it speaking, and what it has to say is uncannily true, perceptive and compassionate." The novel was brilliant, funny, meaningful, said S. N. Behrman. It was probably the most distinguished first novel of the year, said Charles Poore in *Harper's* magazine. The real catch in the *Catcher,* said *Time,* was novelist Salinger himself, who could understand the adolescent mind without displaying one.

Salinger's short stories in the *New Yorker* had already created a stir. In undergraduate circles, and particularly in the women's colleges, this fresh voice, which plainly showed its debt to Ring Lardner, but had its own idiom and message, began to sound prophetic. Salinger was the spokesman of the Ivy League Rebellion during the early Fifties. He had come to express, apparently, the values and aspirations of college youth in a way that nobody since Scott Fitzgerald (the other major influence in his work) had done as well. He is interesting to read for this reason, and because he is a leading light in the *New Yorker* school of writing. (He is probably their *ultimate* artist.) And besides, Salinger's talent is interesting for its own sake.

But just what is the time spirit that he expresses? The *Catch-*

er's hero has been expelled from Pencey Prep as the climax of a long adolescent protest. The history teacher who tries to get at the causes of Holden Caulfield's discontent emerges as a moralistic pedagogue, who picks his nose. ("He was really get-/195/ting the old thumb right in there.") During his farewell lecture, Holden is restless, bored—"I moved my ass a little bit on the bed" —and then suddenly uneasy. "I felt sorry as hell for him all of a sudden. But I just couldn't hang around there any longer." This refrain echoes through the narrative; and the rebellious young hero ends up by being "sorry" for all the jerks, morons, and queers who seem to populate the fashionable and rich preparatory school world.

He is also scornful of all the established conventions as "very big deal." (Another standard refrain in the story.) He seems to be the only truly creative personage in this world, and, though he has failed all his courses except English, he has his own high, almost absolute, standards of literature, at least.

"They gave me *Out of Africa* by Isak Dinesen. I thought it was going to stink, but it didn't. It was a very good book. I'm quite illiterate, but I read a lot." By comparison, *A Farewell to Arms* is really a phony book, so we are told. As in Saul Bellow's work, the very human hero of *The Catcher,* who is a physical weakling, who knows that he is at least half "yellow," is also a symbol of protest against the compulsive virility of the Hemingway school of fiction.

The action of the novel is in fact centered around the athlete Stradlater, who is "a very sexy bastard," and who has borrowed Holden Caulfield's jacket and his girl. Stradlater is "unscrupulous" with girls; he has a very *sincere* voice which he uses to snow them with, while he gives them the time, usually in the back seat of the car. Thinking about all this, Holden gets nervous ("I damn near puked"). In his room, he puts on his pajamas, and the old hunting hat which is his talisman of true rebellion and creativity, and starts out to write the English theme (which Stradlater will use as his own) about his dead brother Allie's baseball mitt. Yet when the athlete returns from his date, full of complacency about Holden's girl and of contempt for Holden's essay, this weakling-hero provokes him into a fight. "Get your dirty stinking moron knees off my chest," says Caulfield to Stradlater. "If I letcha up," says Strad, "willya keep your mouth shut?" "You're a dirty stupid sonuvabitch of a moron," says Holden Caulfield.

Later, nursing a bloody nose as the price of his defiant tongue, he wanders in to old Ackley's room for companionship. "You /196/ could also hear old Ackley snoring. Right through the goddam shower curtains you could hear him. He had sinus trouble and he couldn't breathe too hot when he was asleep. That guy had just about everything. Sinus trouble, pimples, lousy teeth, halitosis, crumby fingernails. You had to feel a little sorry for the crazy sonuvabitch." But he can find no comfort or solace in the room which stinks of dirty socks. Ackley is even more stupid than Stradlater. "Stradlater was a goddam genius next to Ackley." A familiar mood of loneliness and despair descends upon him. "I felt so lonesome, all of sudden, I almost wished I was dead. . . . Boy, did I feel rotten. I felt so damn lonesome." He counts his dough ("I was pretty loaded. My grandmother'd just sent me a wad about a week before.") and says good-by:

When I was all set to go, when I had my bags and all, I stood for a while next to the stairs and took a last look down the goddam corridor. I was sort of crying. I don't know why. I put my red hunting hat on, and turned the peak around to the back, the way I liked it, and then I yelled at the top of my goddam voice, *"Sleep tight, ya morons!"* I'll bet I woke up every bastard on the whole floor. Then I got the hell out. Some stupid guy had thrown peanut shells all over the stairs, and I damn near broke my crazy neck.

These are handsome prose passages, and *The Catcher in the Rye* is eminently readable and quotable in its tragicomic narrative of preadolescent revolt. Compact, taut, and colorful, the first half of the novel presents in brief compass all the petty horrors, the banalities, the final mediocrity of the typical American prep school. Very fine—and not sustained or fulfilled, as fiction. For the later sections of the narrative are simply an episodic account of Holden Caulfield's "lost week end" in New York City which manages to sustain our interest but hardly deepens our understanding.

There are very ambiguous elements, moreover, in the portrait of this sad little screwed-up hero. His urban background is curiously shadowy, like the parents who never quite appear in the story, like the one pure adolescent love affair which is now "ruined" in his memory. The locale of the New York sections is obviously that of a comfortable middle-class urban Jewish society where, however, all the leading figures have become beautifully Anglicized. Holden and Phoebe Caulfield: what perfect American social register names which are presented to us in both a /197/ social and a psychological void! Just as the hero's interest in the ancient Egyptians extends only to the fact that they created mummies, so Salinger's own view of his hero's environment omits any reference to its real nature and dynamics.

Though the book is dedicated to Salinger's mother, the fictional mother in the narrative appears only as a voice through the wall. The touching note of affection between the brother and sister is partly a substitute for the missing child-parent relationships (which might indeed clarify the nature of the neurotic hero), and perhaps even a sentimental evasion of the true emotions in a sibling love. The only real creation (or half-creation) in this world is Holden Caulfield himself. And that "compassion," so much praised in the story, and always expressed in the key phrase, "You had to feel sorry"—for him, for her, for them—also implies the same sense of superiority. If this hero really represents the nonconformist rebellion of the Fifties, he is a rebel without a past, apparently, and without a cause.

The Catcher in the Rye protests, to be sure, against both the academic and social conformity of its period. But what does it argue *for?* When Holden mopes about the New York museum which is almost the true home of his discredited childhood, he remembers the Indian war-canoes "about as long as three goddam Cadillacs in a row." He refuses any longer to participate in the wealthy private boys' schools where "you have to keep making believe you give a damn if the football team loses, and all you do is talk about girls and liquor and sex all day, and everybody sticks together in these dirty little goddam cliques." Fair enough; while he also rejects the notion of a conventional future in which he would work in an office, make a lot of dough, ride in cabs, play

bridge, or go to the movies. But in his own private vision of a
better life, this little catcher in the rye sees only those "thousands
of little children" all playing near the dangerous cliff, "and nobody's around—nobody big, I mean—except me" to rescue them
from their morbid fate.

This is surely the differential revolt of the lonesome rich
child, the conspicuous display of leisure-class emotions, the
wounded affections never quite faced, of the upper-class orphan.
This is the *New Yorker* school of ambiguous finality at its best.
But Holden Caulfield's real trouble, as he is told by the equally
precocious Phoebe is that he doesn't like *any*thing that is hap-
/198/pening. "You don't like any schools. You don't like a million things. You *don't*." This is also the peak of well-to-do and
neurotic anarchism—the one world of cultivated negation in
which all those thousands of innocent, pure little children are
surely as doomed as their would-be and somewhat paranoid savior. "I have a feeling that you're riding for some kind of a terrible, terrible fall," says the last and best teacher in Holden's tor-
mented academic career. But even this prophetic insight is viti-
ated by the fact that Mr. Antolini, too, is one of those flits and
perverty guys from whom the adolescent hero escapes in shame
and fear.

He is still, and forever, the innocent child in the evil and
hostile universe, the child who can never grow up. And no wonder that he hears, in the final pages of the narrative, only a chorus
of obscene sexual epithets which seem to surround the little moment of lyric happiness with his childlike sister. The real achievement of *The Catcher in the Rye* is that it manages so gracefully
to evade just those central questions which it raises, and to preserve both its verbal brilliance and the charm of its emotions
within the scope of its own dubious literary form. It is still Salinger's best work, if a highly artificial one, and the caesuras, the
absences, the ambiguities at the base of this writer's work became
more obvious in his subsequent books. . . . /199/

Salinger and the Search for Love

DAN WAKEFIELD

Fathers and teachers, I ponder "What is Hell?"
I maintain that it is the suffering of being un-
able to love.—Dostoevski

Late one night in a New York apartment a boy who has just been
kicked out of his third prep school is trying to explain his troubles to a former teacher, and the teacher is struggling to give the
boy some hope and advice:

Among other things, you'll find that you're not the first person who
was ever confused and frightened and sickened by human behavior.
You're by no means alone on that score, you'll be excited and *stimulated*
to know. Many, many men have been just as troubled morally and
spiritually as you are right now. Happily, some of them kept records of
their troubles. You'll learn something from them—if you want to. It's
a beautiful reciprocal arrangement. And it isn't education. It's history.
It's poetry.

The boy is Holden Caulfield, the teacher is Mr. Antolini, and
the author of the novel they live in, *The Catcher /68/ in the Rye*,
is J. D. Salinger. The jacket of the novel tells us that Salinger
was born in New York City, attended public schools, a military
academy, and three colleges, and the reader perhaps may imagine that Salinger himself was kicked out of school once and given
such advice as Mr. Antolini gave Holden Caulfield. Whatever our
speculations may be, we know for certain that J. D. Salinger has

"kept a record of his troubles"—a record it is possible to think of not as education but as history and poetry.

The record is essentially the record of a search, and some of the seeds of its later development can be found in the stories that Salinger began to write and publish at the age of fifteen. But the real beginning of the search was marked by the publication of Salinger's first and as yet his only novel and has continued through a series of stories, most of which have appeared in *The New Yorker* magazine. The search begins with the troubled odyssey of sixteen-year-old Holden Caulfield in *The Catcher in the Rye,* and has, through that one novel and a dozen stories, moved from the mere revulsion from "phoniness" to a concept of love so large that it enables Franny Glass and her brother Zooey (in the latest Salinger story, "Zooey") to turn from the desire of withdrawal from the world to an entry, through love, into the midst of life.

Salinger's search has been followed by a great many people, for *The Catcher in the Rye* was acclaimed by book reviewers all across the country on its publication in 1951, made a Book of the Month Club selection, and, since then, along with his book of *Nine Stories,* has been selling steadily and well. The three latest stories, published in *The New Yorker,* were awaited with great anticipation and received as events of the first order by the growing group of Salinger's admirers. It has only been in the past few years, however, that professional literary critics have taken Salinger under their microscopes for examination. Even this belated inspection has been not so much out of interest in his search as it has in him as a species held in high regard by "The Young Generation." Surely this is of interest, but to make it the most important thing in considering Salinger is to distort the meaning of his work.

Out of my own personal experience, which is that of a student of Columbia College in the early fifties who has /69/ spent the last several years in New York, I know that Salinger is indeed regarded highly by many young people. I have heard his work discussed among my friends and acquaintances more than any other contemporary author, and I have heard enough speculation about Salinger himself to feel that there is indeed a "Salinger Myth," as there was in the twenties, though in a different way, a

"Fitzgerald Myth." Certainly any myth alive in our fact-smothered era is of interest, and this one perhaps especially since its nature is so extremely different from the twenties myth. The Fitzgerald myth had its hero in Gatsby-like parties and dunkings in the fountain at Union Square;[1] the Salinger myth has its hero living in a cabin in the woods or going to Japan to study Zen. But in both cases the work of the man is of far more importance than the myth. Limiting Salinger's work to its interest as some kind of "document" that appeals only to people of a certain age and social background is as sensible and rewarding as considering *The Great Gatsby* as a sociological monograph once enjoyed by a now extinct species known as "Flaming Youth."

And yet it seems to follow in the eyes of some older observers that if Salinger is indeed a myth and mentor of many young people, interest in his work is restricted to young people and that this is symptomatic of the fact that it is really childish, sentimental, adolescent, and irrelevant.

Significantly enough, the only critical writer to speak at all in real understanding and appreciation of Salinger's search was one of the group in England labeled "The Angry Young Men"—a group of writers who feel the need for such a search themselves, and who are most inflamed by what they feel is the moral decay of their country. In the "Angry Young Men's" *Declaration,* London drama critic Kenneth Tynan asks:

Do I speak for you when I ask for a society where people care more for what you have learned than for where you have learned it; where people who think and people who work can share the common idiom; where art connects itself instead of separating people; where people feel, as in the new Salinger story, that every fat woman on earth is Jesus Christ . . . ? /70/

He speaks, surely, for all who have not lost hope—or even if they have lost hope, have not lost interest—in the search for love and morality in the present-day world. There is the need for such a search in any time, and certainly in our time. The need has not

[1] The fountain is, in fact, at 59th Street and Fifth Avenue, adjacent to the Plaza Hotel. [Eds.]

changed—and, if anything, has become more acute—since the young writers of the twenties discovered that they were "lost" in a time when, as Fitzgerald put it, all wars were fought, all gods were dead. More wars have been fought, but they have become increasingly depersonalized wars, and the next one that threatens offers the ultimate depersonalization. There have been no new gods, and the old ones have sunk continually deeper in their graves. The inheritors of the "lost" tradition have only produced variations on the theme of being lost, and in attitudes described by the adjectives "beat" and "silent" they have sunk deeper into that state, losing interest even in the possibilities of a search to be "found." The anger expressed by the young English writers is the first sign of interest in revival of such a search, and we have to go back to the time of the simply "lost" to hear a similar desire expressed. It was expressed by a young French writer named Marcel Arland in 1924 when he wrote a piece for the *Nouvelle Revue Française* which better than anything I have read can serve to describe the search going on in the writing of Salinger:

> Morality will be our first concern. I cannot conceive of literature without an ethic. No doctrine can satisfy us, but the total absence of doctrine is a torment to us. . . . Between miracle and suicide, and before one reaches resignation, there is room for an extremely individual literature, dangerous, to be sure, and sometimes lyric and abnormal. . . .

It is not men and women who happen to be past the age of thirty-five who are automatically uninterested in such a concern, but men and women who have, at whatever age, reached resignation. A doctor who spoke at a recent convention of the National Geriatrics Society said that "Age is physiological—not chronological." If we can alter his judgment to read that "Age is moral—not chronological," I think we can better understand the nature of the "youthful" appeal of Salinger's work.

Moral senility can come at any age, or need not come /71/ at all, and we have recently borne painful witness through the Howls of the writers of the "Beat Generation" that moral senility can afflict quite young men and women. This group dismisses the search of Salinger on the grounds that he is "slick" (he writes for *The New Yorker,* and as any sensitive person can tell, it is printed on a slick type of paper). But now that the roar from the motor-cycles of Jack Kerouac's imagination has begun to subside, we find that the highly advertised search of the Beat has ended, at least literarily, not with love but with heroin. The appropriate nature of the symbol can be seen in the fact that the physiological experience of heroin is one of negation (it is the ultimate tran-quilizer), releasing the user during the duration of his "high" from the drive for sex, for love, and for answers. Fortunately for the rest of us, the characters in Salinger's fiction have found no such simple formula as a "fix" for relief from their troubles.

Sixteen-year-old Holden Caulfield was (just like Jack Kerouac) sickened by the material values and the inhumanity of the world around him. That sickness, however, marked the beginning and not the end of the search of Salinger's characters to find an order of morality and a possibility of love within the world. The things that Holden finds so deeply repulsive are things he calls "phony" —and the "phoniness" in every instance is the absence of love, and, often, the substitution of pretense for love. Holden's revul-sion is a meaningful one, for he does not, like the "Beat" think-ers, simply equate material values with some abstract social evil embodied by "Madison Avenue." Holden is repulsed because ma-terial values draw on what little store of love there is in the world and expend it on "things" instead of people.

"Take most people. They're crazy about cars. They worry if they get a little scratch on them, and they're always talking about how many miles they get to a gallon, and if they get a brand-new car already they start thinking about trading it in for one that's even newer. I don't even like *old* cars. I mean they don't even interest me. I'd rather have a goddam horse. A horse is at least human, for God's sake. . . ."

Holden, through the course of his search, is repulsed and frightened, not by what people do to him (he feels /72/ sorry for the teacher who flunks him in history, and when accused of know-ing nothing about the course, says, "I know that, sir. Boy, I know it. You couldn't help it.") but rather by what people do to each other, and to themselves.

There is only pretense, and therefore lack of love, and there-fore human injury, in the actions of the headmaster of one of his former boys' schools who charmed all the "best" parents on Sunday visits, but ". . . if a boy's mother was sort of fat or corny-looking, and if somebody's father was one of those guys that wear those suits with very big shoulders and corny black and white shoes," then "old Haas" the headmaster paid no attention to them.

There is only the pretense of love in the rich alumnus under-taker who comes back to Pennsey [*sic*] Prep to give a chapel speech and tells the boys that they shouldn't be afraid to pray to God:

"He told us we ought to think of Jesus as our buddy and all. He said *he* talked to Jesus all the time. Even when he was driving his car. That killed me. I can just see the big phony bastard shifting into first gear and asking Jesus to send him a few more stiffs. . . ."

When Holden flunks out of school and goes to New York he tries to explain to a girl friend he meets for a date why he thinks all boys' schools are "full of phonies," and what he explains is the cruelty of pretense and of the separation that walls off the possibilities of love:

". . . all you do is study so that you can learn enough to be smart enough to buy a goddam Cadillac someday, and you have to keep making believe you give a damn if the football team loses, and all you do is talk about girls and liquor and sex all day, and everybody sticks together in these dirty little goddam cliques. The guys that are on the basketball team stick together, the goddam intellectuals stick together. Even the guys that belong to the goddam Book of the Month Club stick together. . . ."

In the course of his wanderings around New York, Holden is constantly running into walls that separate people—from each other and from themselves—and shut /73/ out love. He goes to Radio City Music Hall for the Christmas Pageant, and there, as in so many other places, pretense has become institutionalized and emotion therefore paralyzed:

"It's supposed to be religious as hell, I know, and very pretty and all, but I can't see anything religious or pretty, for God's sake, about a bunch of actors carrying crucifixes all over the stage. When they were all finished and started going out the boxes again, you could tell they could hardly wait to get a cigarette or something. . . ."

Holden can only find genuine love in children, who have not yet learned the deadening rituals of pretense. The only person he really can talk to is his ten-year-old sister, Phoebe, and when she listens to his troubles and says that he doesn't like anything, the only thing that he can think of that he really likes is the memory of his dead brother Allie and sitting there talking to Phoebe. As for something he'd like to *be*—there is no job in the world he can think of that fulfills his rigorous requirements of genuine love, and all he can do is create such a job in his imagination:

". . . I keep picturing all these little kids playing some game in this big field of rye and all. Thousands of little kids, and nobody's around— nobody big, I mean—except me. And I'm standing on the edge of some crazy cliff. What I have to do, I have to catch everybody if they start to go over the cliff—I mean if they're running and they don't look where they're going I have to come out from somewhere and *catch* them. That's all I'd do all day. I'd just be the catcher in the rye and all. I know it's crazy, but that's the only thing I'd really like to be. I know it's crazy."

Later on, Holden imagines escaping to a cabin in the woods where "I'd have this rule that nobody could do anything phony when they visited me. If anybody tries to do anything phony they couldn't stay." But the cabin in the woods and the field of rye— those unspoiled places of love and refuge—are not to be found in the real world. Holden can find the world of love only within his imagination, and, /74/ finally breaking down from his strenuous search, ends the recitation of his story in a hospital where he is getting psychiatric care. It is not, however, the end of his search —or of Salinger's. It is the end of one leg of the journey, for Holden and for Salinger, and as far as the future is concerned, Holden perhaps was speaking for Salinger as well as himself, when the psychiatrist asked him if he was going to apply himself when he went back to school in the fall and Holden said:

"It's such a stupid question, in my opinion. I mean how do you know
what you're going to do till you do it? The answer is, you don't."

What Salinger did was carry on his record from sixteen-year-
old Holden's search to the world of adults, as well as children
and adolescents, in *Nine Stories*. Here, too, is the suffering from
the lack of love, from the inability to feel love, and the torment
of it drives the characters to answers of suicide, immersion in
memory and alcohol, and, finally, mysticism. . . . /75/

[Mr. Wakefield goes on to characterize Salinger as "the only new
writer to emerge in America since the second world war who is
writing on what has been the grandest theme of literature: the relationship of man to God, or the lack of God" (p. 79). The remaining ten pages of his essay are largely devoted to an analysis of this
theme in Salinger's later fiction.]

XII

Salinger's Most Sustained Success*

FREDERICK L. GWYNN AND JOSEPH L. BLOTNER

After "Down at the Dinghy" comes "For Esmé" and after "For Esmé" comes Salinger's most sustained success, *The Catcher in the Rye.* This novel's exciting resemblances to *The Adventures of /28/ Huckleberry Finn* have been justly noted by a number of critics—the comic irony, the colloquial language, the picaresque structure, and the theme of anti-phoniness—and it is not inconceivable that some day Holden Caulfield may be as well known an American boy as Huck Finn. For a reader goes through much the same pattern of relishing both boys: first it is the release provided by their rebellion against society, then the inspiration of their honesty against sham, and then the sympathetic awareness of their melancholy roles. After the reader recovers from the releasing joy of Holden's invective (e.g., "Her son was doubtless the biggest bastard that ever went to Pencey, in the whole crumby history of the school") and of his exposure of phoniness (e.g., a Radio City Christmas complete with what has been identified as the movie of James Hilton's *Random Harvest*), he goes on to appreciate the pathos of Holden's loneliness and frustration.

But nervous cynicism and neurosis are not enough for fiction in depth, and the next step for a reader should be to realize that Holden Caulfield is actually a saintly Christian person (there is no need to call him a Christ-figure). True, he has little notion of the love of God, and he thinks that "all the children in our family are atheists." But (1) he himself never does a wrong thing: in-

* Title supplied by the editors.

From *The Fiction of J. D. Salinger* by Frederick L. Gwynn and Joseph L. Blotner. Copyright © 1958 by University of Pittsburgh Press. Reprinted by permission.

stead of commandments, Holden breaks only garage windows (when his brother dies) and the no-smoking rule in the Pencey dormitory. (2) He sacrifices himself in a constant war against evil, even though he has a poignantly Manichean awareness of its ubiquity ("If you had a million years to do it in, you couldn't rub out even *half* the [ubiquitously scrawled dirty words] in the world.") And most importantly, (3) his reward is /29/ to understand that if one considers humanity, one must love it. The text for Holden's behavior is his insistence—oddly enough, to his Quaker friend Childs on absolute primitive Christianity: "Jesus never sent old Judas to Hell. . . . I think any one of the Di*sci*ples would've sent him to Hell and all—and fast, too—but I'll bet anything Jesus didn't do it."

For Jesus and Holden Caulfield truly love their neighbors, especially the poor in goods, appearance, and spirit. Holden not only gives ten dollars to the nuns in the station but also he is depressed by their meagre breakfast and the fact that they will never be "going anywhere swanky for lunch." He worries about where the ducks in Central Park can go when the water freezes, and how wretched his mother would feel if he died—"because she still isn't over my brother Allie yet." He is kind to the repulsive Ackley, with his "Sinus trouble, pimples, lousy teeth, halitosis, crumby fingernails," and he tries to obviate Slagle's envy of his Mark Cross luggage. Most significantly, for an adolescent undergoing the torturing growing pains of sex, he sympathizes with the girl's situation—with the ugly daughter of Pencey's headmaster, with both the ugly girl and the beautiful girl in the nightclub undergoing male treatment from their escorts, with the prostitute Sunny, with the girl whom Luce has enjoyed and now derogates, and especially with Jane Gallagher, the girl whose fear Holden appreciates (she wouldn't move her checker kings out of the back row) and whose virtue he fears Stradlater has taken. And like his Jesus with his Judas, he still forgives Stradlater and the bellboy Maurice who have betrayed and beaten him. Indeed, this is the old-fashioned moral, stated haltingly at the very end /30/ by Holden Caulfield, who wishes to be the Catcher in the Rye suffering little children to come to him and be saved from falling over the cliff. He puts it this way: "About all I know is, I sort of *miss* everybody I told you about. Even old Stradlater and Ackley, for instance. I think I even miss that goddam Maurice. It's funny. Don't ever tell anybody anything. If you do, you start missing everybody." In less concrete words: If you are aware of the human comedy, you must love individual human beings. The ending of *The Catcher in the Rye* is just as artistically weak—and as humanly satisfying—as that of *Huckleberry Finn.* /31/

XIII

J. D. Salinger: Search for Wisdom

GRANVILLE HICKS

Last spring I taught a course in contemporary fiction at New York University. When I was drawing up the reading list, a veteran teacher whom I consulted mildly questioned the inclusion of J. D. Salinger's "The Catcher in the Rye." "It's the one book," he said, "that every undergraduate in America has read." I think he was pretty nearly right about that, but, for my own sake, I'm glad I decided to teach the book. To most of my students, I discovered, Holden Caulfield meant more than Jake Barnes or Jay Gatsby or Augie March or any other character we encountered in the course, and in the discussion of the novel there was a sense of direct involvement such as I felt on no other occasion.

For the college generations of the Fifties, Salinger has the kind of importance that Scott Fitzgerald and Ernest Hemingway had for the young people of the Twenties. He is not a public figure as they were; on the contrary, his zeal for privacy is phenomenal; but he is felt nevertheless as a presence, a significant and congenial presence. There are, I am convinced, millions of young Americans who feel closer to Salinger than to any other writer.

In the first place, he speaks their language. He not only speaks it; he shapes it, just as Hemingway influenced the speech of countless Americans in the Twenties. The talk of his characters is, so to speak, righter than right. The voice of Holden Caulfield is a voice we instantly recognize, and yet there is just that twist of stylistic intensification that always distinguishes good dialogue.

In the second place, he expresses their rebellion. Most of my undergraduates, so far as I could tell, were as nonpolitical as

From *Saturday Review*, XLII, July 25, 1959. Copyright © by *Saturday Review*, Inc. Reprinted by permission of the author and *Saturday Review*.

Holden Caulfield. They spoke of the lack of interest in political and social problems as characteristic of their generation, a phenomenon to be neither praised nor condemned but simply accepted. Yet they were far from complacency, and they delighted in Holden's attacks on meanness, stupidity, and especially phoniness. They admired his intransigence, too, which he so often refers to as his craziness, and rejoiced in his gestures of defiance.

But Holden is not merely a rebel, and this also my students understood. What is strongest in him, as is indicated by the passage that gives the book its title, is compassion. He is not only full of tenderness towards his sister Phoebe and all children; he is touched by persons casually met on his pilgrimage—by the woman on the train, by the girls in the night club, by the nuns in the station—and wants to make them happy. In the end he feels sorry even for those who have hurt him.

I have been talking seriously about a book that on page after page is wildly funny; but it is fundamentally a serious book, as its younger readers know. Holden Caulfield is torn, and nearly destroyed, by the conflict between integrity and love. He is driven by the need not to be less than himself, not to accept what he knows to be base. On the other hand, he is capable of understanding and loving the persons to whom his integrity places him in opposition. The problem of values with which Salinger so persuasively confronts his sixteen-year-old is not exclusively a problem of adolescence.

It is a problem that has continued to engage Salinger, whose literary career has taken a curious turn. Although he has been appearing in magazines for almost twenty years, he has published only two books: "The Catcher in the Rye" in 1951 and "Nine Stories" in 1953. (The twenty-odd stories that were published in magazines between 1940 and 1947 have never been collected.) What is even more extraordinary is that since 1953 he has published only four stories, all of them in *The New Yorker*. It is true that they are all quite long, but even so one can hardly regard him as prolific.

These stories have received a remarkable amount of attention, not only from youthful Salinger fans but also from professional students of literature. As everyone knows, either from reading the

stories or from reading essays about them, they are all concerned
with members of the Glass family. The family was introduced in
"A Perfect Day for Bananafish," which was published in *The
New Yorker* in 1948 and included in "Nine Stories," and two
other stories in that volume belong to the Glass saga. However,
it was not until "Franny" (*The New Yorker,* Jan. 29, 1955) that
Salinger made a full-length study of one of the seven Glass children—Franny is youngest of them—and it was not until "Raise
High the Roof Beam, Carpenters" (Nov. 19, 1955) that he gave
his readers an idea of the family as a whole. In "Zooey" (May 4,
1957) he was even more informative, and in "Seymour: An Introduction" (June 6, 1959) he has gone on building his structure
higher and higher.

There are many things to say about "Seymour," but I want to
concentrate on two. The story is told in the first person by Buddy,
the second oldest of the Glass children, and Salinger has chosen
to identify himself completely with Buddy: for instance, Buddy
describes three stories he has written, and they are three stories
written and signed by J. D. Salinger. This does not entitle us to
assume that Salinger had four brothers and two sisters or appeared on a quiz show or teaches in a women's college, but we
cannot avoid the conclusion that when Buddy speaks on literary
matters he speaks for Salinger. What we discover is that Salinger
is acutely self-conscious, about his writing, about his philosophy,
about his reputation (Buddy alludes to "the bogus information
that I spend six months of the year in a Buddhist monastery and
the other six in a mental institution.") Indeed, self-consciousness
gives the story its peculiar quality, and although the tone is beautifully sustained, as always in Salinger's later work, the self is ex-
ceedingly obtrusive. Buddy was prominent in "Raise High the
Roof Beam, Carpenters," but he wasn't constantly talking about
himself as a writer, and I think that was a better story than this.
(So was "Zooey," if only by virtue of the wonderful bathroom
conversation between Zooey and his mother, which "Seymour"
has nothing to equal.)

On the other hand, as a piece of stylistic virtuosity, the story
does make the reader's hair stand on end, and, what is more, the
reader begins to see Seymour as Salinger wants us to see him. He

was interesting and likable in "A Perfect Day for Banana-/13/ fish," but no more than that. In "Raise High the Roof Beam, Carpenters" and "Zooey" we felt that he was a man of unusual powers, but we saw him only from a distance. Now, in brief glimpses but in the most concrete way, Salinger makes us feel Seymour's brilliance, his high poetic gifts, and above all his capacity for love. "What was he, anyway?" Buddy asks. "A *saint?* Thankfully, it isn't my responsibility to answer that one." But that is exactly what Salinger is trying to create—a contemporary saint—and in the end he convinces me.

Salinger doesn't make things easy for his readers as he moves slowly along his chosen path, but I imagine that the devotees are still with him. The Glass saga can go on for a long time: Salinger intimates that he may do more with Seymour, and about Waker, Walt, and Boo Boo we so far know only enough to be sure we should be glad to know more. On the other hand, Salinger may grow tired of the Glasses, or may be led in a new direction by his constant experimentation with technique. For myself, I shall be glad if he moves away from Buddy's self-consciousness, but, whatever he writes, I look forward to reading it.

When we were discussing "The Catcher in the Rye" in class, there was one dissenting voice, one student who felt that Holden Caulfield's rebellion was too immature and ineffectual to be worth serious consideration. Most of the students loudly disagreed, and I went along with the majority. Holden is not rejecting maturity but is looking for a better model than his elders by and large present. Like the Glasses, though in a less ostentatious way, he is a seeker after wisdom. That Salinger can make the search for wisdom seem important to large numbers of young people is not exactly cause for alarm. /30/

XIV

The Language of *The Catcher in the Rye*

DONALD P. COSTELLO

A study of the language of J. D. Salinger's *The Catcher in the Rye* can be justified not only on the basis of literary interest, but also on the basis of linguistic significance. Today we study *The Adventures of Huckleberry Finn* (with which many critics have compared *The Catcher in the Rye*) not only as a great work of literary art, but as a valuable study in 1884 dialect. In coming decades, *The Catcher in the Rye* will be studied, I feel, not only as a literary work, but also as an example of teenage vernacular in the 1950's. As such, the book will be a significant historical linguistic record of a type of speech rarely made available in permanent form. Its linguistic importance will increase as the American speech it records becomes less current.

Most critics who looked at *The Catcher in the Rye* at the time of its publication thought that its language was a true and authentic rendering of teenage colloquial speech. Reviewers in the Chicago *Sunday Tribune*, the London *Times Literary Supplement*, the *New Republic*, the New York *Herald Tribune Book Review*, the New York *Times,* the *New Yorker*, and the *Saturday Review of Literature* all specifically mentioned the authenticity of the book's language. Various aspects of its language were also discussed in the reviews published in *America,* the *Atlantic,* the *Catholic World,* the *Christian Science Monitor,* the *Library Journal,* the Manchester *Guardian,* the *Nation,* the *New Statesman and Nation,* the New York *Times Book Review, Newsweek,* the *Spectator,* and *Time.*[1] Of these many reviews, only the writers for

From *American Speech*, XXXIV (October 1959). Copyright 1959 by Columbia University Press. Reprinted by permission of the author.

[1] See reviews in *America* LXXV (August 11, 1951), 463, 464; *Atlantic,* CLXXXVIII (1951), 82; *Catholic World,* CLXXIV (1951), 154; Chicago *Sunday*

the *Catholic World* and the *Christian Science Monitor* denied the authenticity of the book's language, but both of these are religious journals which refused to believe that the 'obscenity' was realistic. An examination of the reviews of *The Catcher in the Rye* proves that /172/ the language of Holden Caulfield, the book's sixteen-year-old narrator, struck the ear of the contemporary reader as an accurate rendering of the informal speech of an intelligent, educated, Northeastern American adolescent.[2]

In addition to commenting on its authenticity, critics have often remarked—uneasily—the 'daring,' 'obscene,' 'blasphemous' features of Holden's language. Another commonly noted feature of the book's language has been its comic effect. And yet there has never been an extensive investigation of the language itself. That is what this paper proposes to do.

Even though Holden's language is authentic teenage speech, recording it was certainly not the major intention of Salinger. He was faced with the artistic task of creating an individual char-

---

Tribune, July 15, 1951, Part 4, p. 3; *Christian Science Monitor,* July 19, 1951, p. 9; *Library Journal,* LXXVI (1951), 1125; *Times* [London] *Literary Supplement,* September 7, 1951, p. 561; Manchester *Guardian,* August 10, 1951, p. 4; *Nation* (CLXXIII (September 1, 1951), 176; *New Republic,* CXXXV (July 16, 1951), 20, 21; *New Statesman and Nation,* XLII (August 18, 1951), 185; New York *Herald Tribune Book Review,* July 15, 1951, p. 3; New York *Times Book Review,* July 15, 1951, p. 5; New York *Times,* July 16, 1951, p. 19; *New Yorker,* XXVII (August 11, 1951), 71-76; *Newsweek,* XXXVIII (July 16, 1951), 89, 90; *Saturday Review of Literature,* XXXIV (July 14, 1951), 12, 13; *Spectator,* CLXXXVII (August 17, 1951), 224; *Time,* LVIII (July 16, 1951), 96, 97. /172/

[2] If additional evidence of the authenticity of the book's language is required, one need only look at the phenomenal regard with which *The Catcher in the Rye* is held by today's college students, who were about Holden's age at the time the book was written. In its March 9, 1957, issue the *Nation* published a symposium which attempted to discover the major influences upon the college students of today. Many teachers pointed out the impact of Salinger. Carlos Baker, of Princeton, stated: 'There is still, as there has been for years, a cult of Thomas Wolfe. They have all read J. D. Salinger, Wolfe's closest competitor.' Stanley Kunitz, of Queens College, wrote: 'The only novelist I have heard praised vociferously is J. D. Salinger.' Harvey Curtis Webster, of the University of Louisville, listed Salinger as one of the 'stimulators.' R. J. Kaufman, of the University of Rochester, called *The Catcher in the Rye* 'a book which has completely aroused nearly all of them.' See 'The Careful Young Men,' *Nation,* CLXXXIV (March 9, 1957), 199-214. I have never heard any Salinger partisans among college students doubt the authenticity of the language of their compatriot, Holden. /173/

acter, not with the linguistic task of reproducing the exact speech
of teenagers in general. Yet Holden had to speak a recognizable
teenage language, and at the same time had to be identifiable as
an individual. This difficult task Salinger achieved by giving
Holden an extremely trite and typical teenage speech, overlaid
with strong personal idiosyncrasies. There are two major speech
habits which are Holden's own, which are endlessly repeated
throughout the book, and which are, nevertheless, typical enough
of teenage speech so that Holden can be both typical and individual in his use of them. It is certainly common for teenagers to
end thoughts with a loosely dangling 'and all,' just as it is common for them to add an insistent 'I really did,' 'It really was.'
But Holden uses these phrases to such an overpowering degree
that they become a clear part of the flavor of the book; they become, more, a part of Holden himself, and actually help to characterize him.

Holden's 'and all' and its twins, 'or something,' 'or anything,'
serve no real, consistent linguistic function. They simply give a
sense of looseness of expression and looseness of thought. Often
they signify that Holden knows there is more that could be said
about the issue at hand, but he is not going to bother going into
it: /173/

> ... how my parents were occupied and all before they had me (5.)[3]
> ... they're *nice* and all (5.)
> I'm not going to tell you my whole goddam autobiography or any-
> thing (5.)
> ... splendid and clear-thinking and all (6.)

But just as often the use of such expressions is purely arbitrary,
with no discernible meaning:

> ... he's my *brother* and all (5.)
> ... was in the Revolutionary War and all (6.)
> It was December and all (7.)
> ... no gloves or anything (7.)
> ... right in the pocket and all (7.)

[3] Whenever *The Catcher in the Rye* is substantially quoted in this paper, a
page number will be included in the text immediately after the quotation. The
edition to which the page numbers refer is the Signet paperback reprint.

Donald Barr, writing in the *Commonweal*, finds this habit indicative of Holden's tendency to generalize, to find the all in the one:

Salinger has an ear not only for idiosyncrasies of diction and syntax, but for mental processes. Holden Caulfield's phrase is 'and all'—'She looked so damn *nice,* the way she kept going around and around in her blue coat and all'—as if each experience wore a halo. His fallacy is *ab uno disce omnes;* he abstracts and generalizes wildly.[4]

Heiserman and Miller, in the *Western Humanities Review,* comment specifically upon Holden's second most obvious idiosyncrasy: 'In a phony world Holden feels compelled to reenforce his sincerity and truthfulness constantly with, "It really is" or "It really did." '[5] S. N. Behrman, in the *New Yorker,* finds a double function of these 'perpetual insistences of Holden's.' Behrman thinks they 'reveal his age, even when he is thinking much older,' and, more important, 'he is so aware of the danger of slipping into phoniness himself that he has to repeat over and over "I really mean it," "It really does." '[6] Holden uses this idosyncrasy of insistence almost every time that he makes an affirmation.

Allied to Holden's habit of insistence is his 'if you want to know the truth.' Heiserman and Miller are able to find characterization in this habit too:

The skepticism inherent in that casual phrase, 'if you want to know the truth,' suggesting that as a matter of fact in the world of Holden Caulfield very few people do, characterizes this sixteen-year-old 'crazy mixed up kid' more sharply and vividly than pages of character 'analysis' possibly could.[7] /174/

Holden uses this phrase only after affirmations, just as he uses 'It really does,' but usually after the personal ones, where he is consciously being frank:

[4] Donald Barr, 'Saints, Pilgrims, and Artists,' *Commonweal,* LXVII (October 25, 1957), 90.
[5] Arthur Heiserman and James E. Miller, Jr., 'J. D. Salinger: Some Crazy Cliff,' *Western Humanities Review,* X (1956), 136.
[6] S. N. Behrman, 'The Vision of the Innocent,' *New Yorker,* XXVII (August 11, 1951), 72.
[7] Heiserman and Miller, *op. cit.,* p. 135. /174/

I have no wind, if you want to know the truth. (8.)
I don't even think that bastard had a handkerchief, if you want to
know the truth. (34.)
I'm a pacifist, if you want to know the truth. (44.)
She had quite a lot of sex appeal, too, if you really want to know. (53.)
I was damn near bawling, I felt so damn happy, if you want to know
the truth. (191.)

These personal idiosyncrasies of Holden's speech are in keeping
with general teenage language. Yet they are so much a part of
Holden and of the flavor of the book that they are much of what
makes Holden to be Holden. They are the most memorable feature of the book's language. Although always in character, the
rest of Holden's speech is more typical than individual. The special quality of this language comes from its triteness, its lack of
distinctive qualities.

Holden's informal, schoolboy vernacular is particularly typical
in its 'vulgarity' and 'obscenity.' No one familiar with prep-school
speech could seriously contend that Salinger overplayed his hand
in this respect. On the contrary, Holden's restraints help to characterize him as a sensitive youth who avoids the most strongly
forbidden terms, and who never uses vulgarity in a self-conscious
or phony way to help him be 'one of the boys.' *Fuck,* for example,
is never used as a part of Holden's speech. The word appears in
the novel four times, but only when Holden disapprovingly discusses its wide appearance on walls. The Divine name is used
habitually by Holden only in the comparatively weak *for God's
sake, God,* and *goddam.* The stronger and usually more offensive
for Chrissake or *Jesus* or *Jesus Christ* are used habitually by Ackley and Stradlater; but Holden uses them only when he feels the
need for a strong expression. He almost never uses *for Chrissake*
in an unemotional situation. *Goddam* is Holden's favorite adjective. This word is used with no relationship to its original meaning, or to Holden's attitude toward the word to which it is attached. It simply expresses an emotional feeling toward the object: either favorable, as in 'goddam hunting cap'; or unfavorable,
as in 'ya goddam moron'; or indifferent, as in 'coming in the goddam windows.' *Damn* is used interchangeably with *goddam;* no
differentiation in its meaning is detectable.

Other crude words are also often used in Holden's vocabulary. *Ass* keeps a fairly restricted meaning as a part of the human anatomy, but it is used in a variety of ways. It can refer simply to that specific part of the body ('I moved my ass a little'), or be a part of a trite expression ('freezing my ass off'; in a half-assed way'), or be an expletive ('Game, my ass.'). *Hell* is perhaps the most versatile word in Holden's entire vocabulary; it serves most of the meanings and constructions which Mencken lists in his *American Speech* /175/ article on 'American Profanity.'[8] So far is Holden's use of *hell* from its original meaning that he can use the sentence 'We had a helluva time' to mean that he and Phoebe had a decidedly pleasant time downtown shopping for shoes. The most common function of *hell* is as the second part of a simile, in which a thing can be either 'hot as hell' or, strangely, 'cold as hell'; 'sad as hell' or 'playful as hell'; 'old as hell' or 'pretty as hell.' Like all of these words, *hell* has no close relationship to its original meaning.

Both *bastard* and *sonuvabitch* have also drastically changed in meaning. They no longer, of course, in Holden's vocabulary, have any connection with the accidents of birth. Unless used in a trite simile, *bastard* is a strong word, reserved for things and people Holden particularly dislikes, especially 'phonies.' *Sonuvabitch* has an even stronger meaning to Holden; he uses it only in the deepest anger. When, for example, Holden is furious with Stradlater over his treatment of Jane Gallagher, Holden repeats again and again that he 'kept calling him a moron sonuvabitch' (43).

The use of crude language in *The Catcher in the Rye* increases, as we should expect, when Holden is reporting schoolboy dialogue. When he is directly addressing the reader, Holden's use of such language drops off almost entirely. There is also an increase in this language when any of the characters are excited or angry. Thus, when Holden is apprehensive over Stradlater's treatment of Jane, his *goddams* increase suddenly to seven on a single page (p. 39).

Holden's speech is also typical in his use of slang. I have cata-

[8] See H. L. Mencken, 'American Profanity,' *American Speech*, XIX (1944), 242. /176/

logued over a hundred slang terms used by Holden, and every one of these is in widespread use. Although Holden's slang is rich and colorful, it, of course, being slang, often fails at precise communication. Thus, Holden's *crap* is used in seven different ways. It can mean foolishness, as 'all that David Copperfield kind of crap,' or messy matter, as 'I spilled some crap all over my gray flannel,' or merely miscellaneous matter, as 'I was putting on my galoshes and crap.' It can also carry its basic meaning, animal excreta, as 'there didn't look like there was anything in the park except dog crap,' and it can be used as an adjective meaning anything generally unfavorable, as 'The show was on the crappy side.' Holden uses the phrases *to be a lot of crap* and *to shoot the crap* and *to chuck the crap* all to mean 'to be untrue,' but he can also use *to shoot the crap* to mean simply 'to chat,' with no connotation of untruth, as in 'I certainly wouldn't have minded shooting the crap with old Phoebe for a while.'

Similarly Holden's slang use of *crazy* is both trite and imprecise. 'That drives me crazy' means that he violently dislikes something; yet 'to be crazy about' something means just the opposite. In the same way, to be 'killed' by /176/ something can mean that he was emotionally affected either favorably ('That story just about killed me.') or unfavorably ('Then she turned her back on me again. It nearly killed me.'). This use of *killed* is one of Holden's favorite slang expressions. Heiserman and Miller are, incidentally, certainly incorrect when they conclude: 'Holden always lets us know when he has insight into the absurdity of the endlessly absurd situations which make up the life of a sixteen-year-old by exclaiming, "It killed me." '[9] Holden often uses this expression with no connection to the absurd; he even uses it for his beloved Phoebe. The expression simply indicates a high degree of emotion—any kind. It is hazardous to conclude that any of Holden's slang has a precise and consistent meaning or function. These same critics fall into the same error when they conclude that Holden's use of the adjective *old* serves as 'a term of endearment.'[10] Holden appends this word to almost every character, real or fictional, mentioned in the novel, from the hated 'old

[9] Heiserman and Miller, *op. cit.*, p. 136.
[10] *Ibid.* /177/

Maurice' to 'old Peter Lorre,' to 'old Phoebe,' and even 'old Jesus.' The only pattern that can be discovered in Holden's use of this term is that he usually uses it only after he has previously mentioned the character; he then feels free to append the familiar *old*. All we can conclude from Holden's slang is that it is typical teenage slang: versatile yet narrow, expressive yet unimaginative, imprecise, often crude, and always trite.

Holden has many favorite slang expressions which he overuses. In one place, he admits:

'Boy!' I said. I also say 'Boy!' quite a lot. Partly because I have a lousy vocabulary and partly because I act quite young for my age sometimes. (12.)

But if Holden's slang shows the typically 'lousy vocabulary' of even the educated American teenager, this failing becomes even more obvious when we narrow our view to Holden's choice of adjectives and adverbs. The choice is indeed narrow, with a constant repetition of a few favorite words: *lousy, pretty, crumby, terrific, quite, old, stupid*—all used, as is the habit of teenage vernacular, with little regard to specific meaning. Thus, most of the nouns which are called 'stupid' could not in any logical framework be called 'ignorant,' and, as we have seen, *old* before a proper noun has nothing to do with age.

Another respect in which Holden was correct in accusing himself of having a 'lousy vocabulary' is discovered in the ease with which he falls into trite figures of speech. We have already seen that Holden's most common simile is the worn and meaningless 'as hell', but his often-repeated 'like a madman' and 'like a bastard' are just about as unrelated to a literal meaning and are /177/ easily as unimaginative. Even Holden's nonhabitual figures of speech are usually trite: 'sharp as a tack'; 'hot as a firecracker'; 'laughed like a hyena'; 'I know old Jane like a book'; 'drove off like a bat out of hell'; 'I began to feel like a horse's ass'; 'blind as a bat'; 'I know Central Park like the back of my hand.'

Repetitious and trite as Holden's vocabulary may be, it can, nevertheless, become highly effective. For example, when Holden piles one trite adjective upon another, a strong power of invective is often the result:

He was a goddam stupid moron. (42.)
Get your dirty stinking moron knees off my chest. (43.)
You're a dirty stupid sonuvabitch of a moron. (43.)

And his limited vocabulary can also be used for good comic effect. Holden's constant repetition of identical expressions in countless widely different situations is often hilariously funny.

But all of the humor in Holden's vocabulary does not come from its unimaginative quality. Quite the contrary, some of his figures of speech are entirely original; and these are inspired, dramatically effective, and terribly funny. As always, Salinger's Holden is basically typical, with a strong overlay of the individual:

He started handling my exam paper like it was a turd or something. (13.)
He put my goddam paper down then and looked at me like he'd just beaten the hell out of me in ping-pong or something. (14.)
That guy Morrow was about as sensitive as a goddam toilet seat. (52.)
Old Marty was like dragging the Statue of Liberty around the floor. (69.)

Another aspect in which Holden's language is typical is that it shows the general American characteristic of adaptability—apparently strengthened by his teenage lack of restraint. It is very easy for Holden to turn nouns into adjectives, with the simple addition of a -y: 'perverty,' 'Christmasy,' 'vomity-looking,' 'whory-looking,' 'hoodlumy-looking,' 'show-offy,' 'flitty-looking,' 'dumpy-looking,' 'pimpy,' 'snobby,' 'fisty.' Like all of English, Holden's language shows a versatile combining ability: 'They gave Sally this little blue butt-twitcher of a dress to wear' (117) and 'That magazine was some little cheerer upper' (176). Perhaps the most interesting aspect of the adaptability of Holden's language is his ability to use nouns as adverbs: 'She sings it very Dixieland and whorehouse, and it doesn't sound at all mushy' (105).

As we have seen, Holden shares, in general, the trite repetitive vocabulary which is the typical lot of his age group. But as there are exceptions in his figures of speech, so are there exceptions in his vocabulary itself, in his word stock. An intelligent, well-read ('I'm quite illiterate, but I read a lot'), and educated boy, Holden possesses, and can use when he wants to, many words /178/ which are many a cut above Basic English, including 'ostracized,' 'exhibitionist,' 'unscrupulous,' 'conversationalist,' 'psychic,' 'bourgeois.' Often Holden seems to choose his words consciously, in an effort to communicate to his adult reader clearly and properly, as in such terms as 'lose my virginity,' 'relieve himself,' 'an alcoholic'; for upon occasion, he also uses the more vulgar terms 'to give someone the time,' 'to take a leak,' 'booze hound.' Much of the humor arises, in fact, from Holden's habit of writing on more than one level at the same time. Thus, we have such phrases as 'They give guys the ax quite frequently at Pency'* and 'It has a very good academic rating, Pency' (7). Both sentences show a colloquial idiom with an overlay of consciously selected words.

Such a conscious choice of words seems to indicate that Salinger, in his attempt to create a realistic character in Holden, wanted to make him aware of his speech, as, indeed, a real teenager would be when communicating to the outside world. Another piece of evidence that Holden is conscious of his speech and, more, realizes a difficulty in communication, is found in his habit of direct repetition: 'She likes me a lot. I mean she's quite fond of me.' (141), and 'She can be very snotty sometimes. She can be quite snotty.' (150). Sometimes the repetition is exact: 'He was a very nervous guy—I mean he was a very nervous guy.' (165), and 'I sort of missed them. I mean I sort of missed them.' (169). Sometimes Holden stops specifically to interpret slang terms, as when he wants to communicate the fact that Allie liked Phoebe: 'She killed Allie, too. I mean he liked her, too' (64).

There is still more direct evidence that Holden was conscious of his speech. Many of his comments to the reader are concerned with language. He was aware, for example, of the 'phony' quality of many words and phrases, such as 'grand,' 'prince,' 'traveling incognito,' 'little girls' room,' 'licorice stick,' and 'angels.' Holden is also conscious, of course, of the existence of 'taboo words.' He makes a point of mentioning that the girl from Seattle repeatedly

* Salinger spells it Pencey. [Eds.]

asked him to 'watch your language, if you don't mind' (67), and
that his mother told Phoebe not to say 'lousy' (160). When the
prostitute says 'Like fun you are,' Holden comments:

It was a funny thing to say. It sounded like a real kid. You'd think a
prostitute and all would say 'Like hell you are' or 'Cut the crap' instead
of 'Like fun you are.' (87.)

In grammar, too, as in vocabulary, Holden possesses a certain
self-consciousness. (It is, of course, impossible to imagine a student getting through today's schools without a self-consciousness
with regard to grammar rules.) Holden is, in fact, not only aware
of the existence of 'grammatical errors,' but knows the social ta-
boos that accompany them. He is disturbed by a schoolmate who
is ashamed of his parents' grammar, and he reports that his former /179/ teacher, Mr. Antolini, warned him about picking up
'just enough education to hate people who say, "It's a secret between he and I" ' (168).

Holden is a typical enough teenager to violate the grammar
rules, even though he knows of their social importance. His most
common rule violation is the misuse of *lie* and *lay,* but he also is
careless about relative pronouns ('about a traffic cop that falls
in love'), the double negative ('I hardly didn't even know I was
doing it'), the perfect tenses ('I'd woke him up'), extra words
('like as if all you ever did at Pencey was play polo all the time') ,
pronoun number ('it's pretty disgusting to watch somebody picking their nose'), and pronoun position ('I and this friend of mine,
Mal Brossard'). More remarkable, however, than the instances of
grammar rule violations is Holden's relative 'correctness.'
Holden is always intelligible, and is even 'correct' in many usually difficult constructions. Grammatically speaking, Holden's
language seems to point up the fact that English was the only
subject in which he was not failing. It is interesting to note how
much more 'correct' Holden's speech is than that of Huck Finn.
But then Holden is educated, and since the time of Huck there
had been sixty-seven years of authoritarian schoolmarms working
on the likes of Holden. He has, in fact, been overtaught, so that
he uses many 'hyper' forms:

I used to play tennis with he and Mrs. Antolini quite frequently. (163.)
She'd give Allie or I a push. (64.)
I and Allie used to take her to the park with us. (64.)
I think I probably woke he and his wife up. (157.)

Now that we have examined several aspects of Holden's vocabulary and grammar, it would be well to look at a few examples
of how he puts these elements together into sentences. The structure of Holden's sentences indicates that Salinger thinks of the
book more in terms of spoken speech than written speech. Hold-
en's faulty structure is quite common and typical in vocal expression; I doubt if a student who is 'good in English' would ever
create such sentence structure in writing. A student who showed
the self-consciousness of Holden would not *write* so many fragments, such afterthoughts (e.g., 'It has a very good academic rating, Pency' [7]), or such repetitions (e.g., 'Where I lived at
Pency, I lived in the Ossenburger Memorial Wing of the new
dorms' [18]).

There are other indications that Holden's speech is vocal. In
many places Salinger mildly imitates spoken speech. Sentences
such as 'You could tell old Spencer'd got a big bang out of buy-
ing it' (10) and 'I'd've killed him' (42) are repeated throughout
the book. Yet it is impossible to imagine Holden taking pen in
hand and actually writing 'Spencer'd' or 'I'd've.' Sometimes, too,
emphasized words, or even parts of words, are italicized, as in
'Now /180/ *shut up,* Holden. God damm it—I'm *warn*ing ya' (42).
This is often done with good effect, imitating quite perfectly the
rhythms of speech, as in the typical:

I practically sat down on her *lap,* as a matter of fact. Then she *really*
started to cry, and the next thing I knew, I was kissing her all over—
*any*where—her eyes, her *nose,* her forehead, her eyebrows and all, her
ears—her whole face except her mouth and all. (73.)

The language of *The Catcher in the Rye* is, as we have seen,
an authentic artistic rendering of a type of informal, colloquial,
teenage American spoken speech. It is strongly typical and trite,
yet often somewhat individual; it is crude and slangy and impre-

cise, imitative yet occasionally imaginative, and affected toward standardization by the strong efforts of schools. But authentic and interesting as this language may be, it must be remembered that it exists, in *The Catcher in the Rye,* as only one part of an artistic achievement. The language was not written for itself, but as a part of a greater whole. Like the great Twain work with which it is often compared, a study of *The Catcher in the Rye* repays both the linguist and the literary critic; for as one critic has said, 'In them, 1884 and 1951 speak to us in the idiom and accent of two youthful travelers who have earned their passports to literary immortality.'[11] /181/

[11] Charles Kaplan, 'Holden and Huck: the Odysseys of Youth,' *College English,* XVIII (1956), 80. /181/

The Knighthood of J. D. Salinger

WILLIAM WIEGAND

In his latest work of fiction, J. D. Salinger, speaking through a favorite narrator, makes the following observation about P. B. Shelley, a writer some one-hundred-odd years his senior: "I surely think," he says, "that if I were to ask the sixty-odd girls in my two Writing for Publication courses to quote a line, any line, from 'Ozymandias' or even just to tell what the poem is about, it is doubtful whether ten of them could do either, but I'd bet my unrisen tulips that some fifty of them could tell me that Shelley was all for free love and had one wife who wrote *Frankenstein*, and another who drowned herself."

Probably, it would be another safe bet, and one must assume Salinger knows it, that for every ten of Salinger's fans who know anything about the intellectual basis of Zen, a pet subject of his, or the contents of *The Bhagavad-Gita*, there are at least fifty who know that Holden Caulfield had to go to a psychiatrist ("it killed him, really it did"), and that Franny Glass wasn't pregnant after all. Salinger's Zen is to the faithful like Shelley's Platonism—vague and a little dry. But Holden and Franny—that's different. They are the author's kin, as much kin as Shelley's wives were to Shelley. Information about them is more than mere information; it is intimate lore. And discovering it has led naturally and indiscriminately to the quest for information about the pater-familias, Salinger himself.

Nobody can fail to recognize that this rampant curiosity about the author—"lurid and partly lurid," Salinger calls it—is one of the most interesting aspects of his reputation. Just how intense

From *The New Republic*, CXLI, October 19, 1959. Copyright © by *New Republic*. Reprinted by permission.

the interest is may be hard to gauge, but if his experiences are anything like those of Buddy Glass, the writer through whom Salinger has written much in the last few years, the fifty are already beating a path to his door, planting tire tracks in his rose beds and asking him silly questions about "the endemic American *Zeitgeist*," just as they have done with Buddy.

This is remarkable devotion in a generation as cagey as the present one is supposed to be, and yet it might all be conceded to Salinger gracefully enough (fads being what they are) if the body of Salinger's admirers was confined purely to that undergraduate group which sees that it can follow Holden Caulfield's nice line between colloquial earthiness and colloquial mysticism without feeling either too far In or too far Out. But the group is much larger than that, and some people, outside it, have wondered why. About the only explanation Salinger has offered, as he no doubt recalls all the bad imitations of Holden Caulfield, is Buddy Glass' crack, "I have been knighted for my heart-shaped prose."

Going beyond that answer, certain critics, like Maxwell Geismar and John Aldridge, have tried to explain Salinger's appeal by examining some of his favorite themes. Geismar calls Salinger "the spokesman of the Ivy League rebellion of the early Fifties." "Ivy League" means to Geismar that it is a rebellion founded mostly on a dislike for the fancy prep-school phony who abounds in *Catcher in the Rye* and Salinger's other fiction. For Geismar, and for Aldridge too, the rebellion never quite transcends this adolescent pique at wrong guys and boring teachers. The sympathy of the undergraduate with Salinger can, by this line of reasoning, be reduced to the fact that he doesn't like his roommate any better than Holden does and that he may also share Holden's wish for deafness, or Teddy's wish for death and reincarnation in a quieter world where nobody, for God's sake, is lecturing at him on Western Civilization three or four mornings a week. For Geismar and Aldridge, the "rebellion," thus interpreted, seems irresponsible and "adolescent."

It is hard to argue with their opinion, except to observe that the derogation of "adolescent" has also been applied at different times to Goethe, Schiller, Sterne, Byron, Shelley, Keats, Fitzger-

ald, Wolfe, Hemingway and others. The trouble with such a reduction is that it tends to cancel out Geismar's equally interesting
opinion that Salinger is "the ultimate artist of *The New Yorker*
school of writing," a compliment which ought to have some bearing on our question. Beyond that, their assessment does not do
much about telling why the "lurid or partly lurid" curiosity that
has always distinguished the interest in Shelley turns today to
somebody like Salinger rather than to other writers who are concerned with adolescent and pre-adolescent characters.

Salinger's subject matter is not unique, nor are his positions
quite as intelligible as the talk about rebellion would indicate.
He has undercut almost every position he has taken, so much so
lately that to call him the spokesman for anything seems bold.
Probably, if we could find the True Blue Salingerite, that ideal
reader who would remain staunchly superior to any *ad hoc* image
of Salinger, he would be no more addicted to rebellion than he
would be to Zen. He would, I think, be likely to say that he is
interested in Salinger for no better reason than that Salinger's
characters are so uncomfortably alive that one has a kind of irrational desire to keep after them and see if something can't be
worked out. If pressed, he might guess further that Salinger made
them uncomfortable quite deliberately, and that there is an apparently conscious development toward isolating and then en-
larging upon the discomforts of the people he is writing about.

This may be put in terms of two propositions; first, that Salinger is offering something different, something presumably more
provocative than other writers of his "school"—certainly a good
reason for popularity. And, second, that he becomes increasingly
interesting to follow because he has changed /19/ (and is chang-
ing) his own methods after a conscious pattern.

The first proposition is fairly easy to demonstrate. Compare
any of Salinger's stories—they all deal more or less with the in-
digestible past—and the work of most of the other writers of Reminiscence fiction in *The New Yorker* and the little quarterlies.
The difference is in the half-embarrassed attitude of Salinger's
characters ("I did something very stupid and embarrassing." "Why

do I go on like this?" "I'm a madman, really I am."). This is a
bit more than a trademark; the writers of conventional Reminiscence avoid any tinge of self-consciousness like the plague.
While they may be just as jealous of their hunting caps and
crocus-yellow neckties as Holden Caulfield and Buddy Glass are,
they make it all sound blithely natural and healthy. Where Salinger lurks off in the shadow of his banana tree, they plant themselves under a spreading chestnut, anyway something more solid
and less sickly-green. They may experience the same reaction
against Today, the same cherishing of Yesterday, but seldom see
any implications in so much nostalgia.

The second proposition may be a little subtler. All writers develop in some fashion or other, but Salinger's development has
been especially interesting. As with a singer who evolves a style
slowly, much of the pleasure of the audience comes from knowing the stages in his growth.

Salinger's method has depended all along on a close personal
touch with the reader, the shy advance and retreat, the candor
about making mistakes, and the tacit assurance that his defenses
will be seen through; but in its most recent manifestation it feels
for the reader's very heartbeat, tries to catch every flicker of interest or disaffection. By reaching for this kind of communion, it
must promise, above all, candor in the difficult writer-reader relationship. Many readers find this concern for staying honest with
them particularly appealing; they truly believe (and why not?)
that Salinger is trying to get at a more intimate and accurate vision of things than if he took one of the short cuts of form where
truths become so facile that they seem more like lies.

Why can this be regarded as a "development"? Because in
Salinger's early work, even the best, there was the tendency to
take these short cuts, to slide through by means of an easy symbol or two, to settle for one of the standard explanations, or appearances of explanation. There, Salinger was criticizing a formulated and formulable society, and his writing derived from some
wing of the proletarian tradition in which the gulf between the
"lover" and the corrupted bourgeoisie causes most of the suffering of the protagonist. For example, the "banana fever" which

afflicts Seymour in the 1948 story, "A Perfect Day for Bananafish" is a result, as far as we can tell, of his wife's failure of imagination as in the contrast between her telephone conversation with her mother, and Seymour's scene on the beach where he describes to a little girl the plight of a creature bloated with experience which weighs him down in a society he cannot escape.

But after *Catcher in the Rye,* an impulse which was latent in the early work began to assert itself. It was an impulse to deal cautiously, but exclusively, with the emotional graph of a single personality: No moments of sudden truth to give the nice terminal epiphany, but rather a series of tentative illuminations, which confess, explicitly and implicitly, the speaker's lack of any all-encompassing revelation. In "Teddy" and "Franny," the strain of having to contrive a well-made story had started to show, and afterwards Salinger began his experiment with the longer novella. His distrust of what he calls "beginning-middle-end" fiction stemmed then most probably from his awareness of the easy facility not only of the work of others, but of his own. ("Pretty Mouth and Green My Eyes" may have seemed terse and calculable; "A Perfect Day for Bananafish" almost too tidily abstruse.) When Salinger returns to Seymour Glass in the middle-Fifties in order to do him right, Buddy Glass, Seymour's brother, is moved in to afford a kind of analysis that completely rejects conventional structural formula. Also, in the course of the three most recent stories, the social context in which Seymour moved has been largely forsaken.

At the same time, Salinger has found new ways to keep the reader oriented. While he violates most of the rules of the well-made story as well as the usually sacrosanct convention of self-effacement of the author, he still retains certain organizing principles. In "Seymour: an Introduction," the device is one familiar in lyric poetry. As the poets have catalogued the charms of their ladies, in "Seymour" Buddy takes up one at a time the pertinent characteristics and activities of his brother. A rather droll solution, it nevertheless provides a goal for the story; namely, to make the reader feel Seymour less as a saint and more as a human being. If I pull myself together, Buddy says, Seymour who has killed himself may yet be reconstructed—his eyes, his nose, his ears may rematerialize, even his words may be heard without the echo of the tomb. He is not a dead saint, Buddy tells us, and we don't want to think of him as ectoplasm; hence, a tormenting effort to describe his features, his clothes, his poems—anything to make him imperishable.

One by one, the items are ticked off. The poems may be the most embarrassing part of it; they are the hope held in reserve, the means of making Seymour immortal. They are the magic elixir which Buddy keeps half-concealed in the pocket of his coat. He does not really trust the elixir's effectiveness, so he rationalizes his failure to have had the poems published. The reader may not like them, so he advertises their merits in advance. The English Departments may not like them so he prepares to deny their denials of Seymour's immortality.

The consequences of this method are considerable for in the course of the story, Buddy becomes almost indistinguishable from Seymour. Buddy himself notices this. The object-observed has become the observer. All the air has been pumped out of the bell-jar, time and space continuums are sacrificed, and Buddy and Seymour react so intuitively to each other that there is no reverberation. Consequently, the description of the relationship is so great an effort that Buddy breaks into a cold sweat or sinks to the floor, or falls ill for weeks in the torture of trying to present a report without any of the ordinary points of reference or means of control.

The objective of the story then in a manner fails. If Seymour in fever was in danger of becoming a saint, Buddy, who identifies too much, has no better /20/ luck avoiding the same impression of Seymour in health. No longer the bananafish, Seymour is here metamorphosed into a "curlew sandpiper." He is faster than the Fastest Runner in the World; he makes his profoundest observations in the twilight. He is ephemeral, and no matter how many homely anecdotes are told about him, he has grown too diffuse to look at in the daytime; his talents have become supernatural. Only reincarnation ("and here the first blushes will be the reader's, not mine") could bring him down to earth again, and Buddy knows it, knowing the agonizing failure of his heart-shaped prose to do the job.

To use the word "failure" about the story itself is, however, probably almost meaningless to the true Salingerite, for there is a great difference between a failure of purpose ("Does the writer accomplish what he set out to do?") and a failure of effect. In the tradition in which Salinger is now writing, effect is attained not through achieving any goal, any resolution, but rather by getting the effort toward the goal down on the page. However vague that may seem as a criterion, the technical equipment required to meet it with intelligence, integrity, and variety is great. Salinger has submitted to the challenge with particular rigor in the last three stories where the dramatic action in the present has grown increasingly less, and in "Seymour" becomes almost totally expressed in the drama of the individual consciousness, anchored by incidental reports of Buddy's getting up, going to class, getting sick. The past is funneled through by means of letters and personal journals, but remains a part of the struggle of the present.

Corollary to this, it has been important for his enduring appeal that Salinger's narrative procedure has not been associative or "stream of consciousness," a conventional modern reaction against over-rigid form. His syntax is sophisticated and lucid, and in spite of the destruction of the time continuum, he proposes his objectives and makes his digressions (if we want a fictional forebear) with an aplomb like Sterne's, whose techniques those of "Seymour" perhaps most resemble.

Compare, for example, this from *Tristram Shandy:*

". . . It is one comfort at least to me that I lost some four-score ounces of blood this week in a most uncritical fever which attacked me at the beginning of this chapter; so that I still have some hope remaining, it may be in the serous or globular parts of the blood and in the subtle aura of the brain. . . ."

with Salinger's:

". . . I'm really not up to anything that *intime* just here. (I'm keeping especially close tabs on myself, in fact. It seems to me that this composition has never been in more danger than right now of taking on precisely the informality of underwear.) I've announced a major delay between paragraphs by way of informing the reader that I'm just freshly risen from nine weeks in bed with acute hepatitis. . . ."

There are dangers in this kind of writing. Sometimes it verges on whimsy, and certainly it can lead to cultishness, as it did with Sterne or with Byron and Shelley, all of whom on occasions got *intime* with their readers. Also, and particularly with temperaments like Salinger's, it may depend too much on wit to relieve and to steady it. When the humor shows signs of exhaustion and despair, as Byron's and Sterne's did at times, as Salinger's does in "Seymour," the writer may be in trouble.

The body of Salinger's work has been an exploration chiefly of the problem of loss and mutability, free from theories about how a solution may be found. Inasmuch as poets have largely lost interest in such quests since about the time of Tennyson's *In Memoriam* and that it has made few real inroads into English or American fiction (unlike French and German) since Tennyson, the Salinger vogue is not surprising. It answers a need for a different kind of treatment of experience.

When Buddy Glass asks, "How can I record what I've just recorded and still be happy?" he doesn't answer the question. But there are hints that he is happy with his persistence, and that many of his readers who are up to anything *intime* are happy with it too. /21/

XVI

The Salinger Industry

GEORGE STEINER

Writing in *The Nation* in March 1957, Mr. David L. Stevenson expressed surprise at the fact that Salinger is "rarely acknowledged by the official guardians of our literary virtue." He can now rest assured. The heavy guns are in action along the entire critical front. Salinger's unique role in contemporary letters has been accorded full recognition:

Salinger is probably the most avidly read author of any serious pretensions in his generation. (Arthur Mizener, *Harpers*, February, 1959)

There are, I am convinced, millions of young Americans who feel closer to Salinger than to any other writer. (Granville Hicks, *Saturday Review*, July 25, 1959)

The only Post-War fiction unanimously approved by contemporary literate American youth consists of about five hundred pages by Jerome David Salinger. (F. L. Gwynn and J. L. Blotner, *The Fiction of J. D. Salinger*, University of Pittsburgh Press, 1958)

Obviously, critics are interested to find out why this should be so. Salinger has caught with uncanny precision the speech and thought-rhythms of the young. "The talk of his characters is, so to speak, righter than right" (Hicks). He can make a kind of poetry of "the simplest occasion," giving the shapes of art to the swift, raw, undigested materials of urban and college life (Mizener). The crisis of a Salinger fable makes the reader aware of how we are "members all of the lonely crowd" (Stevenson). Salinger is

From *The Nation*, CLXXXXIX, November 14, 1959. Copyright 1959 by The Nation Associates. Reprinted by permission.

the spokesman for the corner-of-the-mouth rebelliousness of the
postwar generation; he expresses the "Ivy League Rebellion of
the Fifties" (Maxwell Geismar). He speaks for the nonconform-
ists who resist the old betrayals of rhetoric and illusion. As Ibsen
would put it, he rejects the false "claims of the ideal" (William
Wiegand, *Chicago Review,* II).

One might have thought that that was more than enough to
account for the success of a good minor writer with an audience
which is, by any traditional tokens, largely illiterate. But no.
Where the Higher Criticism is at work more portentous issues
are invoked. Writing in the *Western Humanities Review* (Spring,
1956), Professors Heiserman and Miller tell us that *The Catcher
in the Rye* belongs to an ancient narrative tradition, "perhaps
the most profound in western fiction":

> It is, of course, the tradition of the Quest. We use the medieval term
> because it signifies a seeking after what is tremendous, greater than the
> love of a woman. . . . Holden's Quest takes him outside society; yet the
> grail he seeks is the world and the grail is full of love. . . . Huck Finn had
> the Mississippi and at the end of the Mississippi he had the wild /360/
> west beyond Arkansas. The hero of *The Waste Land* had Shantih, the
> peace which passes human understanding. Bloom had Molly and his own
> ignorance; Dedalus had Paris and Zurich. But for Holden, there is no
> place to go.

In the course of exegesis, Salinger's young lout is also compared
with Alyosha Karamazov, Aeneas, Ulysses, Gatsby, Ishmael, Hans
Castorp and Dostoevsky's Idiot, and always rather to his own advantage.

With Salinger firmly enthroned in the critical pantheon, the
gates were open to the happy hunt for literary influences and
analogues. In the *American Quarterly* (IX, 1957), Professor Edgar Branch rightly pointed out the extent to which *The Catcher*
is related to *Huckleberry Finn.* "Holden is truly a kind of latter-
day, urbanized Huck." Fair enough, and the comparison itself is
high praise for any modern novel. But we plunge deeper: "Salinger's viewpoint also draws upon a mystical sense merely inchoate
in Mark Twain's imagination" (poor fellow); it has an "awe-

some relevance to our collective civilized fate." A piece by Martin Green in the *Chicago Review* (Winter, 1958) starts out more modestly. Green shrewdly observes that there is between the heroes of Salinger and those of Kingsley Amis a suggestive similarity. Both, as Kenneth Tynan had seen earlier, reflect angry youth and an abdication from politics and idealism. But again, the summits beckon:

Modern literature—the literature of Hemingway, Faulkner, Robert Penn Warren, Greene, Waugh, McCullers, Bowen, Buechner, etc.—I trust is now over. I trust that in these two new writers we see at last a positive, life-giving alternative. . . . Salinger also *creates* life.

In short: Salinger's tales are "comic masterpieces" (Charles Kaplan, *College English,* XVIII, 1956), and they may safely be compared with the classic in literature. The scholarly apparatus which such stature implies is also forthcoming. Professors Gwynn and Blotner provide a "Check-List of J. D. Salinger's Fiction" and a list of "Critical Studies of Salinger's Fiction." They devote a learned monograph to their man and come up with a pronouncement which caps the entire Salinger Industry:

The problem he [Salinger] has set himself in this last period is no less than the utilization of transcendental mysticism in satiric fiction, something (as far as we know) never attempted before by an American writer, and by only a few in Western literature.

Roll of drums; exeunt Cervantes, Chekhov and other lesser souls.

In themselves, all these pomposities and exaggerations are of no great importance. But they do point to some of the things that are seriously wrong with contemporary American criticism.

First of all, they get Salinger's work badly out of focus and could do him a great deal of harm if he were so misguided as to read them (most probably he does not). Mr. Jerome David Salinger is neither Molière nor Chekhov. He is not yet Mark Twain (and by a long shot). Why should he be? He is a gifted and entertaining writer with one excellent short novel and a number of memorable stories to his credit. He has a marvelous ear for the semiliterate meanderings of the adolescent mind. He has caught and made articulate the nervous, quizzical, rough-edged spirit of the moment. He very obviously touches on major or traditional motifs: the failure of the bridges that are meant to link young and old, the mending power of a general, non-sexual love between human beings (something between friendship and compassion). "For Esmé—with Love and Squalor" is a wonderfully moving story, perhaps the best study to come out of the war of the way in which the greater facts of hatred play havoc in the private soul. "The Laughing Man" and "Down at the Dinghy" are fine sketches of the bruised, complicated world of children. But neither holds a candle to Joyce's *Araby* or to the studies of childhood in Dostoevsky. Of late, Salinger has begun parodying Salinger. His most recent chronicle of the Glass family is a piece of shapeless self-indulgence (*The New Yorker* is notoriously vulnerable to the delights of sheer length). The writer himself, moreover, is interest-/361/ing. He has adopted a T. E. Lawrence technique of partial concealment. He does not sign books at Brentano's nor teach creative writing at Black Mountain. "I was with the Fourth Division during the war. I almost always write about very young people." That's about all he wants us to know.

Salinger's virtues account for part of his vast appeal. But only for part. The rest is less exalted. The young like to read about the young. Salinger writes *briefly* (no need to lug home a big book or something, Lord help us, not available in paperback). He demands of his readers nothing in the way of literacy or political interest (in my time, college bull-sessions raged over *Doctor Faustus;* but that meant having heard of Hitler or Nietzsche or being dimly aware of a past writer called Goethe). Salinger flatters the very ignorance and moral shallowness of his young readers. He suggests to them that formal ignorance, political apathy and a vague *tristesse* are positive virtues. They open the heart to mystic intimations of love. This is where his cunning and somewhat shoddy use of Zen comes in. Zen is in fashion. People who lack even the rudiments of knowledge needed to read Dante or the nerve required by Schopenhauer, snatch up the latest paperback on Zen. "Salinger's constant allusions to the Bhagavad Gita, Sri Ramakrishna, Chuang-tsu, and the rest are only efforts to find alternate ways of expressing what his stories are about," says

Mizener. I wonder. They are more likely a shrewd insight into the kind of half-culture which the present college generation revels in. Twelfth-century madrigals are bound to come soon into the lives of Franny or Zooey or the late lamented Seymour.

These are the main facts. Why is literary criticism so determined to get them out of proportion?

First, there is a matter of language. Having added to the legacy of Germanic scholarship the jargon of the New Criticism, many American academic critics are no longer able to write with plainness or understatement. They have a vested interest in the complex and the sublime. (Hence Messrs. Heiserman and Miller's capitalized Quest and their pious statement, "We use the medieval term.". . .) A new, probably rather minor achievement comes along, and at once critical language soars to sublimity. The result is a serious devaluation of critical coin. If one writes about Salinger as do Gwynn and Blotner, just how is one to write about Cervantes or Turgenev? The entire sense of discrimination between values which should be implicit in a critic's language goes lost.

Secondly, there is a matter of economics. The young assistant or associate professor must publish in order to get advancement or to obtain one of those Fulbrights, Guggenheims or Fords which mark the ascent to Parnassus. Now suppose he is still faintly alive and does not care to write yet another paper on imagery in Pope or cancel-sheets in Melville. He wants to test his critical sense against a contemporary work. He does not know enough French or German to write about European masters. What is he to do? He turns to the American scene. The giants are no longer about. Faulkner is making tape recordings and Hemingway is adding further gore to *Death in the Afternoon* (surely one of the dullest books in our time). Along comes a small though clearly interesting fish like Salinger and out go the whaling fleets. The academic critic can do his piece with few footnotes, it will be accepted by critical reviews or little magazines, and it is another tally on the sheet of his career.

American literary criticism has become a vast machine in constant need of new raw material. There are too many critical jour-

nals, too many seminars, too many summer schools and fellow-
ships for critics. One is reminded of the ambitions of Marcia, a
character in the New York *Herald Tribune* comic strip, *Miss
Peach*. Asked what she wished to become in life, the little brute
answered, "A critic." And whom would she criticize? "Every man,
woman, and child in the United States." There has never been,
and cannot be, enough good literature produced at any given
moment to supply a critical industry so massive and serious. The
immediate past, moreover, has been a classic period for critics.
With Eliot, /362/ Pound, Leavis, Edmund Wilson, Trilling,
Blackmur, Tate and Yvor Winters in the field, just how much use
is there in writing yet another essay on Dante or Shakespeare or
Yeats? The quarry of greatness having been exhaustively mined,
younger critics turn their big guns on to the smaller targets.

All this has serious consequences. There is, at the moment, a
gross devaluation of standards (the Cozzens ecstasy of a few sea-
sons back is a case in point). If criticism does not serve to distinguish what is great from what is competent, it is not carrying out
its proper task. If it conspires to suggest that transcendent values
are made articulate in anything quite as loose and glossy as the
maunderings of Zooey, it is betraying its responsibilities. Of
course, Salinger is a most skillful and original writer. Of course,
he is worth discussing and praising. But not in terms appropriate
to the master poets of the world, not with all the pomp and circumstance of final estimation. By all means, let us have Esmé,
Daumier-Smith and all the Glasses. But let us not regard them as
the house of Atreus reborn. /363/

XVII

Must Writers Be Characters?

HARVEY SWADOS

. . . We are suffering from what might be called the cult of personality in American letters. No doubt it will immediately be objected that this is mere obfuscation, confusing the popular acclaim of middlebrow spokesmen (who, as Louella Parsons serves the movie-going public, serve their public with news of Hemingway's chest measurements and William Faulkner's alcoholic propensities) with the serious appraisals of established literary critics. Let us anticipate this objection by examining some of the current enthusiasms of our literary critics, and contrasting them with some of the omissions.

If there are any two American writers of the current generation who have been more written about in recent years than any others, they are surely J. D. Salinger and Norman Mailer. It seems to me not at all irrelevant that the first of these has so sedulously avoided publicity that he has aroused the liveliest curiosity about himself, and that the second has frankly and unremittingly sought to gain what the metaphysicians of advertising would define as maximum exposure to his reader-potential.

Salinger, the Greta Garbo of American letters, is now in his early forties and is the author of one novel, "The Catcher in the Rye," a book of short stories, and a number of as yet uncollected stories, mostly dealing with the travails of the Glass family. That is all we are supposed to know, and it should be enough. Unquestionably he is a clever and knowledgeable writer who concerns himself with a somewhat restricted segment of American society,

From *Saturday Review*, XLIII, October 1, 1960, pp. 12-14, 50. Reprinted by permission of *Saturday Review* and of James Brown Associates, Inc.

and who has a first-rate ear for the mannerisms of American speech, particularly those peculiar to the young. Once this has been said, we find ourselves shifting, so to speak, from one foot to the other. And yet such has been the outpouring of articles, essays, and speculations on J. D. Salinger that the Salinger bibliography might lead one unfamiliar with his work to think that it consisted, not of one bittersweet novel and some short stories, but of an *oeuvre* comparable to William Faulkner's twenty-odd books.

What is more, this outpouring has come not so much from the middle-brows as it has from the groves of academe and from those not accustomed to trifling with merely popular writers. Can there be a college literary magazine in the land which has not had /12/ its Salinger piece? By now it has become as obligatory as the Pound exegesis or the James explication. Why?

For one thing, these critics seem much impressed with Salinger's increasing popularity abroad as a spokesman—he begins to approach the universal acceptance of Hemingway, which in itself is awesome. Yet we have not been subjected so far to a spate of studies of Dashiell Hammett simply because he is much admired in France, or of Jack London simply because he is adored in Russia. We may reasonably suspect, therefore, that other considerations are involved. In addition to the fact of his popularity abroad, these critics are apparently much moved by Salinger's manifest and continuing appeal to youth and by the evidence in his work that he is attempting to compose a Christian parable.

Both these factors, the touching appeal of his work to the young and his painfully self-conscious effort to be Deep, are of course closely interrelated. But those of us who can, if we are honest, recall all too easily our adolescent infatuation with Thomas Wolfe (because he seemed to be speaking directly to us, and speaking too of the really profound things in life) must, I am afraid, be reduced in our maturity to stammering embarrassment for the author and for his apologists when we are asked in all seriousness to consider Salinger, like Wolfe, as a profoundly reflective philosophical novelist. No, it seems more likely that there exists in the minds of those who make such claims a connection between Salinger's supposed profundity and his tantalizing physical inaccessibility. The legend of mysterious private suffering cohabiting with a singularly Christian literary morality is self-generating and self-perpetuating; it is also conducive to excited appraisals of a writer's importance based finally on what must be regarded as extraliterary considerations. . . . /13/

. . . This massive concentration on a handful of writers (for reasons all too often nonliterary), coupled with a massive exclusion of most other writers from consideration, can result in a ludicrously distorted picture of the American literary situation. Recently a leading editor observed at a literary symposium that the past decade's fiction had been "dominated by adolescents." Presumably what he meant was that the beats had made the most noise and had therefore drowned out such writers as Baldwin, Bellow, Malamud, Ellison, Bourjaily, Morris, and other serious novelists who had come to maturity during the Fifties. But who did "dominate" the fiction of the decade? If it was the beats, as the editor implied, and not the really serious creative people, then we may be justified in asserting that the editors and critics are, as Norman Mailer has shrewdly observed of American audiences in general, "incapable of confronting a book unless it is successful." . . . /14/

. . . It should not be thought that this is a nostalgic plea for a return to a past in which novelists were all seriously considered, earnestly discussed, and warmly appreciated during their lifetimes. Such a past never existed. But surely we have a responsibility to plead for a better future. I speak now not as an occasional critic, but as a novelist concerned about his fellow writers as well as his fellow readers, when I propose that the critics and the publishers who regard themselves by definition as the caretakers of our culture, but function in reality as drum-beaters for an arbitrarily limited galaxy of stars and hence as vulgar hucksters for the cult of personality, be required to assume what should be their true responsibility: to make more accessible to us all those writers who do not, in the words of Manes Sperber, "look for adventures, but for an encounter with consciousness; not for the dream, but for the awakening." /50/

XVIII

COMMUNITY CRITICS . . . AND CENSORS

Soon after *The Catcher in the Rye* had begun to acquire a critical reputation as a modern classic and had become readily available in an inexpensive paperback edition (first published by Signet in March 1953), the book appeared on lists of required reading, first, apparently, in college and university classes in English and later in some high school classes. In still other high schools it was included on "recommended" or "supplementary" reading lists as an optional choice for individual reading.

One consequence of using the novel in schools and colleges was the sudden emergence of protests alleging immorality, obscenity, or even subversiveness. In Texas, for example, a Houston lawyer, whose daughter had been assigned the novel in an English class at the University of Texas, threatened to remove the girl from the University:

. . . The aggrieved father sent copies to the governor, the chancellor of the university, and a number of state officials. The state senator from Houston threatened to read passages from the book on the senate floor to show the sort of thing they teach in Austin. The lawyer-father said Salinger used language "no sane person would use" and accused the university of "corrupting the moral fibers of our youth." He added that the novel "is not a hard-core Communist-type book, but it encourages a lessening of spiritual values which in turn leads to communism."[1]

Demands for removal of the book from high school reading lists (or from the open shelves of public libraries) were voiced in Miami, Florida; Santa Ana, California; Salt Lake City, Utah; Louisville, Kentucky; and in other cities. At least one high school

[1] Willie Morris, "Houston's Superpatriots," *Harper's Magazine*, October 1961, p. 50.

teacher was dismissed from her position for assigning the novel (Louisville) and another teacher was reprimanded and transferred to another assignment (San Jose, California).[2]

In the following section of this book we present three essays concerning *The Catcher* and the censors. In the first essay, "Not Suitable for Temple City," the editors relate the novel's fortunes in the high school of a California community. The second, "Catcher and Mice" by Everett T. Moore, reprinted from *ALA Bulletin*, the official publication of the American Library Association, reports similar controversies involving schools and libraries elsewhere. The third essay, "Raise High the Barriers, Censor," by Edward P. J. Corbett is an examination of various charges made against the novel together with arguments in its defense.

1

Not Suitable for Temple City

THE EDITORS

Temple City, California, is a suburban community fifteen miles northeast of the Los Angeles City Hall. Like many of the adjoining communities in the San Gabriel Valley (Arcadia, San Gabriel, San Marino, Pasadena), Temple City is tied economically to what is often called the Greater Los Angeles Metropolitan Area. Like these other suburbs, it stoutly maintains some vestiges of independence from the metropolis, such as its own city government and its own public school system. Both the elementary schools

---

[2] For details of these and other instances see *Newsletter on Intellectual Freedom* (published for the American Library Association by the Freedom of Information Center, School of Journalism, University of Missouri), e.g., the issues of June 1960, June 1961, and July 1962.

and the single high school of the community are under the juris-
diction of a local school board known as the Temple City Unified
School District.

Although *The Catcher in the Rye* was not an assigned text in
Temple City High School, the book had been included in a list
of novels prepared by eleventh grade English teachers as suggested supplementary reading for an occasional student working
for extra credit. Early in 1962 Salinger's novel became the subject of controversy at a meeting of the Temple City Board of
Education. The controversy was reported in the Pasadena *Star-
News* on February 7, 1962, in this news story by Mrs. Kate Sex-
ton, a staff writer:

TEMPLE CITY—The school board Monday night [February 5] voted to
abolish the list of selected novels used by some teachers of 11th grade
English as a guide to reading for extra credit.

The action, recommended by Clarice Manshardt, district director of
curriculum, closed the door, at least temporarily, on the storm of controversy which arose over the list a month ago.

It also disappointed critics of some 26 books on the list who had hoped
to see the list retained with the 26 novels deleted.

The novels they singled out as objectionable had already been annotated by school staff compilers as "M," difficult and suitable only for
mature readers; "P," requiring parents' permission for reading; and
"MP," a combination of both.

"Catcher in the Rye" by J. D. Salinger, although not annotated,
came in for specific criticism. . . .

Principals in the formal discussion were Howard B. Beckner, super-
intendent of schools; Miss Manshardt; Robert DeMille and Mrs. Arthur
Crippen, objecting parents, and board members Harlos Gross, Robert
Moses, Virginia Harker, Stewart Klass and Mrs. Glassco.

Miss Manshardt gained board approval of substituting closer teacher-
pupil-parent communication for the list which she said has had a "very
limited" use in English classes.

She proposed that hereafter teachers of all grade levels answer questions about books suitable to each level and make assignments in light
of the students' needs.

"This should produce a livelier and more personal job of teaching,"
she added, "and any parent should exercise the control which he sees
as his right over his child's selection of a book not required for class
credit."

"But," she asked, "do parents know how many books not on this list our young people are reading? Some of them would raise your eyebrows. We find them in the bushes around school."

Mrs. Crippen . . . mother of two high school students, read passages from a three-page typed statement:

"I fail to understand the need to use any books that need defending when our literary heritage has given us thousands of good books from which to choose and that are far more constructive in their use of English and certainly will build better vocabularies than some that have been previously recommended. . . .

"A sound principle with regard to books for the young must be: Only the best is good enough. For there is an immense idealism hidden beneath the blunt or the unposed concern of youth.

"When literary creations bring into focus abundant examples of immorality, perversion, varied crimes; literary creations ripping away at God-created institutions of family, society, government; literary creations ranging through the cycle of all known moral and intellectual disorder, then the authors of such literary creations have adopted a criminal approach to their responsibilities as authors."

Mrs. Crippen later admitted to a reporter that her statement incorporated views and statements of "many other persons," but declined to name the collaborators. . . .

Several questions about the book list came to his mind, DeMille's statement began.

"Are all the books on the list representative of good literature?"

"Has a criteria [sic] for the selection of significant books been established?"

"Does the committee preparing the list judge the books from their own personal review of the book or are they prone to use the sometimes biased analysis of proclaimed reviewers?"

"Is the criteria [sic] of these reviewers the same as that used by the department?"

"Is the material contained in the books of high school and not college level?"

DeMille said he found "Catcher in the Rye" uninteresting, rambling and a chore to read, "certainly not one you would reread."

"The language . . . is crude, profane and obscene; not what you would expect of a boy given the advantages of private schools. Much of the language is unfamiliar to many of our young people.

"We . . . protest the many blasphemies, unpatriotic attitudes, reference to prostitution and sexual affairs. There are continuous slurs with a down-grading of our home life, teaching profession, religion and so forth.

"With reservations, we feel this book might better have a place in a college graduate course in abnormal psychology or sociology."

Novels annotated "M," "P," or "MP" on the selected list include "Crime and Punishment" by Dostoyevsky, "Madame Bovary" by Flaubert, "The Scarlet Letter" by Hawthorne, "Brave New World" by Huxley, "Moon and Sixpence" by Maugham, "1984" by Orwell, "Grapes of Wrath" by Steinbeck, "Candide" by Voltaire and "Nana" by Zola.[3]

For the next month the columns of the *Star-News* reflected, almost daily, reactions to the continuing controversy in Temple City. On February 11 the newspaper ran an editorial condemning the pressures for censorship as disgraceful anti-intellectualism and speculating as to the possible existence of an organized minority with politically ultraconservative views.

In response to the editorial the following letter from Mrs. Crippen, one of the "objecting parents," appeared in the newspaper's "Letters to the Editor" column:

The misunderstanding as to the books objected to in the editorial, "The Scope of Reading" (Feb. 11) is understandable; however, not wishing to appear "anti-intellectual" nor having an "inadequate recognition of the classics of literature," may I quote from my communications to the English Department and the Board of Education of Temple City.

"Thus with some question and considerable concern, I review our eleventh grade supplemental reading lists and find such authors as Steinbeck, Arthur Miller, Tennessee Williams, and Salinger. On one list are 'Tortilla Flat,' 'Grapes of Wrath,' 'Cannery Row' and 'Catcher in the Rye.' 'Catcher in the Rye' takes the Lord's name in vain 295 times and uses blatant blasphemy 587 times in 187 pages of text. One instructor gives credit for 'Cat on a Hot Tin Roof' and 'Of Mice and Men.' Gentlemen, do these represent the culture of America and our contribution to the advancement of civilization? Or are they merely 'best sellers' of the day or the writings of frustrated men seemingly obsessed with the abnormal and debauchery?" . . .

In a statement following the letter the editor commented, in part, as follows:

[3] From the Pasadena (California) *Star-News*, February 7, 1962. Reprinted by permission.

. . . In the statement she read to the board Mrs. Crippen indicated she categorically opposed the inclusion of any book that "needs defending." She did not then specify which works or authors she thought unsuitable. . . . Board records show that in a statement preceding her presentation at the meeting Mrs. Crippen said, "The board should have a policy that books of any kind that anyone thinks are controversial would be eliminated from the list."

Subsequent letters to the editor appeared at the rate of at least two or three per day. On one day the entire "Letters" column was given over to the Temple City controversy. One writer (a resident of another suburb) called *The Catcher in the Rye* "a trashy book" and said, among other things, "I can't see why our kids should read about a boy getting himself kicked out of school. The book is filled with swear words and no decent person wants to read swear words." Another made the point that the novel might perhaps be suitable for college students, but ". . . the interpretation we place upon reading material at 19 is rarely the same as that when we were 16, and therein lies my quarrel with placing 'Catcher' on required lists for high school students." One woman not only complained about the immorality of the novel (which, she said, she had not read and certainly did not intend to), but also exhibited an unintentionally comic confusion between J. D. Salinger and Pierre Salinger, press secretary to President Kennedy, for, she insisted, a man who wrote a book like *The Catcher* should be immediately discharged from the President's service.

A number of letter writers, it should be pointed out, composed thoughtful defenses of *The Catcher*. One mother, for example, after describing the significance she found in the novel, said, "I sincerely hope that people with minds unable to penetrate a book's meaning beneath the surface of its style (in this case the idiom of a teen-age boy) are not going to set themselves up as censors of reading for MY children." Another writer exonerated the book from the charges of obscenity and blasphemy; drawing parallels between the language of *The Catcher* and that of the Bible and Shakespeare, he argued: "Should we ban Shakespeare because of the vulgarity in some of his scenes? Of course not!

There's nobility and inspiration in his plays. There is nobility and inspiration in Salinger."

The final official word from Temple City, however, was a statement by the superintendent of schools, who said:

> ... Let's set the record straight! The Board did not approve or defend "Catcher in the Rye," nor did it formally ban it (a loud denunciation would only have led to more reading of the book). Incidentally I expressed my distaste for it in writing to Mrs. Crippen and Mrs. DeMille (two of the objectors) before the board meeting. It should be noted that this book has not been in our library nor has it been used as a textbook of any sort. . . .
>
> How could the Board better answer objectors than to say: (1) That hereafter no list recommending specific books will be issued. (Remember lists already out could hardly be recovered.) (2) That teachers are to be responsible for the counseling and guidance of students on book selections and suitable reading material. (3) That parents have the right, and should accept some responsibility for the guidance of their sons and daughters in the matter of outside reading. . . .

The superintendent added the opinion that the controversy at the meeting of the school board may have come from "those who had deliberately planned to place the Board in a difficult situation." Furthermore, he suggested, "The affair was not a spontaneous expression of concern but had been carefully planned, and the crowd included certain chronic critics who proclaim that 'This is a republic not a democracy.'"

Copies of the novel are still to be seen occasionally in the paperback book racks of Temple City's drugstores and supermarkets, and it may be that, from time to time, a copy is bought by a high school student. But the English teachers in Temple City High School are evidently unlikely to recommend the novel to their students.

———————————— 2 ————————————

Catcher and Mice

EVERETT T. MOORE

Some of the parents and other citizens who have been objecting to *The Catcher in the Rye* as recommended reading for high school students may themselves have read no farther than the second page of J. D. Salinger's novel, where young Holden Caulfield takes a disenchanted look at his own school, from which he has just been expelled. Although Pencey Prep advertises that "since 1888 we have been molding boys into splendid, clear-thinking young men," Holden thinks this is "strictly for the birds."

"They don't do any damn more *molding* at Pencey than they do at any other school," says Holden. "And I didn't know anybody there that was splendid and clear-thinking and all. Maybe two guys. If that many. And they probably *came* to Pencey that way."

Inelegance of language and a precociously earthy view of life on the part of our hero have apparently offended many adults who would rather their youngsters were given a blander diet. But their efforts to discourage interest in this book—which has delighted discerning teachers and perceptive students alike—have been running into the difficulties censors usually encounter sooner or later: the book becomes more popular than ever. Its paperback edition has occupied a strong position on best-seller lists for some time.

Within the past year or so *The Catcher in the Rye* has been in trouble—or has got teachers in trouble for assigning or recommending it—in such places as Tulsa, Oklahoma, Louisville, and San Jose and Marin County in California.

From *ALA Bulletin,* March 1961. Reprinted by permission of the American Library Association.

In Tulsa, a high school English teacher assigned the book to her eleventh-grade English class. Eight parents protested and demanded the teacher be fired. She was given a reprieve, but the book was banned.

In Louisville, a tenth-grade English teacher who assigned *The Catcher* to a class of boys was told he would be released at the end of the year.

In San Jose, a high school removed the Salinger book from its supplementary reading list for the twelfth-year advanced English course, along with Hemingway's *The Sun Also Rises*, Huxley's *Brave New World*, Wolfe's *Look Homeward, Angel*, and Saroyan's *The Human Comedy*. The teacher who had compiled the list was transferred out of the school.

In Marin County, California, officials of the Tamalpais Union High School District received a complaint last November from a Baptist minister in Larkspur, the Rev. Michael Barkowska, about the use of *The Catcher in the Rye* and Steinbeck's *Of Mice and Men* in the schools. "They bring reproach upon the name of God," he said, and contain "profanity, lewd words, and poor English." The minister said he had read only excerpts from the books, because he found the language so sickening that he could not continue.

Twenty persons joined the minister in signing a petition to the board of trustees of the high school district denouncing use of the two books in Redwood High School, where they were on a list of recommended reading for eleventh-year English students. School officials said the books were also available in the libraries of two other schools in the district.

Several weeks later, after the matter had received publicity (Herb Caen had noted in the San Francisco *Chronicle* that "Another book-burning hassle is in the making over in Marin . . ."), the minister added another list of twenty-five signatures to the petition, including seven more ministers.

Two ministers, however, issued open letters opposing the efforts to ban the books from the school libraries. The Rev. Samuel A. Wright, of the Unitarian Church in San Rafael, said he thought the Rev. Mr. Barkowska was "dead wrong," praised Salinger's book as "one of the better aids in helping change the path of young men on the road to delinquency," and said the Steinbeck novel "has become a classic." The other minister, the pastor of the Holy City Apocalyptic Church, in the Santa Cruz mountains, several counties away, thought no good would come of the drive to suppress the two books. The director of education of the Episcopal Diocese of San Francisco, Canon Trevor A. Hoy, joined in the defense of the books. He wrote the directors of the high school district that the attempt to ban them was "irresponsible and hasty censorship."

The geographical setting of the case was of more than passing interest to Californians, for Larkspur, in Marin County, was the home of Mrs. Anne Smart, who in 1954 had led a fight to have fifteen books banned from the Tamalpais Union High School District as subversive and obscene. She had withdrawn the books from /229/ one of the high school libraries and turned them over to the county grand jury, which declared that they had been "definitely placed in our school libraries to plant the seeds of communism in the minds of our children." Included were *Emotional Problems of Living,* by English and Pearson, Steinbeck's *A Russian Journal,* Embree's *Thirteen Against the Odds,* McWilliams' *Brothers Under the Skin,* and *American Argument,* by Pearl Buck and Eslanda Robeson. The fifteen were only samples, Mrs. Smart reminded her followers, of the many books she had found to be obscene or immoral. On that occasion the trustees of the school district had rejected the findings of the grand jury and declared that all fifteen books should be retained in the school libraries.

Last December the trustees of the same school district voted to deny the petition for removal of *The Catcher in the Rye* and *Of Mice and Men* from Marin County high school libraries. The San Francisco *Chronicle,* in an editorial headed "Good Sense in Marin," said, "Not every school board would have moxie enough to stand up against the sanctimony of a passel of parsons setting out to protect other people's children from literature they disapprove of."

There is no evidence in press reports that Mrs. Smart had any part in inspiring the attack on the Salinger and Steinbeck books in Marin County. Nor is there evidence of any generally circu-

lated lists that are inspiring would-be censors in such widely separated points as Tulsa, Louisville, and Marin to concentrate on
much the same group of "objectionable" books.

In perhaps most communities of the United States, teachers of
English who assign or recommend the reading of such a book as
The Catcher in the Rye, and their librarians who stock the book,
are risking censure from parents or others who have strong objections to exposing youngsters to this kind of literature. What
backing are they likely to have from their administrators?

At the conference last fall of the New England Association of
Teachers of English, the chairman of a meeting on "Censorship
and the Teacher of English" asked how many teachers in the
room felt their school administration would back them in a crisis.
Only eight out of about sixty said they did. The rest thought they
would be "thrown to the wolves" if they assigned reading that
aroused some parent or pressure group.

As reported in the *Secondary Principal's Letter* (Arthur C.
Croft Publications, New London, Connecticut), December 1960,
the question had been asked after Thomas Aquila, Principal of
North Haven High School, had said, "I feel English teachers are
putting themselves in the position where their freedom to teach
is in jeopardy. I'm even more upset at the complacency with
which teachers are taking a pushing around." Asked how he copes
with pressure from irate parents, citizens, or religious and civic
groups he said, "Principals should anticipate a visit from the
bookburners in whatever form they may take. They should be
sure they have read books being assigned by teachers."

"If you haven't read the book," Mr. Aquila continued, "you're
immediately in trouble. . . . Once the bookburners have you on
the run, you're done for." He said that when parents complained
about a book he first established he had read the book by telling
why he thought it had literary merit. Then he told them that if
they did not want their children to read it that was all right with
him, but the other students were going to. "This method usually
brings results, especially with status-seeking parents who want
their children to be on a par with their peers," he said.

Holden Caulfield, late of Pencey Prep, might have found such
a snob appeal "very depressing," but teachers and librarians may

manage to find some comfort in any effort to preserve their freedom of action. What will mean more to them in the long run will
be the kind of strong community support that was demonstrated
by the school board in Marin County. /230/

—————————————— 3 ——————————————

Raise High the Barriers, Censors

EDWARD P. J. CORBETT

About six years ago, at a Modern Language Association convention, a group of professors were discussing job openings, as is their
wont at such gatherings. One of the teachers mentioned an offer
he had had from a West Coast college. A pipe-smoker in the
group blurted out: "For heaven's sake, stay away from *that* place.
They recently fired a man for requiring his freshman students to
read *The Catcher in the Rye*."

That firing may have been the earliest instance of a teacher
getting into serious trouble over J. D. Salinger's book. Since that
time, reports of irate protests from school boards, principals, librarians and parents have multiplied. The most publicized recent
stir about the book was the reprimand that Mrs. Beatrice Levin
received from her principal for introducing *The Catcher in the
Rye* to her 16-year-old students at Edison High School in Tulsa,
Okla. Scores of subsequent letters to the editor revealed other
bans on the book in schools and libraries. Curiously enough, the
same kind of censure was once visited upon the book to which

From *America*, CIV (January 7, 1961), 441-44. Reprinted by permission from
America, National Catholic Weekly Review, 920 Broadway, New York 10, N.Y.

The Catcher in the Rye has most often been compared—Mark Twain's *Huckleberry Finn.*

Adult attempts to keep *The Catcher in the Rye* out of the hands of young people will undoubtedly increase, for it is the one novel that young people of postwar generation have been reading and discussing avidly. I had firsthand evidence of students' reactions when *The Catcher in the Rye* was one of the three novels (the other two were Huxley's *Brave New World* and Conrad's *Under Western Eyes*) eligible for review two years ago in the Jesuit English Contest, an annual event among ten Midwestern Jesuit colleges and universities. At least 90 per cent of our students elected to write on Salinger's book. In fact, I have never witnessed on our campus as much eager discussion about a book as there was about *The Catcher in the Rye.* There were a few repercussions from adults outside the university, but these subsided when the question was raised: "Would the Jesuit Educational Association assign a book that was going to corrupt young people?"

To the many people who have come to love the book and its hero, Holden Caulfield, all this controversy is puzzling and disturbing. They regard even the suggestion that the book needs defending as sacrilegious—almost as though they were being asked to vindicate the Constitution. Although their feelings of outrage are understandable, I feel that in view of the vast and continuing popularity of the book the objections should be confronted and appraised. My arguments in defense of *The Catcher in the Rye* are the common ones, quite familiar to those acquainted with other controversies about "forbidden" books.

The language of the book is crude, profane, obscene. This is the objection most frequently cited when the book has been banned. From one point of view, this objection is the easiest to answer; from another point of view, it is the hardest to answer.

Considered in isolation, the language *is* crude and profane. It would be difficult to argue, however, that such language is unfamiliar to our young people or that it is rougher than the language they are accustomed to hear in the streets among their acquaintances. But there is no question about it, a vulgar expression seen in print is much more shocking than one that is spoken. Lewd scribblings on sidewalks or on the walls of rest-rooms catch our attention and unsettle our sensibilities; and they become most shocking when they are seen in the sanctity of the printed page. Traditionally, novelists have been keenly aware of the shock value of printed profanities. Stephen Leacock has a delightful essay in which he reviews the many circumlocutions and typographical devices that novelists since the 18th century have employed to avoid the use of shocking expressions.

Granting the shock potential of such language, especially to youngsters, must we also grant it a corrupting influence? To deny that words can shape our attitudes and influence our actions would be to deny the rhetorical power of language. But to maintain that four-letter words of themselves are obscene and can corrupt is another matter. Interestingly enough, most reports about the banning of this novel have told that some principal or librarian or parent hastily paged through the book and spotted several four-letter words. That was evidence enough; the book must go. It is natural, although not always prudent, for adults to want to protect the young from shock. And this concern may be sufficient justification for adults wanting to keep the book out of the hands of grade-school children or the more immature high school students. But one of the unfortunate results of banning the book for this reason is that the very action of banning creates the impression that the book is nasty and highly corrosive of morals.

As has happened in many censorship actions in the /441/ past, parts are judged in isolation from the whole. The soundest defense that can be advanced for the language of this novel is a defense based on the art of the novel. Such a defense could be stated like this: Given the point of view from which the novel is told, and given the kind of character that figures as the hero, no other language was possible. The integrity of the novel demanded such language.

But even when readers have been willing to concede that the bold language is a necessary part of the novel, they have expressed doubts about the authenticity of Holden's language. Teen-age girls, I find, are especially skeptical about the authenticity of the language. "Prep-school boys just don't talk like that," they say. It is a tribute, perhaps, to the gentlemanliness of adolescent boys that when they are in the company of girls they temper their language. But, whatever the girls may think, prep-school boys do on occasion talk as Holden talks. As a matter of fact. Holden' patois is remarkably restrained in comparison with the blue-streak vernacular of his real-life counterparts. Holden's profanity becomes most pronounced in moments of emotional tension; at other times his language is notably tempered—slangy, ungrammatical, rambling, yes, but almost boyishly pure. Donald P. Costello, who made a study of the language of *The Catcher in the Rye* for the journal *American Speech* (October, 1959), concluded that Salinger had given "an accurate rendering of the informal speech of an intelligent, educated, Northeastern American adolescent." "No one familiar with prep school speech," Costello goes on to say, "could seriously contend that Salinger overplayed his hand in this respect."

Holden's swearing is so habitual, so unintentional, so ritualistic that it takes on a quality of innocence. Holden is characterized by a desperate bravado; he is constantly seeking to appear older than he really is. Despite that trait, however, Holden's profanity does not stem from the same motivation that prompts other adolescents to swear—the urge to seem "one of the boys." His profanity is so much ingrained by habit into the fabric of his speech that he is wholly unaware of how rough his language is. Twice his little sister Phoebe reminds him to stop swearing so much. Holden doesn't even pause to apologize for his language; he doesn't even advert to the fact that his sister has reprimanded him. And it is not because he has become callous, for this is the same boy who flew into a rage when he saw the obscenity scribbled on a wall where it might be seen by little children.

Some of the episodes in the book are scandalous. The episode commonly cited as being unfit for adolescents to read is the one about the prostitute in the hotel room. A case could be made out for the view that young people should not be exposed to such descriptions. It would be much the same case that one makes out in support of the view that children of a certain age should not be allowed to play with matches. But a convincing case cannot be, and never has been, made out for the view that vice should never be portrayed in a novel.

One shouldn't have to remind readers of what Cardinal Newman once said, that we cannot have a sinless literature about a sinful people. That reminder, however, has to be made whenever a censorship controversy comes up. The proper distinction in this matter is that no novel is immoral merely because vice is represented in it. Immorality creeps in as a result of the author's attitude toward the vice he is portraying and his manner of rendering the scene.

Let us consider the scene in question according to this norm in order to test the validity of the charge that it is scandalous. First of all, neither the novelist nor his character regards the assignation with the prostitute as proper or even as morally indifferent. The word *sin* is not part of Holden's vocabulary, but throughout the episode Holden is acutely aware that the situation in which he finds himself is producing an uncomfortable tension, a tormenting conflict, within him. And that vague awareness of disturbance, of something being "wrong," even if the character doesn't assign the label "sin" to it, is enough to preserve the moral tone of the scene in question.

Some readers seem to forget, too, that Holden didn't seek this encounter with the prostitute. He was trapped into it; he was a victim, again, of his own bravado. "It was against my principles and all," he says, "but I was feeling so depressed I didn't even *think*." Nor does he go through with the act. Embarrassment, nervousness, inexperience—all play a part in his rejection of the girl. But what influences his decision most, without his being aware of it, is his pity for the girl. That emotion is triggered by the sight of her green dress. It is that pity which introduces a moral note into Holden's choice. Nor does Salinger render this scene with the kind of explicit, erotic detail that satisfies the pruriency of readers who take a lickerish delight in pornography. All of the scenes about sexual matters are tastefully, even beautifully, treated. Is it any wonder that devotees of the novel are shocked by the suggestion that some of the scenes are scandalous? /442/

Holden, constantly protesting against phoniness, is a phony himself. With this objection we move close to a charge against the novel that is damaging because it is based on sounder premises than the other two objections. No doubt about it, Salinger likes this boy, and he wants his readers to like the boy, too. If it could be shown that Salinger, despite his intentions, failed to create a sympathetic character, all the current fuss about the novel would be rendered superfluous, because the novel would eventually fall of its own dead weight.

Holden uses the word *phony* or some derivative of it at least 44 times. *Phoniness* is the generic term that Holden uses to cover all manifestations of cant, hypocrisy and speciosity. He is genuinely disturbed by such manifestations, so much so that, to use his own forthright term, he wants to "puke." The reason why he finds the nuns, his sister Phoebe and children in general so refreshing is that they are free of this phoniness.

But, as a number of people charge, Holden is himself a phony. He is an inveterate liar; he frequently masquerades as someone he is not; he fulminates against foibles of which he himself is guilty; he frequently vents his spleen about his friends, despite the fact that he seems to be advocating the need for charity. Maxwell Geismar puts this objection most pointedly when he says: "*The Catcher in the Rye* protests, to be sure, against both the academic and social conformity of its period. But what does it argue *for?*" Because of this inconsistency between what Holden wants other people to be and what he is himself, many readers find the boy a far from sympathetic character and declare that he is no model for our young people to emulate.

These readers have accurately described what Holden *does*, but they miss the point about what he *is*. Holden is the classic portrait of "the crazy, mixed-up kid," but with this significant difference: there is about him a solid substratum of goodness, genuineness and sensitivity. It is just this conflict between the surface and the substratum that makes the reading of the novel such a fascinating, pathetic and intensely moral experience. Because Holden is more intelligent and more sensitive than his confreres, he has arrived prematurely at the agonizing transition between adolescence and adulthood. He is precocious but badly seasoned. An affectionate boy, yearning for love and moorings, he has been cut off during most of his teen-age years from the haven of his family. Whatever religious training he has been exposed to has failed to touch him or served to confuse him. Accordingly, he is a young man adrift in an adult world that buffets and bewilders him.

The most salient mark of Holden's immaturity is his inability to discriminate. His values are sound enough, but he views everything out of proportion. Most of the manners and mores that Holden observes and scorns are not as monstrous as Holden makes them out to be. His very style of speech, with its extraordinary propensity for hyperbole, is evidence of this lack of a sense of proportion. Because he will not discriminate, he is moving dangerously close to that most tragic of all states, negation. His sister Phoebe tells him: "You don't like *any*thing that's happening." Holden's reaction to this charge gives the first glimmer of hope that he may seek the self-knowledge which can save him.

Holden must get to know himself. As Mr. Antolini, his former teacher, tells him: "You're going to have to find out where you want to go." But Holden needs most of all to develop a sense of humor. One of the most startling paradoxes about this book is that although it is immensely funny, there is not an ounce of humor in Holden himself. With the development of a sense of humor will come the maturity that can straighten him out. He will begin to see himself as others see him.

The lovely little scene near the end of the book in which Phoebe is going around and around on the carrousel can be regarded as an objective correlative of Holden's condition at the end of his ordeal by disillusionment. Up to this point, Holden has pursued his odyssey in a more or less straight line; but in the end, in his confusion and heartsickness, he is swirling around in a dizzying maelstrom. In the final chapter, however, it would appear that Holden has had his salutary epiphany. "I sort of *miss* everybody I told about," he says. Here is the beginning of wisdom. The reader is left with the feeling that Holden, because his values are fundamentally sound, will turn out all right.

I suspect that adults who object to Holden on the grounds of his apparent phoniness are betraying their own uneasiness. Holden is not like the adolescents in the magazine ads—the smiling, crew-cut, loafer-shod teen-agers wrapped up in the cocoon of suburban togetherness. He makes the adults of my generation uncomfortable because he exposes so much of what is meretricious in our way of life.

In defending *The Catcher in the Rye*, one is liable to the danger of exaggerating J. D. Salinger's achievement and potential. As George Steiner has warned in the *Nation* (Nov. 14, 1959), there is a vigorous "Salinger industry" under way now, which could put Salinger's work badly out of focus. Judged in the company of other post-war fiction, *The Catcher in the Rye* is an extraordinary novel. His earlier short stories, especially "For Esmé—with Love and Squalor," are truly distinguished. But the last two long, diffuse stories to appear in the *New Yorker*, "Zooey" and "Seymour," have been something of a disappointment. They are fascinating as experiments with the short-story form, but they strike me as being an accumulation of finger exercises rather than the finished symphony. If we admirers of Salinger can keep our heads about us, maybe we can make it possible for Salinger to build on the promise of his earlier work.

In the meantime, some concession must be made, I suppose, to the vigilantes who want to keep *The Catcher in the Rye* out of the hands of the very young. Future controversy will probably center on just what age an adolescent must be before he is ready for this book. That may prove to be a futile dispute. But I would hope that any decisions about the book would be influenced by the consideration, not that this is an immoral, corrupting book—for it is certainly not—but that it is a subtle, sophisticated novel that requires an experienced, mature reader. Above all, let the self-appointed censors *read* the novel before they raise the barriers. /443/

Kings in the Back Row: Meaning Through Structure, A Reading of Salinger's *The Catcher in the Rye**

CARL F. STRAUCH

I

The impressive accumulation of critical views on Salinger's *The Catcher in the Rye* is a tribute not only to the exciting qualities of the book but also to the awareness and resourcefulness of academic commentators. It has been compared to other fictional treatments of the crushing moral problems of sensitive American adolescents confronted by a hostile society. Critics, for the most part, have lavished an affectionate understanding upon a Holden Caulfield who regards his fellows with religious compassion and at the same time, out of his own durable honesty, reacts against the phony in both institutions and people. On this score there has been, so far as I know, only one conservative protest, wholly unconvincing, against Salinger's alleged Rousseauistic philosophy.[1] In another quarter *The Catcher* has been regarded as itself a conservative protest, along with *The Great Gatsby, H. M. Pulham, Esq.,* and the work of William Faulkner, against the anarchic drift of society and the shortcomings of the "natural man"; but in this view *The Catcher* is dismissed as providing a merely negative answer to the question of social chaos, and the conclusion of the novel can hardly serve "as a creed to live by."[2] If such

From *Wisconsin Studies in Contemporary Literature,* II (Winter 1961), 5-30. Reprinted by permission.

[* At the time this article was published much of the Salinger criticism had begun to be directed toward *Franny and Zooey* and other later stories. We have therefore placed this essay out of strict chronological order so that it might be read as part of the general discussions of *The Catcher in the Rye.*—Eds.]

[1] Albert Fowler, "Alien in the Rye," *Modern Age,* I (Fall, 1957), 193-197.

[2] Hugh Maclean, "Conservatism in Modern American Fiction," *College English,* XV (March, 1954), 315-325. See pp. 321-322 especially.

an undiscerning approach amounts to a begging of the question, several rewarding insights, on the other hand, have emerged from detailed analysis of parallels in narrative pattern and characterization in *Huck Finn* and *The Catcher;* and one judges that such expansive comparisons between Huck and Holden require correction only in several premature unfavorable impressions of Holden.[3] A profitable view has arisen from the exploration of the epic motifs of alienation and quest; and from this vantage point Holden is observed to keep company not only with Huck Finn but also with Ulysses, Aeneas, Ishmael, Alyosha, Stephen Dedalus, and /5/ Hans Castorp.[4] Still another view discloses Holden as an American Don Quixote, indulging with rare gestures of the spirit in "behavior that sings" and thus, in spite of his adolescent disaffiliation, affirming values of truth and imagination.[5]

There is, nevertheless, some critical unhappiness with a Holden who refuses to mature and with a distinctly unsatisfactory conclusion to the novel; and on both counts *The Catcher* suffers in comparison with *Huck Finn.* If Holden displays a superiority over Huck in certain traits of character, his neurotic psychology, intensified by sexual conflicts from which Huck was free and aggravated by a vulgar, dehumanized society, leads the boy to the psychoanalytical couch in a thoroughly pessimistic novel, whereas *Huck Finn* ends on a resolute note of courage in Huck's rejection of his society with his escape into the farther West.[6]

Thus we may summarize a commentary at once elaborate,

[3] Edgar Branch, "Mark Twain and J. D. Salinger: A Study in Literary Continuity," *American Quarterly,* IX (Summer, 1957), 144-158. /5/

[4] Arthur Heiserman and James E. Miller, Jr., "J. D. Salinger: Some Crazy Cliff," *Western Humanities Review,* X (Spring, 1956) , 129-137.

[5] Ihab H. Hassan, "Rare Quixotic Gesture: The Fiction of J. D. Salinger," *The Western Review,* XXI (Summer, 1957) , 261-280.

[6] See especially Branch, pp. 147 *et passim.* For Branch Holden is "the sex-conscious boy who yearns for the uncomplicated state of Huck" (p. 147); the carrousel scene represents "a dynamic moment of happy, static immaturity" (p. 149) ; "the underlying despair of Salinger's book is that a privileged adolescent wants to act immaturely" (p. 150) . For Heiserman and Miller, Holden "seeks the role of a child" (p. 131). This is substantially the view in Leslie A. Fiedler's *Love and Death in the American Novel* (New York, 1960). But see Charles H. Kegel's brief reply to Heiserman and Miller: "Incommunicability in Salinger's *The Catcher in the Rye,*" *Western Humanities Review,* XI (Winter, 1957), 188-190. This excellent note fails, unfortunately, to present the full complexity of the problem; but Kegel does see that Holden matures. /6/

precise, and generally correct as far as it goes; and yet all these approaches, however sophisticated the insight, remain discursively short of the critical goal because they fail to acknowledge the terms for understanding that the novel itself, as a work of art, has furnished. Except in scattered and fragmentary flashes, it has thus far escaped attention that Salinger sharply accentuates the portrayal of Holden with a symbolic structure of language, motif, episode, and character; and when the complex patterns are discovered, the effect is to concentrate our scrutiny on a masterpiece that moves effortlessly on the colloquial surface and at the same time uncovers, with hypnotic compulsion, a psychological drama of unrelenting terror and final beauty.

If Holden's suffering is the measure as well as the product, in part, of the outrageous assault on private innocence by social depravity, it does not follow that Salinger's philosophy is Rousseau-istic. If we acknowledge that a personality has been split to the very core, such a discovery does not support the view that Holden, unlike the resourceful Huck, wishes to remain immature. Nor, as we shall learn, does the conclusion of *The Catcher* present a "creed" of any kind in the sense demanded by one critic; and the conclusion, furthermore, is neither pessimistic nor, for that matter, ironical in any sense perceived thus far. An immature Holden is not being delivered up to the unmerciful process of adjustment to a society he detests. The irony is profounder than that because the meaning is profounder: a Holden who has accepted both the mood and the act of responsibility with Phoebe does /6/ not require psychoanalytical therapy, for he has miraculously wrought his own cure and has thus spiritually escaped the social rigidities that would be imposed upon him. The conclusion is, therefore, optimistic and affirmative, not in any credal sense but in terms of the unconquerable resources of personality.

Now, the thesis of the present study is that all or most of this psychological and philosophical insight can be gained only through a recognition of the interlocking metaphorical structure of *The Catcher*. We may thus perceive that Salinger has employed neurotic deterioration, symbolical death, spiritual awakening, and psychological self-cure as the inspiration and burden of an elaborate pattern—verbal, thematic, and episodic, that yields the mean-

ing as the discursive examination of Holden's character and problem out of metaphoric context can never do. Structure *is* meaning.

As a start, the readiest way of understanding *The Catcher* lies
in an awareness of the dualism or ambivalence of language, for
Holden employs both the slob and the literate idiom. He mingles
them so nicely, however, and with such colloquial ease that the
alternating modes have heretofore escaped attention; and however we look at the two languages, each is, in effect, employed
both realistically and metaphorically. Holden's slob speech is obviously justified as a realistic narrative device, since it is the idiom
of the American male; yet from the psychological point of view,
it becomes the boy's self-protective, verbalized acceptance of the
slob values of his prep school contemporaries. He thus may justify
himself in his overt being and may hope to secure immunity from
attack and rationalize his "belonging"; slob language, therefore,
hits off two important social themes—security and status. But the
psychological intent becomes symbolical portent when we see that
the mass idiom emphasizes a significant distinction between two
worlds—the phony world of corrupt materialism and Holden's
private world of innocence, which, in its corporate love, embraces
a secret goldfish, Holden's dead brother Allie, his sister Phoebe
(all children, in fact), Jane Gallagher, nuns, and animals (duck
and zoo animals, the Doberman that belonged to Jane's family,
and the dog that Olivier-Hamlet patted on the head). For his
private world Holden uses a literate and expressive English, and
so the profounder psychological and symbolical purposes of slob
language may be detected only as that idiom functions in polar-
ized relationship with the other. We need not /7/ labor the point
that the full range of Salinger's portrayal would never be disclosed without an awareness of the ambivalence of language.

The literary Salinger has, of course, created a literate and even
literary and artistic Holden, capable of acute aesthetic as well as
moral judgments. Thus, Ernie, the piano player in Greenwich
Village, was phony in his mingled real snobbery and false humility, and the Lunts overdid their acting and were *too* good. It
is such a perceptive Holden that opens the narrative on a confessional note—"all that David Copperfield kind of crap"; and it

may be observed in passing, as a literary parallel, that if Dickens portrays a young Victorian immoralist, Steerforth, Salinger gives us Stradlater, a "secret slob" and "sexy bastard." Holden's literary taste provides depth of background for a boy who said of himself, "I'm quite illiterate, but I read a lot." Favorite authors are his own brother D. B., Ring Lardner, and Thomas Hardy. Holden dismisses Hemingway as phony but approves of Fitzgerald's *The Great Gatsby*, from which, amusingly, he has borrowed Gatsby's nonchalant and phony habit of address—"old sport"; thus Holden refers to "old Spencer," "old Mrs. Morrow," "old Ernie," "old Phoebe." If this literary borrowing represents merely Holden's linguistic "horsing around," there is, on the other hand, real bite to his reporting Allie's verdict that Emily Dickinson was a better war poet than Rupert Brooke, the idea being that imagination imparts meaning to experience; and the discerning reader will keep this in mind as a gloss for Holden's concluding observation on his traumatic adventures.

Presumably, Holden's literary judgments are as perceptive as Allie's. Holden "wouldn't mind calling...up" Isak Dinesen, the author of *Out of Africa;* and his reason, open to readers of the Danish noblewoman, springs from his own suffering, for a writer so warmly understanding of children and animals would make an appropriate *confidante.* The slob Holden is more prominent, but the literate Holden is more intrinsic, for like Isak Dinesen he can use language to express sensitive insights and humane joys. As we proceed we shall note that although some of the literary sophistication is solely for background, a few works enter into and reenforce the moral, psychological, and symbolic range of *The Catcher.*

The literary precision with which Holden employs slob language for a public world that is varyingly indifferent and cruel and usually phony and literate speech for his private world emerges beautifully /8/ when he explains how he met Jane Gallagher: "The way I met her, this Doberman pinscher she had used to come over and *relieve* himself on our lawn, and my mother got very irritated about it. She called up Jane's mother and made a big *stink* about it. My mother can make a very big *stink* about that kind of stuff" (italics mine).

Once we have recognized the ambivalence of language we are prepared to discover Salinger's elaborate use of several kinds of pattern that support and help to develop the narrative. The first verbal pattern to be examined stands in an ironic and mutually illuminating relationship with the image of the secret goldfish at the head of the narrative symbolizing Holden and his secret world. In D. B.'s short story "The Secret Goldfish" the boy would not let others see the goldfish "because he'd bought it with his own money." Holden likewise was to pay in far more than money for his secret world; and as a further parallel, nobody ever saw (or cared to see) this secret world, although Holden invites inspection in the confessional mode, "if you really want to hear about it." This mode is maintained throughout with frequent interpolations of "if you want to know the truth" or "if you really want to know." As the story uncovers more and more of Holden's dilemma, these phrasings, although employed in the most casual manner, transcend their merely conversational usage and become psychologically portentous. The inference is that society, including his own parents, has no desire to recognize the truth about Holden or its own obsessions. In the middle of the tale Holden learns from the psychoanalytical snob, Carl Luce, that his father had helped him to "adjust"; and the blunted resolution of the narrative on the Freudian couch represents society's final humiliating indifference to truth. Recognition of the truth would embrace the love and compassion that it has no time for but that Holden himself not only lavishes on his secret world but extends to the public world in episodes and reflections rounded off with a minor verbal pattern, "You felt sort of sorry for her" or "I felt sorry as hell for him." The confessional mode embraces still another verbal pattern put variously, "People never notice anything," "He wasn't even listening," "People never believe you," and morons "never want to discuss anything." The failure in communication could not be more bleakly confirmed; and there is an immense irony in the contrast between Holden's telling the truth and the indifference surrounding him. Note, then, that the confessional mode, developed by several verbal patterns, provides /9/ a beautifully formulated enclosing structure for the tale—with the symbolic image of the secret goldfish at the start and at the end the equally symbolic talking couch.

Two other patterns ironically reenforce the confessional mode. At Pencey Dr. Thurmer had talked to Holden "about Life being a game," and Mr. Spencer added for the truant's benefit, "Life *is* a game that one plays according to the rules." Toward the end Mr. Antolini sustained the cliché in his overblown rhetoric. Considering Holden's own honesty and the indifference of his seniors, "playing the game" becomes a grisly farce; and there is further irony in the fact that Holden is himself fervently devoted to the concept, first in his treasuring Allie's baseball mitt and then in his confiding in Phoebe that he would like to be a catcher in the rye to save children from falling off "some crazy cliff." And does he not wear his red hunting hat backwards like a catcher? Mr. Antolini, who speaks to Holden from a sophisticated height and warns him of a "terrible, terrible fall," a "special kind of fall," is capable, in these psychological terms, of no more than talk, for he arrived too late to catch young Castle, who jumped out the window to escape the persecution of his contemporaries. The second pattern furnishes an ironical grace note or two. At the beginning of the tale Holden thought that Mr. Spencer yelled "Good luck" at him, and toward the close a teacher in Phoebe's school wished him "good luck." Unrelenting in its vision of the double-dealing of society, *The Catcher* portrays teachers as sentimentalists and guardians of an exploded ethic; and one of them, Antolini, is a linguistic phony. In these enclosing patterns, then, the reverberations of irony appear to be endless, and the structure of language and motif is all the more impressive because everything is presented in such an artless and colloquial fashion.

II

If the design thus far disclosed may be construed as the motif of unsportsmanlike sportsmanship and if the social corollary is that by playing the game (but what *are* the rules?) one may achieve security and status, it remains to be said that society reduces Holden to an ambivalence of acceptance and rejection, of boastful claims and humiliating admissions that are, in effect, destructive of the integrity of his personality. Holden seeks status with his contemporaries by talking slob language, but he shows the same impulse with his elders in more /10/ subtle fashion. With "old" Spencer he readily condemns himself as a moron and suggests plausibly that his trouble with school-work must arise from his passing through a phase. If his remark that he is "probably the biggest sex maniac you ever saw" represents the sting of conscience, his pursuit of sex with the prostitute is patently for adolescent status; and he immediately admits, with his engaging candor, that he is a virgin. So nervously aware of status is he that he is careful to preserve it for others. His roommate Slagle had inexpensive suitcases, and Holden therefore hid his own leather luggage under his bed "so that old Slagle wouldn't get a goddam inferiority complex about it." But Holden's acceptance of status is mere lip-service, and the intrinsic Holden emerges in the remark that he "wouldn't go to one of those Ivy League colleges if [he] was *dying*, for God's sake" and in his rejection of law because a lawyer, like his father, would not know whether he was being phony.

If society were no worse than a somewhat difficult but rational enough arrangement for status-seeking and if a person had merely to pay a stiff psychological price in adjustment for the rewards, Holden's frequent charge of "phony" might be dismissed. But the matter goes far deeper than that: society, in the repulsive form of Stradlater, subjects Holden to humiliations that pass beyond the legitimacies of playing the game. Holden's career discloses intensified patterns of ambivalence—withdrawal and aggression, guilt feelings, fantasies of mutilation, the death-wish; and the reason lies almost as much in the social encounter as in the death of his brother Allie. A society that ignores or rejects his gesture for understanding, that preempts his possessions, body, and mind, that invades and violates his inner being—such a society is not only status-seeking; it is actively and crudely anthropophagus and psychophagus. The vision of ugliness in *The Catcher* challenges anything else in the same genre. From the window of his New York hotel room, as from a box in a theatre, Holden witnesses an example of transvestism and sees a man and a woman spitting water or highballs in each other's face; "they were in hysterics the whole time, like it was the funniest thing that ever happened." The violent contrast between such a society and Holden's private world produces the psychological ambivalence mentioned above; hence, also, the importance of certain verbal patterns that may be identified by their key words—"madman," "crazy," "kill," and "yellow." /11/

As we pursue the "madman" pattern through its emotive transmutations we can see how Salinger loads his narrative with verbalisms that by themselves impart a pervasively psychological tone. Thus although there is nothing particularly significant in the description of the snow as "still coming down like a madman," in the Stradlater episode we detect a note of hysteria when Holden says that "he went right on smoking like a madman." On three separate occasions he "apologized like a madman"—first, to one of the three girls whom he picked up in the hotel; secondly, to the nuns for blowing smoke in their faces; thirdly, to Sally Hayes for his rude behavior. In his hotel room the prostitute "looked at [him] like [he] was a madman." It is obvious from these few examples that in a highly charged emotional context the verbalism slips out of the innocuously colloquial into the psychologically meaningful; and in these moments, furthermore, the verbal patterns converge and intensify the encounter, as may be noted with the "madman" and "crazy" patterns in the scenes with Stradlater and Sally Hayes.

The somewhat less than twenty pages of chapters four and six, the Stradlater episode, provide a brilliant instance of Salinger's technical virtuosity. Here we have convincing evidence that this completely selfish and indifferent young animal did push Holden, in his already neurotic state, down the nightmarish incline toward the psychoanalytical couch. Unlike Ackley, who was a slob, visible to all, in his personal habits, Stradlater was "a secret slob," impressive in his appearance for public show (he was handsome in a Year Book way), but filthy in his private habits. His razor "was always rusty as hell and full of lather and hairs and crap." He was "madly in love with himself" and spent half his life in

front of a mirror, and he could never whistle in tune. Since it is
the despoiling and humiliation of Holden Caulfield, the cynically
indifferent invasion and stripping bare of his person, property,
and secret imaginative world that is the burden of this episode,
we note with fascinated attention how Stradlater possesses himself of all things that are Holden's, one after another. He uses
Holden's Vitalis on his "gorgeous locks," he borrows Holden's
hounds-tooth jacket for his date, and yawning all the while, he
expects Holden to write his theme for him. A sovereign indifference to all about him is Stradlater's salient characteristic. He
could not be bothered to get Jane Gallagher's first name right;
he called her Jean. When Holden, with his studious /12/ care for
the other person, asked whether Jane had enjoyed the game,
Stradlater didn't know. A bitter humiliation for Holden is that
he must ask this gorgeous phony, who has made a theme-slave of
him, not to tell Jane that he is being expelled from Pencey; most
galling for the reader is Holden's admission that Stradlater probably won't tell "mostly...because he wasn't too interested."

It is, however, the imminently dangerous quality of sex that is
frightening. In chapter four when Holden heard that Stradlater
was to have a date with Jane Gallagher, he "nearly dropped
dead" and "nearly went crazy," and in chapter six, through all
the mounting ordeal, he "went right on smoking like a madman."
The psychological significance of these verbalisms is unmistakable, for Stradlater has invaded Holden's secret world and violated
a symbol of innocence and respect. Indeed, in the elaborate pattern of this episode, Stradlater, the "secret slob," matched Holden's secret world with his own, for when Holden was driven to
ask the crude but important question, he announced with all
the taunting impudence of his kind, "That's a professional secret, buddy."

When Holden recalls for this "sexy bastard" how he had met
Jane and goes on to say that he used to play checkers with her,
Stradlater's contemptuous comment is, "*Checkers,* for Chrissake!"
This girl, who had had a "lousy childhood" with a booze hound
for stepfather running "around the goddam house naked," always
kept her kings in the back row. As Holden put it, "She just liked

the way they looked when they were all in the back row." Half
earnestly, half facetiously, he requests Stradlater to ask Jane
whether she still keeps her kings in the back row; the symbolism
of this imagery, portraying defense against sexual attack, is the
central motif of the episode. Stradlater cannot, of course, know
what a shocking and menacing figure he has become, for on the
simple realistic level the request is merely casual reminiscence;
but in the psychological context danger signals have begun flut-
tering in Holden's mind. If the request may be construed as
Holden's desire to send Jane a secret warning against the slob
who would himself be the bearer of the message, this defensive
gesture, nevertheless, cannot issue in decisive action, and it remains no less symbolical than Holden's wearing his red hunting
hat "with the peak around to the back and all." But these gestures
indicate, so early in the narrative, that Holden is unconsciously
preparing for his subsequent role as a catcher in the /13/ rye. In
chapter six the futile best that he can do is to invite a beating at
Stradlater's hands, and after the struggle he cannot, for a while,
find the hat. All the protective gestures have dissolved in impotence, and with his nose "bleeding all over the place" Holden
has had a thorough lesson in the game of life.

This lesson is all the more pathetic because in chapter five we
have the first full glimpse of Holden's secret world and hence
some indication of how, given a chance, Holden would play the
game. The subject of his theme is his dead brother Allie's out-
fielder's mitt that has "poems written all over the fingers and
pocket and everywhere." The mitt symbolically indicates that
Holden would like to play the game with sensitivity and imagination, and Stradlater's crude rejection of the theme is itself a symbolic gesture, and a final one, shutting off all hope of communication. Holden tears the theme into pieces. But it should be
added that, like Jane's kings in the back row, Holden's private
world is impotent, and the effort at self-revelation in the theme
is of a piece with this futility. His rapidly worsening neurotic
condition has frozen him in this posture of feebleness, and indeed
Holden must take Antolini's "special kind of fall" and disappear
into the museum room where the mummies are and thus sym-

bolically encounter death before he may be reborn to an active defense of his world. But this is to anticipate; meanwhile, on the night of his humiliation, several hours later and many hours before the precious Antolini disgorged his wisdom, Holden reflected, "It just drove me stark staring mad when I thought about her and Stradlater parked somewhere in that fat-assed Ed Banky's car [Stradlater is the conscienceless, universal borrower]. Every time I thought about it, I felt like jumping out the window." Holden's fantasying about suicide (and young Castle *did* jump) provides final evidence of frozen impotence, and action is not outwardly directed but inwardly as an impulse toward self-destruction.

The "crazy" pattern continues throughout the middle portion of the book and reaches a climax in the Sally Hayes episode; thereafter, since Holden's neurosis has by then been established, it occurs less frequently, and other patterns come into prominence. Meanwhile in the lobby of the New York hotel Holden's obsessive imagination presents a picture to him of Stradlater with Jane that "almost drove [him] crazy." After the incident with the prostitute and Maurice, Holden's violent fantasying (of which, more later) compels him to say, "But I'm crazy. I swear to God I am." The literary talk with the nuns provides some /14/ relief before the scene with Sally Hayes, but even here Holden's reflections are violent, though interestingly varied from the obsession with Jane. The talk is about *Romeo and Juliet;* his favorite character, Mercutio, leads him to the private comment, "The thing is, it drives me crazy if somebody gets killed—especially somebody very smart and entertaining and all...."It is part of Salinger's intricately patterned structure that Holden's favorite character in the play should have been killed in a duel and that Holden himself was the manager of the Pencey fencing team and had "left all the foils and equipment and stuff on the goddam subway." Of greater import is the recollection of Allie in Holden's words about Mercutio, "somebody very smart and entertaining and all." Furthermore, this brief literary interlude brings together the "crazy" and "kill" patterns; and in a moment we shall pursue the latter.

The episode with Sally Hayes provides an explosive self-revelation, in which Holden (we have previously noted his apologizing "like a madman") admits that he is crazy and swears to God that he is a madman. What is a madman? Earlier in the fight with Stradlater Holden was "practically yelling"; and here Sally must ask him twice to stop shouting. Certainly, in his neurotic condition, Holden is scarcely master of himself, and yet, for the reader's sake if not for Sally's, he expresses his urge to withdraw from society with some semblance of rational discourse. His proposal that Sally and he escape to New England on his small bank account is, of course, fatuous; but what lies behind the proposal is not fatuous, and Salinger, indeed, permits us to penetrate the moral quality of Holden's secret world. Earlier that world was presented largely in terms of pathetic sentiment and instinctive honesty, but now our view of it is compellingly moral. Whereas Holden is nervously protective in the Stradlater episode, he is now aggressive and attacks modern urban life and mores. He protests that he doesn't like automobiles, even *"old* cars." "I'd rather have a goddam horse. A horse is at least *human,* for God's sake." As Holden sees matters, life has become so inhumanly mechanized that in his secret world animals move up a notch to assume the status of humans. Swift would approve such misanthropy.

III

We observe, then, that the "madman" and "crazy" patterns are employed most effectively in episodes, chiefly in the first two thirds of /15/ the book, that reveal Holden's neurotic condition and, as above, his sense of alienation. The psychological substratum is the frightening ambivalence of fantasy, with all the highly charged emotional responses flashing back and forth between the negative and positive poles; and we must now explore this dominant pattern.

Holden's fantasy begins at the obvious and apparently extroverted level of "horsing around." With Ackley Holden pretends to be a "blind guy," saying, "Mother darling, give me your *hand.* Why won't you give me your *hand?"* Considering the view we get later of parental care *in absentia* or by remote control, and considering, furthermore, what has already been disclosed of the highly wrought design of *The Catcher,* we should not fail to note, so early in the novel, the motif of mutilation and the implied charge that a mother has not provided guidance and owes her son the hand that he has broken; with Holden the extroverted simply does not exist. Ackley's response is, "You're nuts, I swear to God." Ackley calls Holden's hat a "deer shooting hat," and Holden facetiously retorts, "I shoot people in this hat"; and once again, in the sequel, the facetious may be seen to envelop aggressive tendencies. The hat, indeed, is the central symbol of Holden's fantasy and so of the book—not only, as here, for aggression, but later for his humanitarian role, faintly foreshadowed, as we have already noted, in the Stradlater episode; and a third symbolic function of the hat is to hit off Holden's quest, which is in a large measure hysterical flight, as he rushes about New York before he comes home to Phoebe. Aggression and withdrawal follow each other rapidly in the opening scenes, the first with Stradlater when Holden leaps on him "like a goddam panther," and the second when he wakes up Ackley and asks about joining a monastery.

In his hotel room, after "old Sunny," the prostitute, has gone, he talks "sort of out loud" to Allie and expresses guilt feelings about his having refused to take Allie with him and a friend on a luncheon bike-trip because Allie was just a child. Since Allie's death, whenever Holden becomes depressed, he tries to make up for this past cruelty by saying that he may go along. Here, then, in his guilt feelings we have an explanation of why Holden broke his hand against the garage windows, and we may trace all the elements of his fantasying to this psychological cause. Mutilation is itself the physical symbol of a psychological state of self-accusation and self-laceration. Hence, when /16/ Holden, after discovering that he cannot pray, reflects that next to Jesus the character in the Bible that he likes best is the lunatic that lived in the tombs and cut himself with stones, we observe a consistent psychological development of the motif of mutilation and, linked to it, the death-wish; and recalling the verbal patterns of "madman" and "crazy" we note further that Holden identifies himself with a madman. In *Mark* V:1–20, we are told of the lunatic that broke all chains and fetters, for no man could tame him. Jesus drove

the spirits that possessed him into the swine and told him to go
home to his friends. If we are to comprehend what really happens in *The Catcher* we must attribute prime importance to this
little scene of about two pages at the head of chapter fourteen;
for Holden will subsequently break his morbid psychological fetters, he will go home to Phoebe, and, in a manner of speaking, he
will be able to pray.

Before all this may occur, however, society in the form of
Maurice, the "elevator guy," intrudes for his shake-down and
sadistic treatment of Holden, who, in consequence, is plunged
into his most elaborate fantasy of mutilation, death-wish, and
aggression. He pretends that in a gun fight with Maurice he receives a bullet in his abdomen, and Jane Gallagher bandages
him and holds a cigarette for him to smoke as he bleeds. "The
goddam movies. They can ruin you. I'm not kidding." The function of Hollywood is to glamorize and distort and, in consequence, to disparage private suffering for an entranced national
audience. This view is scarcely fresh-minted in *The Catcher,* but
it is substantially Holden's criticism in the comment above when
he realizes that he has given his own genuine difficulty the *ersatz*
Hollywood form.

As the supreme national incarnation of the phony, Hollywood
(and by extension, California) figures prominently in the tale
from first to last, for it provides another enclosing pattern. We
learn quite early that D. B. has prostituted himself by going to
Hollywood to write scenarios; and at the end we see Holden in
the clutches of a California psychoanalyst, who is interested not
in the cause of suffering, not even in the person suffering, but
rather in the "desirable" social result of adjustment. The suffering, in any case, would not have arisen or assumed such neurotic
proportions had there been parental care instead of a nomadic
existence at expensive prep schools. As Phoebe tells Holden,
"Daddy can't come. He has to fly to California." /17/

When Holden visits Radio City he is confronted by a phony
image of withdrawal and escape matching his own genuine urge.
Indeed, the fantasy projected upon the screen also matches his
own most persistent fantasy of mutilation, for the hero, "this
English guy," who is a Duke, suffers from the mutilation of am-

nesia. Furthermore, the adult audience is sentimentally phony, for sitting next to Holden is a woman who, weeping copiously, refuses to take her boy to the lavatory but keeps him squirming in his seat. "She was about as kindhearted as a goddam wolf." If Holden is sick and escapes into fantasy, so too the nation; and although it may be going too far to suggest that a movie touched off Holden's recovery, it is nonetheless true that in the last third of the narrative the emphasis is on maturity and an affirmative, curative psychology.

Following the movie, Holden meets Carl Luce in the Wicker Bar of the Seton Hotel, where Holden, at his most amusingly raffish, "horses around" conversationally to the boredom and vexation of his older prep school friend, who has taken up with Eastern philosophy and a Chinese mistress rather older than himself. Three separate times Luce is driven to comment on Holden's immaturity: "Same old Caulfield. When are you going to grow up?" After Luce has gone Holden starts "that stupid business with the bullets in [his] guts again," but quite likely the phony movie and Luce's rather exalted talk have helped to take some of the steam out of "that stupid business." Certainly, the reader is being prepared for a turning point. Before Holden leaves the hotel he is told five times to go home; the psychological direction of the novel, under the narrative surface, is by now unmistakable. Although Luce "couldn't care less, frankly" about Holden's growing up, Holden will mature, and in the terms supplied subsequently by Antolini out of Stekel: "The mark of the immature man is that he wants to die nobly for a cause, while the mark of the mature man is that he wants to live humbly for one."[7]

[7] Wilhelm Stekel (1868-1940), the colleague of Freud and Jung, was the author of numerous works, based on his own practice, in which infantilism and maturity are a frequent subject of interpretation and comment. Worthy of special mention here is the English translation by James S. Van Teslaar of his *Peculiarities of Behavior: Wandering Mania, Dipsomania, Pyromania and Allied Impulsive Acts* (New York, 2 vols., 1924 and 1943). I do not find Antolini's quotation in this or other works by Stekel, though there are passages in several volumes, in particular the *Autobiography* (New York, 1950), that hit off the same idea. Interestingly, Stekel is mentioned in Dashiell Hammett's *The Thin Man* (1943), in which two adolescents, Dorothy and Gilbert Wynant, exhibit psychological problems arising out of the social chaos around them similar to those of Jane Gallagher and Holden Caulfield. Among other parallels are the "lousy childhood" of Dorothy and Jane (involving a stepfather)

IV

The visit to Central Park and then home to Phoebe must be regarded as the two halves of a single, unfolding psychological experience; they provide the hinge on which *The Catcher* moves. Holden had started thinking about the ducks during his talk with "old" Spencer; and in New York he asked two cab drivers about what the ducks did /18/ in such wintry weather. Holden knew the park "like the back of [his] hand," for as a child he had roller-skated and ridden his bike there. But now, searching for the lagoon, he is lost, and, as he says, "it kept getting darker and darker and spookier and spookier." The park has become *terra incognita*. When at last he finds the lagoon there are no ducks. Meanwhile he has dropped and broken the *Shirley Bean* record that he had bought for Phoebe, but he carefully gathers up the pieces into his pocket. He sits down on a park bench and shivers "like a bastard" because back at the hotel he had sloshed water over his head, and "little hunks of ice" had formed on his back hair. He thinks of himself as dying of pneumonia and by easy stages gets on to Allie, whom, significantly, he seems to regard as alive, out there in the cemetery surrounded by "dead guys and tombstones." It nearly drives him crazy to think that visitors could run to their cars when it rained, but Allie could not. To relieve his distress Holden skips what little change he has over the lagoon "where it wasn't frozen." Finally, the thought of Phoebe gives him courage to live. "So I got the hell out of the park, and went home."

The psychological and thematic components of this little scene are profoundly rich and yet beautifully simple. Central Park represents Holden's Dark Tower, Dark Night of the Soul, and Waste-land; the paradise of his childhood is bleak, and the ducks that, in his fantasy, he has substituted for the human, have vanished. In effect, Holden is finished with childhood and is prepared for the burdens of maturity. But all the same he gathers up the pieces

---

and the wandering mania of Dorothy and Holden. Considering the critical emphasis on comparisons between Huck Finn and Holden, it may be plausibly urged that *The Thin Man* is just as acceptable a prototype for *The Catcher* as is *Huck Finn.* /18/

to be treasured, and in a final act of childhood profligacy—skipping coins over the lagoon—he symbolically rejects the materialism of the adult world that he is about to enter.

The apartment episode with Phoebe is so brilliant and so densely packed that we must examine it in two stages, here largely from Holden's point of view and later from Phoebe's. The meeting between brother and sister is presented as a conspiracy, for Holden enters the building under false pretenses and slips into his own apartment "quiet as hell." "I really should've been a crook." The anti-social bond is confirmed when Phoebe tells Holden that she has the part of Benedict Arnold in a Christmas play and when he gives her his symbolical hunting hat. They are rebels and seekers both.

Almost the first thing that Holden notices in D. B.'s room where Phoebe usually sleeps when D. B. is away is her fantasying with her /19/ middle name, which she changes frequently, the present one being "Weatherfield." The various kinds of fantasy have an important role in *The Catcher* and, in alliance with other motifs, hint at the philosophical question of the narrative: "What is the nature of reality?" From this point onward the novel converges upon the answer. Meanwhile, Phoebe's fantasying "killed" Holden; and in this and later scenes with children his mood is good humored, indulgent, and parental. The word "kill" is used throughout the novel in colloquial fashion, as here; but presently it reflects a rising hysteria when Phoebe exclaims again and again about Holden's leaving school, "Daddy'll *kill* you." Paradoxically, the terror exists not for Holden but for Phoebe, and the boy who had been fleeing from one physical and psychological terror after another now finds himself in the role of the elder who must reassure his young sister that nobody is going to kill him.

The spotlight is, furthermore, powerfully focused upon Holden's problem when Phoebe acts out a killing. She had seen a movie about a mercy killing; a doctor compassionately put a crippled child (on his way up to the apartment Holden, continuing his mutilation fantasy, had been "limping like a bastard") out of its misery by smothering it with a blanket. In symbolic mimicry Phoebe places her pillow over her head and resists Holden's plea to come out from under. Here, indeed, is killing—

"mercy" killing, and assuredly one way of dealing with children. But it would be a "mercy" also to save children, to catch them as they are about to fall off "some crazy cliff," and this is the humanitarian solution that Holden expresses to Phoebe. The antisocial conspiracy has blossomed into a benevolent and protective order. Antolini's thesis, coming belatedly as it does, merely renders conceptually the courage and maturity that Holden, with his imaginative heart, had discovered in the stolen moments of domestic affection and security with Phoebe. Salinger is intimating that for the imaginatively endowed the living experience may become the source of precept and rule. The point is that Holden is way ahead of his elders.

Holden's image of salvation is a compound of his own anecdote to Phoebe of how James Castle plunged to his death and of the snatch of song Holden had heard, "If a body catch a body coming through the rye." From this point onward, however, there is a bifurcation in his development, for he is paradoxically headed for both physical capture and psychological escape. Holden's verbal slip with the song (and /20/ Phoebe corrects him) is a *leitmotif* for his mood of utter weariness as he leaves the apartment; he had entered as a "crook," and now he "didn't give much of a damn any more if they caught [him]." The weariness is evident, furthermore, in his being unable to concentrate both with Phoebe and with Antolini as a sense of the rigidity of life overwhelms him. With a last immense and frightened effort he rushes from Antolini's apartment, escaping what in his fevered imagination he takes to be Antolini's perverted advances on the living room couch, before society finally flings him upon the Procrustes bed of adjustment. Such a development being clearly established, we may follow Holden's escape into freedom.

Now Holden's fantasying will not be neurotically defensive, but rationally motivated and ethically directed; and the death-wish will disappear. On his walk up to Phoebe's school Holden fantasies about going west; he would pretend to be a deaf-mute, and if anybody wanted to talk to him the person would have to write the conversation on a piece of paper. Whereas earlier in his effort to communicate with society, as in the theme he wrote for Stradlater, society rejected him, he now rejects society. If there is to be no communication it is of his own free, rational choice and not a piece of neurotic withdrawal. At Phoebe's school he sees the obscene word twice inscribed on corridor walls; but now, if he says that it drives him almost crazy, it does so not with a neurotic and inwardly directed thrust, but in an outward direction in defense of Phoebe and other children, for he says that he could kill whoever did it.

On the way up Fifth Avenue Holden has a recurrence of a feeling expressed at the beginning: "I felt like I was sort of disappearing," he had said after crossing a road. Once again he feels that he will never get to the other side of the street; he breaks out into a sweat, and he talks to Allie, begging him not to let him disappear. When he has successfully negotiated a crossing he thanks Allie, who thus assumes his function as a guide, like Virgil for Dante, into the lower regions of the dead, as we are about to see. Hence, in the tremendous culmination of the narrative, the "yellow" pattern has a significance that is effectively all-embracing, and it advances our perceptions beyond the threshold of awareness permitted by the other verbal patterns.

From the start Holden is convinced that by either standard—society's or his own, he is a coward. On returning to his hotel from the /21/ Village through the cold night he thinks of his stolen gloves. He calls himself "one of these very yellow guys" and by way of proof explains his likely elaborate and cowardly handling of the affair had he known who the thief was. He would not offer fight, and he would therefore be "partly yellow" since, as he admits, "If you're supposed to sock somebody in the jaw" you should. But his trouble is that he "can't stand looking at the other guy's face"; and this, he concludes, as a veiled revelation to the perceptive reader, is a "funny kind of yellowness." Later when the prostitute and the "elevator guy" knock on his door Holden confesses that he is "pretty scared" and "very yellow about those things." These first two instances show the coercive social standard, but the third, in the apartment with Phoebe, gives us Holden's self-condemnation when he admits that he "was too yellow not to join" a secret fraternity. The final instance, unmistakably illuminating the climax of the book, shows that he is not a coward and that, in effect, he essentially has business to transact only with himself, and he must therefore stop running. In the museum of art when Holden walks down "this very narrow sort of hall" leading to the room containing the mummies, one of the two boys with him bolts and runs, the other says, "He's got a yella streak a mile wide," and then he also flees. Not Holden but society is yellow.

Since Holden's neurosis includes feelings of insecurity stemming from Allie's death and from Jane Gallagher's "lousy childhood" (like his own) and since both Allie and Jane have become inextricably bound together in his mind, Holden conquers the two-fold hysteria at one and the same moment. There is sexual imagery in "this very narrow sort of hall" and the room containing the mummies, especially since the obscene word is written "with a red crayon...right under the glass part of the wall." Once again as in Phoebe's school he reacts with weariness over the corruption of this world and solemnly reflects that if he ever dies and is buried, his tombstone will bear the ugly legend. Here, at last, the identity of the fear of death and the fear of sex is made clear, and these fears are to be seen, actually, as a pervasive fear of violence to body or spirit and the ensuing mutilation. If in the Stradlater episode and throughout the rest of the novel Holden is an innocent, he is so, not so much in terms of our popular literary tradition, but rather in a classical, Christian, or psychoanalytical schema. His very fears yield proof that his innocence represents a harmony of attributes /22/ and drives—intellectual, emotional, and physical, so that in the proper regulation of them harm will result neither for the person nor for others.[8] Holden's obsession about faces indicates this fastidious care; the Egyptians tried to conquer the final violence of death by mummification so that, as Holden says, the face "would not rot." In Holden's encounter it is important that the spirit should not rot.

For insight into the psychologically symbolic meaning of the museum episode we turn once again to the structure of the novel. Allie's death has been such a traumatic experience that all Hol-

---

[8] By a "psychoanalytical schema" I mean, of course, psychotherapy with the sole purpose of exploring the psychological disturbance and restoring the invalid to his original health; I exclude the sociological motivation of "adjustment" to supposedly "desirable" social ends. /23/

den knows is death, for when "old" Spencer, who makes him
"sound dead," confronts him with the unsatisfactory results of
the history examination, it is clear that his historical knowledge
is limited to the subject of mummification. It is to this knowledge,
at the close of the book, that he returns with a sense of how "nice
and peaceful" it all is. The psychological journey from the fear
of death to a calm acceptance of it is further highlighted at the
beginning when we learn that Mr. Ossenburger, the mortician,
has donated the dormitory wing named for him in which Holden
has his room.

Holden's victorious encounter with death reveals psychological
maturity, spiritual mastery, and the animal faith and resiliency of
youth. The charmingly offhand and rather awesome conditional
statement, "If I ever die" reminds the reader that in the last quarter of the book it is so difficult for Holden to think of Allie as
dead that Phoebe must underscore the fact, "Allie's *dead*." Yet
although Holden masters his neurosis he also falls victim to society, for in alternating stress the novel continuously presents two
mingled actions—his own inner dealings with himself and society's brutal effect upon him. After his visit to the mummies
Holden goes to the lavatory and proceeds to faint, i.e., symbolically dies; and his comment is that he was lucky in falling as he
did because he "could've killed" himself. The parallelism with
the earlier Stradlater episode leaps instantly to the mind, for
then, as we recall, Holden "nearly dropped *dead*"; and that
scene also took place in a lavatory—a fit symbol, in both instances,
for a scatological society. Significantly, he feels better immediately after; and he is reborn into a new world of secure feelings
and emotions, with himself fulfilling the office of catcher in his
mature view of Phoebe. Thereafter the psychoanalytical couch
can mean little to him, far less than Antolini's couch, to which it
is thematically related. /23/

V

The dense contrapuntal effect of the verbal patterns is, finally,
enhanced by one that keeps a persistent drum beat in the background until the full thematic range of *The Catcher* is disclosed.
If Holden symbolically and psychologically dies only to be reborn

into the world of Phoebe's innocence and love, he has all through
the novel been announcing the theme of regeneration in the
"wake up" pattern. After the Stradlater episode Holden wakes up
Ackley, then another schoolmate Woodruff (to sell him a typewriter), and as a derisive parting shot, "every bastard on the
whole floor" with his yell, "*Sleep tight, ya morons!*" In New York
he wakes up or provides the occasion for having wakened up
Faith Cavendish (striptease), Sunny (prostitute: "I was *sleepin'*
when that crazy Maurice woke me up"), Sally, Phoebe, and the
Antolinis. To round out the pattern, Holden's father "won't wake
up even if hit over the head with a chair." Obviously, the thematic
implication of the pattern transcends both the episodes and the
characters involved; in moral as well as psychological terms Salinger is suggesting that a brutalized society requires regeneration
and must arouse itself from its mechanistic sloth.

In a development that parallels the "wake up" pattern Salinger
shows that Holden, of course, must wake up in his own way; and
it has been the thesis of this reading of *The Catcher* that he does
effect his own psychological regeneration. Jane Gallagher's kings
in the back row symbolize, as we have already noted, the impotence of Holden's secret world, for kings should range freely over
the checkerboard. Similarly Holden has interpreted the Museum
of Natural History in terms compatible with his own rigid posture. "The best thing, though, in that museum was that everything always stayed right where it was." But the exhibit in the
Indian Room, of which Holden is especially fond, with its portrayal of a vanished life, simply mirrors his own death-wish and
the death-like quality of his secret world. Actually, Holden's secret world fails the boy not only outwardly in the encounter with
society, but also inwardly in his retreat from circumstance, for it
is effectively sealed off, so that, as with the outside world, there is
here likewise no communication. The pattern that discloses this
aspect of Holden's isolation is "giving old Jane a buzz." Early in
the novel Holden thinks of phoning Jane's mother; twice thereafter he thinks of phoning Jane, but instead phones Sally. On two
separate occasions phoning Jane /24/ is part of his fantasy. Toward the close of the novel he thinks of phoning her before going
out west, but this bit of fantasy does not reveal a need for her,

since, as we have observed, Holden's mood has become rational and volitional. But in the violent Hollywood fantasy earlier in the middle of the book, Holden does phone Jane, and she does come to succor him; any comfort, however, that the boy might derive from Jane, who is one of the two nodal images in his private world (the other being Allie), is immediately destroyed by the *ersatz* sentimental form of the fantasy. Equally significant for Salinger's purpose in underscoring the psychological remoteness of the image of Jane is the one time when Holden does actually phone her: there is no answer. His own world fails to respond. Thereafter come the visit to Central Park, the return home to Phoebe, and a concomitant spiritual recovery.

We now approach the second and, possibly, profounder level of interpretation for the apartment scene. Phoebe wakes up easily; and after this moment of incitation the currents of life may flow, and the rigid, frozen posture yield to the genial warmth of the natural and simple. We become aware of the benevolent and protective order of rebels and seekers, symbolized by the hunting hat and underscored by Holden's parental view of Phoebe, through all the devices of language, gesture, image, and symbol; but to comprehend the deeper level of significance (where we are enabled, perhaps, to answer the question, "What is the nature of reality?") we must rely, in this scene, almost entirely on image and gesture, with little help from speech; and in the final, cryptic chapter this submerged level is brought to the surface of conscious thought in the manner of a riddle. As it is, the profoundest language of the moment we are reexamining lies in the occult and dramatic postures of a charmingly expressive girl.

Neurotic fixations give clues to healthy, natural emotional needs; and Holden, in his trance-like satisfaction with everything in its place in the Indian Room, is instinctively reacting against the chaos outside and inside himself. Things must be in their place; but the constellation must be living and dynamic, not dead, and life must have a magnetic center around which the affairs of life will arrange themselves. For Holden Phoebe provides that center.

From Alice Holmberg Phoebe had learned how to cross her legs in the Yogi manner, hold her breath, and by concentrating exert the influence of mind over matter. In this position, "smack in the middle of /25/ the bed," Phoebe represents the still, contemplative center of life; at the same time she is listening to dance music, and with the impulsiveness of the child she offers to dance with Holden. In this manner Salinger indicates the viable relationship between the contemplative and the active participation in the dance of life—a spiritual perception that is as ancient as the *Bhagavad-Gita*. Although the humanitarian role of saviour that Holden assigns himself stands in the foreground, we must nevertheless not fail to see that Phoebe is the essential source; and if Holden, on the path up out of spiritual dilemma and crisis, must find the verbal and conceptual means of expressing his innermost needs, Phoebe, as easily as she wakes up, expresses an even more fundamental insight through symbolic gesture. The charm of the scene, when fully comprehended from this point of view, lies in the mingling of the naive and childlike with the spiritually occult, in the immense discrepancy between means (a child) and ends (spiritual insight); for adults it is a rather puzzling and even terrifying charm, when they acknowledge it, discoverable in fairy tales and some of the teachings of Jesus.

The source of this dualism or polarity of contemplation and activity lies in the intuitive wisdom of the unfettered personality freely acknowledging that the best satisfaction of human nature lies in what Emerson called the law of undulation. Part of this larger spontaneity is the recognition that much of the mastery of life comes through indirection, and hence the preference for the expressive act over precept. Holden, for example, comments that although he had taught Phoebe how to dance when she was "a tiny little kid," "you can't teach somebody how to *really* dance." A far more dramatic defense of personality against restrictions comes in the following scene at Antolini's apartment when, out of a heightened awareness of his approaching crisis, Holden argues his schoolboy point that digressions should be allowed in Oral Expression; "what I mean is, lots of time you don't *know* what interests you most till you start talking about something that *doesn't* interest you most." Holden liked it when somebody got excited about something.

In Holden's maturing there is no repudiation of childhood or

even of the secret world. In the organic processes of life the continuity between childhood and maturity, need not, must not be
severed. If the child is father of the man, as Wordsworth said, assuredly society /26/ at large and parents in particular have
scarcely encouraged this teen-aged boy, well over six feet, with a
crippled right hand and the right side of his head full of "millions of gray hairs," to think of his days in Wordsworthian fashion
as "bound each to each by natural piety." For that reason his secret world, when released from the death-like enchantment of
neurosis, may well have been, ultimately, the real source of his
salvation. Certainly in the daylight return to Central Park with
Phoebe Holden experienced the natural piety that Wordsworth
celebrated, being at once child and parent with her, both in the
zoo (he need no longer search for the ducks) and at the carrousel,
watching Phoebe go round and round, another symbol for the
circular activity of life. Here the sense of continuity that Holden
demands in his surroundings, as we have noted in his feeling for
the exhibit in the Indian Room—the harmonious relation between the private person and the public world, receives a living
affirmation when he comments with so much satisfaction that the
carrousel "played that same song about fifty years ago when *I* was
a little kid." When, to the adult reader's further amusement, Holden, like any apprehensive parent, says that Phoebe will have to
take her chances with falling off the horse when reaching for the
ring, the boy has added a cubit to his psychological stature.

The short concluding chapter, far from being the lame and defective appendage to a charming book that some think it, is like
so much else in *The Catcher,* a triumph of technical virtuosity.
In this reading of the novel the conclusion is blunted, and interestingly so, only because we cannot say what society will do to impose adjustment upon a boy who has effected his own secret cure;
and we therefore close the narrative not with psychoanalytical
questions, but ethical. In rejecting the formalism of psychoanalytical technique for the spontaneous personality Salinger follows
D. H. Lawrence; and in boldly proposing that the resources of
personality are sufficient for self-recovery and discovery, his book
will stand comparison with Herman Hesse's *Steppenwolf,* whose
protagonist, Harry Haller, rises above his own neurosis in a dis-

covery, based on Buddhistic thought, that the potentialities of the
soul are limitless. Altogether, in this reading the answer to the
question, "What is the nature of reality?" is both complex and
simple, residing in the living, organic relation between childhood
and maturity, continuity and change, the contemplative and the
active, the external world and the inner spirit. This reality is not
a philosophical /27/ abstraction, but an existentialist datum of
physical and emotional experience. Since the action of *The
Catcher* takes place against the background of the approaching
Christmas holidays, the answer is again suggested in the implied
contrast between the birth of Jesus and the Egyptian art of mummification.

In the chapter under consideration, as well as in a number of
short stories, Salinger has found his rationale in Buddhistic
thought. The blunted conclusion is to be understood not only as
a realistic narrative device but also as the paradoxical product of
a tremendous leap in thought. In Zen Buddhism the koan or riddle lifts one above the level of the conceptualizing intelligence to
that of immediate insight, as in the famous koan that Salinger affixed to his *Nine Stories:* "We know the sound of two hands clapping. But what is the sound of one hand clapping?" The Zen riddle presents an intellectual impasse "beyond assertion and denial"; and if the master's answer to the disciple's question often
seems impertinent and even frivolous the purpose is to turn the
question back upon the disciple to sharpen his awareness of "life's
elusiveness and indefinability." As one authority puts it, "Thus
when the disciple comes to the final point where the Koan absolutely refuses to be grasped, he comes also to the realization that
life can never be grasped, never possessed or made to stay still.
Whereupon he 'lets go,' and this letting go is the acceptance of
life *as* life, as that which cannot be made another's property,
which is always free and spontaneous and unlimited."[9]

Once again there is an immense discrepancy between means (a
child) and ends (spiritual insight). When the psychoanalyst (in
the role of disciple) asks Holden (the master) whether he in-
tends to apply himself at school, and Holden replies that he

[9] Alan W. Watts, *The Way of Zen* (New York, 1957), pp. 70, 75. See also
Christmas Humphreys, *Zen Buddhism* (London, 1958), pp. 124-131. /28/

doesn't know because you don't know "what you're going to do till you do it," the surface impression is that of a typically unsatisfactory answer from a teen-ager. When D. B. asks him what he thinks about "all this stuff [he] just finished telling...about" and Holden replies that he does not know what to think, the surface impression is the same. Finally, Holden proposes a riddle. He says that he misses everybody, even Stradlater, Ackley, and "that goddam Maurice." "Don't ever tell anybody anything. If you do, you start missing everybody." Here is a shock to the conceptualizing, precept-laden intelligence, a puzzle or paradox that will not yield to logical analysis but that, on the contrary, sends /28/ the mind back over the experience recorded, even into the depths of the unconscious where both the malady and the cure lay. In the large, Whitmanesque acceptance of evil there is affirmation of the life-process as the personality "lets go"; and such Zen riddling is easily translatable into existentialist understanding.

In its emphasis on the conflict between the organic and the mechanistic, the secret and the public, reality and appearance, awakening and death, *The Catcher* hits off the strongest Romantic affirmations from Goethe and Wordsworth down to Lawrence, Joyce, and Hesse. Whether at Walden Pond, at Weissnichtwo, or in New York hot spots, the problem of personality remains; one surmises that, after a century and more, as *A Portrait of the Artist* and *Steppenwolf* likewise indicate, the struggle has become intensified. At the close of *The Catcher* the gap between society and the individual has widened perceptibly; and far from repudiating Holden's secret world, Salinger has added a secret of psychological depth. A mechanistic society, represented just as much by Antolini as by the psychoanalyst, may with the glib teacher continue to ignore the boy and talk of "what kind of thoughts your particular size mind should be wearing"; we may all comfort ourselves with the reflection that, after all, Holden is another bothersome case of arrested development, albeit rather charming in a pathetic and oafish manner.

No doubt Salinger has overdrawn the portrayal, but a work of literature is not a statistic, it is a special vision. In its pathetic and sentimental tone *The Catcher* faithfully reflects the surface of

American life, and insofar, therefore, as it lacks intellectual substance and a valid universality based on a cultural heritage, it falls far below the Romantic masterpieces to which I have made passing reference. But as I have tried to make clear, *The Catcher* is strongest where these are strongest. Whatever the dreadful odds, the human spirit, though slain, refuses to stay dead; it is forever hearing the cock crow, forever responding to the Everlasting Yea. So in *The Catcher;* and the blunted, ambiguous ending mingles with this affirmation the doubt whether now at last, in the long travail of the spirit, the odds have not become too dreadful. If, as this reading interprets the book, the scales tip in favor of the affirmation, it is so because the history of youth is almost always hopeful. /29/

XX

Fit Audience

FRANK KERMODE

What meaning, if any, can one attach to the expression 'a key book of the present decade'? It is used as a blurb in a new reprint of Mr. J. D. Salinger's famous novel,[1] which was first published in 1951. Whoever remembers the book will suppose that this is a serious claim, implying perhaps that *The Catcher,* as well as being extremely successful, is a work of art existing in some more or less profound relationship with the 'spirit of the age.' It is, anyway, quite different from saying that *No Orchids for Miss Blandish* is a key book. On the other hand, there is an equally clear distinction between this book and such key novels as *Ulysses* or *A Passage to India.* For it is elementary that, although these books have been read by very large numbers of people, one may reasonably distinguish between a smaller, 'true' audience and bigger audiences which read them quite differently, and were formerly a fortuitous addition to the 'highbrow' public. But although Salinger is certainly a 'highbrow' novelist, it would be unreal to speak of his audience, large though it is, as divided in this way. What we now have is a new reader who is not only common but pretty sharp. This new reader is also a pampered consumer, so that the goods supplied him rapidly grow obsolete; which may explain why I found *The Catcher* somewhat less enchanting on a second reading.

It is, of course, a book of extraordinary accomplishment; I don't know how one reviewer came to call it 'untidy.' Nothing inept, nothing that does not look good and work well as long as

From *The Spectator,* CC (May 30, 1958), 705-706. Reprinted by permission of *The Spectator,* London.

[1] *The Catcher in the Rye* (Penguin Books, 2s. 6d.). /705/

it is needed, will satisfy this new public. Structural virtuosity is now taken for granted, particularly in American novels. This one is designed for readers who can see a wood, and paths in a wood, as well as sturdy, primitive trees—a large, roughly calculable audience: fit audience though many.

At the level of its untidy story, the book is about an adolescent crisis. A boy runs away from his expensive school because he is an academic failure and finds intolerable the company of so many phoneys. He passes a lost weekend in New York, mostly in phoney hotels, night clubs and theatres, avoids going to bed with a prostitute and is beaten up by her ponce, meets some phoney friends, talks to taxi-drivers, wonders endearingly where the ducks from Central Park Lake go in winter, secretly visits his kid sister, indulges various fantasies of much charm and finally falls ill with exhaustion. He tells his story in a naive sophisticated dialect, partly in the Homeric Runyon tradition, partly something more modern. Repetitive, indecent, often very funny, it is wonderfully sustained by the author, who achieves all those ancient effects to be got from a hero who is in some ways inferior, and in others superior, to the reader. (His wisdom is natural, ours artificial.) The effect is comfortably compassionate; the boy, ungifted and isolated as he thinks himself to be, is getting his last pre-adult look at the adult world, our world, into which he is being irresistibly projected. He can't stand the adolescent world either; clean, good children turn into pimply shavers with dirty minds. For sex is what alters the goodness of children. Of the girls Holden Caulfield knows, one is nice and lovable—for her he admits no sexual feeling, though her date with a crumby seducer helps to work him up to this crisis; one is a prostitute, operating in a hotel which is a comic emblem of the perverted adult world; and one is an arty phoney. Growing up is moving out of crumby phoneyness into perverted phoneyness. These phoneys, they come in at the goddam window, using words like 'grand' and 'marvellous,' reading and writing stories about 'phoney lean-jawed guys named David...and a lot of phoney girls named Marcia that are always lighting all the goddam Davids' pipes for them.' Successful people, even the Lunts, turn into phoneys because of all the phoneys who adore them. Holden, near enough to Nature to spot this, is himself knowingly infected by the false attitudes of the movies, the greatest single source of phoneyness. Only children are free of it, especially dead children.

This much you get from listening to the boy, and it sounds untidy. What Mr. Salinger adds is design. Holden is betrayed at the outset by a schoolmaster (phoney-crumby) and at the end by another (phoney-perverted). The only time his parents come into the story, he has to remain motionless in the dark with his sister. The boy's slang is used to suggest patterns he cannot be aware of: whatever pleases him 'kills' him, sends him off to join his dead brother; almost everybody, even the disappointed whore, is 'old so-and-so,' and 'old' suggests the past and stability. More important, the book has its big, focal passages, wonderfully contrived. Holden hears a little neglected boy singing, 'If a body catch a body, etc.' This kills him. Then he helps a little girl in Central Park to fasten her skates. Next he walks to the Museum of Natural History, which he loved as a child; it seemed 'the only nice, dry cosy place in the world.' Nothing changed there among the stuffed Indians and Eskimos; except *you*. You changed every time you went in. The thought that his little sister must also feel that whenever she went in depresses him; so he tries to help some kids on a see-saw, but they don't want him around. When he reaches the museum he won't go in. This is a beautiful little parable, and part of my point is that nobody will miss it. Another is the climactic scene when Holden is waiting for his sister to come out of school. Full of rage at the '—— yous' written on the school walls, he goes into the Egyptian Room of the museum and explains to a couple of scared children why the mummies don't rot. Of course, he likes mummies; though the kids, naturally, don't. But even in there, in the congenial atmosphere of undecaying death, somebody has written '—— you' on the wall. There is nowhere free from crumbiness and sex. He retreats into his catcher fantasy as Phoebe rides the carousel; and then into illness.

This is only a hint of the complexity of Mr. Salinger's 'highbrow' plotting. There is much more; consider the perfectly 'placed' discussion between the boy and his sister in which he tells her about the phoneys at school. She complains that he doesn't like *anything*, and challenges him to mention something he does. After a struggle, he speaks of two casually encountered nuns, a boy who threw himself out of a window, and his dead brother. He daren't grow up, for fear of turning into a phoney; but behind him Eden is shut for ever.

Why, then, with all this to admire, do I find something phoney in the book itself? Not because there is 'faking,' as Mr. Forster calls it. In his sense, 'faking' doesn't lead one directly to some pre-fabricated attitude, and this does happen in *The Catcher*. The mixed-up kid totters on the brink of a society which is corrupt in a conventional way; its evils are fashionably known to be such, and don't have to be proved, made valid in the book. Similarly, the adult view of adolescence, insinuated by skilful faking, is agreeable to a predictable public taste. Again, we like to look at the book and see the Libido having a bad time while the Death Wish does well, as in the museum scenes; but I don't feel that this situation occurs in the book as it were by natural growth, any more than sub-threshold advertising grows on film. *The Catcher* has a built-in death wish; it is what the consumer needs, just as he might ask that a toothpaste taste good *and* contain a smart prophylactic against pyorrhœa. The predictable consumer-reaction is a double one; how good! and how clever! The boy's attitudes to religion, authority, art, sex and so on are what smart people would like other people to have, but cannot have them-selves because of their superior understanding. They hold to-gether in a single thought purity and mess, and feel good. The author's success springs from his having, with perfect understand-ing, supplied their demand for this kind of satisfaction.

It is this rapport between author and public, or high-class rab-blement, that would have astonished Joyce. Its presence in *The Catcher* may be roughly established by comparison with Keith Waterhouse's *There is a Happy Land,* obviously influenced by Salinger. It is in some ways a more genuine book; the growth of a positive evil out of the sordid innocence of a proletarian child-hood is worked out in a way that prevents anybody feeling supe-rior about it. But it isn't a 'key' book, because it is not designed for the smart-common reader. These may seem hard sayings, when /705/ *The Catcher* has given me so much pleasure. But I speak as a consumer myself, asking why the book, a few years on, seems so much less impressive. The answer seems to be that new needs are readily engendered in us, and readily supplied. Books will not last us any longer than motorcars. Of the rabblement from which we came, we retain one characteristic, its fickleness. What pleases us will not keep, of its very nature. Joyce was right not to seek his readers in the walks of the *bestia trionfante,* Forster to stand by his aristocracy. Mr. Salinger is not like them. Since few men will write for nobody, this fine artist writes for the sharp common reader. /706/

XXI

Salinger's *The Catcher in the Rye:* The Isolated Youth and His Struggle to Communicate

HANS BUNGERT

[Sections I and II, omitted here, provide for the European audience material familiar to the American reader: Salinger biography, the reception of *The Catcher in the Rye* in America, and a summary of the plot. The text of the remainder of the article is printed without excisions, except for some alterations or omissions in the footnotes. Note: The page numbers of the German text, indicated between slashes, are approximate rather than exact since the requirements of translation do not permit precise equivalents in breaks between words or phrases.]

III

The preceding sketch of the novel is sufficient to show that the book deals with the estrangement of the individual from society, a theme which has been exploited time and again in the modern American novel. /210/ Holden Caulfield is an outsider like Gatsby, Joe Christmas, Thomas Sutpen.

What makes Holden different from the other outsiders, first of all, is his youth. He is in that unhappy phase of life, that transitional stage, where he has outgrown the relatively well-ordered world of his childhood and must find his way in the world of adults. Quite a few of his actions and behavior patterns can therefore be explained—at the simplest level of interpretation—

From Hans Bungert, "J. D. Salingers The Catcher in the Rye: Isolation und Kommunikationsversuche des Jugendlichen," *Die Neueren Sprachen*, 1960, pp. 208-217. By permission. Translated from the German expressly for this book by Prof. Wulf Griessbach, Los Angeles State College.

according to the usual categories of adolescent development. Salinger's own knowledge of psychology and, furthermore, of psychoanalysis—evident in both his novel and his short stories—justifies the use of these categories. Holden's alarm at mankind is the kind of experience which is to some degree characteristic of a boy his age who is trying to orient himself. The astute Mr. Antolini may have this in mind when he explains to Holden: ". . . you'll find that you're not the first person who was ever confused and frightened and even sickened by human behavior" (p. 170).[1] In the opinion of psychologists an increase in the desire to communicate, as exhibited by Holden, is also typical of adolescence and so is the boy's final recognition that the "I" is ultimately an island.

This kind of analysis in psychological terms, however, is so elementary that it is at best only a starting point in the interpretation of Holden's character. More significant in recognizing Holden as an outsider is to consider his individuality, his distinct personality, which clearly sets him apart from other boys his age. Unlike his schoolmates Stradlater and Ackley, Holden possesses a refined moral instinct, an unusually critical but also creative intellect, a lively imagination, a passion for asking questions and, above all, a great desire for contact and love. His susceptibility to what is spiritually and morally beautiful in a world that has so little beauty and an excess of ugliness—this is what makes him so desperately vulnerable. He is—in the terms of I. H. Hassan—the "Responsive Outsider" confronted by the "Assertive Vulgarian." This "Assertive Vulgarian," a Stradlater for example, knows little of what troubles Holden, both because of lack of feeling and intellection and /211/ because of unscrupulous aggressiveness. Stradlater has no difficulty at all in adapting himself to his environment and can only be puzzled when confronted with any sign of nonconformity; for example, he shouts at Holden: "You don't do *one damn thing* the way you're supposed to" (p. 40)— this after Holden had written for him a composition deviating from the assigned topic.

[1] [Page references cited throughout have been changed, for the reader's convenience, to those of the Signet paperback.—Eds.]

Holden Caulfield faces a society in which there seems to be no place for him, particularly since it is a society structured essentially to accommodate adults. Denaturalized, perverted, rooted in an insatiable materialism, modern American civilization must inevitably strike a seeker of values like Holden as unapproachable and repelling. The blatant disregard for values surrounds him and renders both communication and contact difficult exactly where one might expect them to be most easily achieved—within his own family. Holden's brother D. B., for so many years his mentor and the author of significant literary works, prostitutes himself writing movie scripts in Hollywood. Lawyers, such as Holden's own father, have no interest in saving the lives of innocent people (according to Holden this is what they should do) but only seek fame, wealth, and social status.

Whatever is originally true, genuine, natural is transformed by this society into something false and corrupt. By virtue of his inner integrity Holden intuitively recognizes the phonies everywhere; he witnesses the triumph of lies and hypocrisy. Charity work becomes a social event for wealthy ladies, philanthropy becomes a means of self-glorification for successful businessmen.

Life in the modern metropolis, whose "emotional starvation and brittleness" F. I. Carpenter has justly discerned in Salinger's novel, is completely mechanized, automatized, denaturalized. Holden laments the dependence on taxis and buses and resents having to use the elevator "when you just want to go outside" (p. 119). The automobile is the center about which everything revolves, and consequently education, as Holden sees it, is nothing but "study so that you can learn enough to be smart enough to be able to buy a goddam Cadillac some day" (p. 119). The only way in which Holden can picture his own future in this conformist society is ". . . working in some office, making a lot of dough, and riding to work in cabs and Madison Avenue buses, and reading newspapers, and playing bridge all the time, and going to the movies and seeing a lot of stupid shorts and coming attractions and newsreels" (p. 121).

Looking at society as perceived through the eyes of an adolescent, Salinger has painted a devastating picture. The clearly ap-

parent contradiction between the morally unimpaired, which
Holden instinctively feels and seeks, and the omnipresent corrupt
and polluted, between value and lack of value, between the ideal
and the real, makes it all the more /212/ surprising that *The
Catcher in the Rye* is in no way a satire; rather than satire, the
novel is permeated with a deep sense of humor placing the work
very close indeed to *Huckleberry Finn*.

IV

Holden Caulfield has been called "one of the loneliest characters in fiction." In truth the loneliness of this boy is depressing.
Holden's feelings and thoughts isolate him from his vulgar,
clique-ridden schoolmates, from his teachers, from the strangers
and friends whom he meets during his wanderings in Manhattan
and who live in a world different from his. He is keenly aware of
his loneliness. Again and again there burst from him statements
like: "I felt so lonesome, all of a sudden. I almost wished I was
dead" (p. 46); "I got feeling so lonesome and rotten . . ." (p. 47);
"It made me too sad and lonesome" (p. 49); ". . . it was so quiet
and lonesome out . . . I kept wishing I could go home . . ." (p. 75);
". . . I was feeling sort of lousy. Depressed and all. I almost wished
I was dead" (p. 83).

The element of isolation in the novel is emphasized in many
ways. The timing of the action itself intensifies the isolation
through contrast, for Holden is alone and an outcast in the days
just before Christmas, a festival of love and human fellowship.
The scenes of action, too, underline the mood of isolation: the
school dormitory deathly quiet at late hours, deserted streets and
hotel lobbies, Central Park on a wintry night. Imagery of various
kinds again emphasizes the element of loneliness. Throughout
the novel Holden keeps asking what is going to happen to the
ducks when the lake in Central Park is frozen over, when their
little world, their life-sustaining refuge, is closed to them. His
question serves simultaneously to illustrate Holden's sympathy
with helpless creatures. The little boy whom Holden watches
trotting alongside the edge of the street, singing and humming,

is also shut out of his environment. Although the traffic of the great city roars past him, his heedless parents only centimeters away from him are in another world. Another child's basic drive to communicate is frustrated when his mother bursts into tears over the events depicted in the illusory world of the movie and ignores his urgent needs. This symbolism of loneliness culminates in Holden's conception of the American West /213/, the place to which in fantasy he would escape; by pretending to be a deaf-mute he even hopes to exclude the possibility of "goddam stupid useless conversations" (p. 179).

The image of Holden's dead brother Allie—abandoned alone in his grave at the first sign of rain when the visitors hurriedly leave the cemetery for their cars, turn on the radio, and drive to some warm, cozy restaurant—leads into the realm of death sym-bolism, the importance of which must not be overlooked, and which has already been pointed out by E. Branch. Death, as sym-bolized for instance by the Egyptian mummies in the museum, has a considerable fascination for Holden as a realm of stillness, purity, and peace. More than once Holden wishes he were dead, and after one particularly trying experience he even toys with the idea of suicide. Yet Harrison Smith's assumption that it was only his sister Phoebe who prevented Holden from committing suicide[1] probably goes too far. In abandoning the idea of suicide the boy is not influenced by anyone else but only by aesthetic considerations and by the fear of violating his intimately personal sphere: he does not want "a bunch of stupid rubbernecks" to stare at his corpse.

Holden does not, therefore, turn to death as a possible means of escape from civilization. Instead he seriously considers another kind of flight—leaving the big city and leading a simple, natural, genuine life far away in the country. Like Huck Finn he wants to "light out for the Territory." One of the most dramatic and at the same time one of the funniest episodes in the novel is that in which his plan—which is also an attempt to find a way to the *other*, the *you*—comes to naught. For when Holden tries to per-suade his girl friend Sally to join him in escape, she exhibits a

[1] "Manhattan Ulysses, Junior," *Saturday Review*, July 14, 1951, p. 12. /214/

complete lack of understanding of his unconventional ideas. Even a new version of his plan also fails, and this time it is Phoebe who interferes.

Thus Holden does not find happiness in a simple, natural world, a world he imagines as uncorrupted, pure, and secure, but —and this characterizes the frustration and the rootlessness of this twentieth-century Ulysses—he ends up on the couch of the psychoanalyst.

Try as he may to be a nonconformist, Holden's own core reaches down into the very civilization he hopes to leave behind. Hence his constant efforts to escape from the feeling of being an island within this civilization /214/ and his efforts to have his questions answered by fellow-men. A considerable part of the novel is taken up with his repeated attempts at communicating, most of the time with little success. Often, in spite of his desperate efforts, he can find no partner in conversation. Whenever a conversation does in fact materialize, Holden's own trend of thought is frequently either misunderstood or ignored, for he cannot get through to the others: Sally Hayes is too narrow-minded and superficial, Stradlater lacks feeling and interest, Carl Luce is too egocentric and intellectually smug.

Communication is difficult, if not impossible, chiefly because Holden and the various representatives of a society from which he finds himself estranged inhabit quite separate worlds. The distance between these two worlds is vividly expressed through the image of the telephone Holden so frequently resorts to as a medium of communication between himself and the others.

Moreover, the difficulty of communication is a topic which occupies a central position not only in *The Catcher in the Rye* but also in Salinger's short stories. The topic finds its stylistic expression, as I. H. Hassan has pointed out, in the fragmentary sentences used by many characters, in the frequency of such expressions as "I don't know" and "you know," and—if one wishes to add to Hassan's observations—in the frequency of questions and of questions answered by questions.

What distinguishes Holden Caulfield from his close literary relative Huck Finn is, among other things, the fact that because of his age Holden has to wrestle with sexual problems and has to learn about his relationship to the other sex. "Sex is something I just don't understand," he exclaims with concern (p. 59). Again and again he is drawn by his need for contact to the girls who are such a mystery to him. But here, too, he fails to establish contact with an understanding other, a you. His attempt to find something in common with Sally Hayes, a prototype of the "phonies," is bound to fail. When in despair he seeks the company of a prostitute, he finds physical contact impossible, not to mention spiritual understanding; the only result of the experience is a feeling of having soiled himself. Among the girls of his acquaintance only Jane Gallagher has the inherent prerequisites for a genuine partnership. In the past Holden had experienced happy moments of spiritual harmony, of wordless understanding, with her. But now he cannot reach her; he is fearful that her date with Stradlater, the "sexy bastard," has forfeited her purity and thus dragged her down into the world of vulgarity and ugliness.

In his isolation he finds refuge in the realm of imagination and playfulness. Behaving in an irrational manner /215/ he finds one way of letting off steam, and the unexpectedness of his behavior is one source of the novel's humor. The "horsing around," the harmless lies, the play-acting—these are simultaneously his protection from an emotional breakdown and his protest against the mechanized, prosaic, non-imaginative present day. The red hunter's cap he repeatedly puts on is the most notable symbol of his need for protection and of his rebellion.

Contact with other human beings is not always blocked, however. Even in this false and ugly world there are enclaves of purity and sincerity. The two nuns Holden meets live in such an enclave. He admires them, feels himself inwardly related to them, likes them, and manages to have a satisfactory exchange of ideas with them. This is one of the encounters in which he can forget his attitude of defense and contempt and can reveal his love for fellow-men without fear of getting hurt. This love, directed above all towards the helpless and the suffering, is so strong that Holden has not unjustly been called a "saintly Christian person."[2] It is so all-embracing a love that one of his comments at the end of the novel includes everybody, even the "phonies": "About all I know is, I sort of *miss* everybody I told about" (p. 192).

Children, especially, live in an enclave of unimpaired purity. Even during very brief meetings, Holden has no trouble establishing contact with them since he understands the psyche of the child intuitively. His talks with his ten-year-old sister, Phoebe, who is precocious like almost all children in Salinger's works, are therefore the high points in experiencing true contact. The close brother-sister relationship between him and Phoebe is a point of stability in his turbulent life, the character of which is misunderstood if one disposes of it—as Maxwell Geismar does—as "perhaps even a sentimental evasion of the true emotions in a sibling love."[3]

Holden would like to see the innocence and the purity of childhood preserved. "Certain things should stay the way they are," he says (p. 111), like those life-size figures in the glass cases of the museum which never change their positions.

Not many people, however, are as concerned about preserving purity as Holden, who even refrains from throwing a snowball out into the unspoiled whiteness of fresh snow. On the contrary, dangers threaten innocence everywhere, /216/ as symbolized by the obscene inscriptions everywhere which disturb the mind of the child and which could not be erased during a life lasting millions of years.

This struggle for preserving the purity and security of childhood is to Holden the only thing which makes life worth living. He would like to be "The Catcher in the Rye" and save thousands of small children, playing in a field of rye, from falling into the nearby abyss, the very one into which he has already fallen, or is falling at this very moment: ". . . if they're running and they don't look where they're going I have to come out from somewhere to *catch* them" (p. 156).

[2] Gwynn and Blotner, p. 29.

[3] Maxwell Geismar, *American Moderns: From Rebellion to Conformity*, p. 198. /216/

In connection with this picture of a desirable purpose in life one more point should be made. The image derives from Robert Burns whose poem "Coming Through the Rye" puts it this way in line nine: "Gin a body meet a body." The substitution of "catch" for "meet" documents, as E. Branch states, Holden's need of "human intimacy" but also points to Holden's yearning for a life of activity and awareness, and this is emphasized in the American edition by putting the word in italics.

Naturally, Holden Caulfield knows that his desire for the preservation of the absolutely pure and beautiful cannot be fulfilled, that it is just as much an illusion as his own return to lost childhood. What remains is the nostalgic love for children, a love which seems to be Salinger's own when he writes in his autobiographical sketch: "Some of my best friends are children. In fact, all of my best friends are children. It's almost unbearable to me to realize that my book [i.e., *The Catcher in the Rye*] will be kept on a shelf out of their reach."[4]

[4] *Twentieth-Century Authors,* First Suppement, p. 859. /217/

precocious: exhibiting mature qualities at an early age.

XXII

Soviet Critics on J. D. Salinger's Novel, *The Catcher in the Rye*

KONSTANTIN CHUGUNOV

There is no disputing the popularity of J. D. Salinger's novel *The Catcher in the Rye* in the United States. Some critics, Alfred Kazin for instance, regard him as a classic of 20th-century literature worthy to rank with Mark Twain, Ernest Hemingway and Sinclair Lewis. Elena Romanova, a Soviet critic, after visiting the United States in 1960 wrote in the *Literaturnaya Gazeta* that whenever her conversation with American students turned to literature, the question of Salinger's novel was immediately brought up.

Whether he is a classic or not, one thing is quite clear: the appearance of his novel was a great event in the literary life of the United States.

The Russian translation of the novel was published in the Soviet magazine *Foreign Literature* in November 1960, but comments by Soviet critics still appear in the press. I can truly say that no other book by an American writer published in recent years aroused such a response in our country. Moscow's leading newspapers and magazines alone—including *Foreign Literature, Novy Mir, Znamya, Voprosi Literaturi, Literaturnaya Gazeta, Literatura i Zhizn* and *Komsomolskaya Pravda*—published more than a dozen articles and critical reviews devoted to the novel.

The general opinion is that Salinger is a very talented writer, and his novel an outstanding work of fiction that makes a deep impression on the reader. The famous Soviet writer Vera Panova says in her afterword to the Russian translation: "Every episode is evidence of the maturity of the writer's talent. At first sight it

From *Soviet Literature*, No. 5, 1962, pp. 182-184.

seems that the novel is written in a loose style, but it soon becomes apparent that it is a subtle work of a real master. Outwardly simple, the novel has a complex inner mechanism that evokes a vortex of thoughts and emotions."

Salinger has identified himself with his principal character to such an extent that one almost does not feel his presence there. It seems that it is sixteen-year-old Holden Caulfield who is the author, simply and frankly relating the story of his misadventures.

The novel is not long but covers a great deal of ground. It contains nothing superfluous, nothing that could interfere with the flow of the main theme. Salinger's descriptions are laconic but very precise. Such are, for instance, the pictures of New York life. The enormous city looks strikingly colourless as if it reflects Holden's gloomy and depressed mood. "It was just very cold and nobody around anywhere," says Holden. /182/

In *New York Herald Tribune Books* Salinger said about himself: "I have trouble writing simply and naturally. I am a dash man and not a miler." But everyone knows how well-trained a dash man must be in order to run "naturally"!

Georgi Vladimov, a talented young Soviet critic and author, says: "No movement of Holden Caulfield is false and no phrase in the novel strikes a wrong note."

Holden's naive coarseness is rather amusing sometimes, but at the same time the boy arouses sympathy by his great sincerity, honesty and kindness.

Salinger makes excellent use of first-person narrative and of dialogue. This applies not only to *The Catcher in the Rye,* but also to his short stories, two of which *For Esmé—with Love and Squalor* and *A Perfect Day for Bananafish* were published in Soviet magazines in 1961.

Holden's language is raw, even vulgar, and is cluttered up with slang, but this does not prevent the author from reproducing the finest nuances of Holden's moods.

Inna Levidova, the author of several works on American literature, writes: "The book . . . gives a very precise representation of the typical meagre and monotonous, but sometimes very amusing language of a green youth. . . . It is slang of course, but slang that does not kill the individuality of the narrator. And behind all this one can clearly see Holden's great inner purity and honesty. It is these features, in fact, that give a dramatic tension to the book and raise it above the usual aping of childishness."

Soviet critics agree that the chief merits of the book are the descriptions of modern American life, and the honesty of the writer.

The world surrounding Holden is barren and dreary. The boy is tragically alone among tired, spiritually bankrupt people. He cannot find a place for himself in this life. "Holden feels that he is the only sane being among psychopaths and living corpses," says Georgi Vladimov. "Where is he going, what makes him cling to life? He cannot answer these questions, just as he cannot say what is his attitude towards war: he does not know whose side to take, he knows only that the American army 'was practically as full of bastards as the nazis were,' and the best thing, therefore, would be 'to sit right the hell on top' of the atomic bomb. . . . Holden's only unfailing attachment is little children and among them, first of all, his sister Phoebe."

Holden is a rebel. He revolts against the world of grown-ups. But his revolt takes the form of an escape from this world. He does not want to become grown-up himself.

We feel sorry for the boy. It is hard to believe that his blind revolt will end in nothing and that he will find himself in the company of such loathsome people as Ossenburger and James Castle's murderers.

Soviet critics do not agree with everything in Salinger's novel. One of them asks, for instance: "Isn't the very fact that Salinger has chosen such a fragile vessel for keeping his moral ideals in, that his sympathies lie with his hero, a kind but weak-spirited and wretched person, a sign of the writer's social and ideological narrow-mindedness?"

A well-known critic, Evgenia Knipovich, says that Holden "could, no doubt, define his attitude towards the world more concretely, if the author had not taken so much care of him and left him to his abstract and pathetic day-dreams. . . . *The Catcher in the Rye* is typical of works by Western writers who use for their motto Shakespeare's phrase 'a plague on both your houses'

—a plague on the 'rights' and on the 'lefts,' on the Whites and on the Reds, and on the struggle between them." /183/

Among the grown-up personages of the novel Holden's former teacher, Antolini, produces a favourable impression. It is he who picked up Holden's schoolmate after he had been beaten by hooligans and had thrown himself out of a window; he opened the door of his house to Holden when he came to him half-frozen and desperate in the middle of the night. Antolini's actions and manner of talking show him as an honest and noble man, but he is also spiritually broken and seeks consolation in heavy drinking. Besides, Holden suspects him of being a homosexual, and panic-stricken flees from his house. And it is here that critic Inna Levidova puts the question: Couldn't Holden Caulfield possibly come across one honest and clever man who wouldn't be dipsomaniac or a homosexual at the same time? The answer is: yes, he certainly could, but that wasn't the author's intention, apparently.

"*The Catcher in the Rye,*" writes Alexander Dymshits in *Literaturnaya Gazeta,* "is a frightening book, for it reflects the spiritual bankruptcy of modern America. . . . This is the most valuable thing about the book and not its end where the author tries to make the reader believe in the possibility of an 'independent' moral rebirth of his hero."

However, these criticisms do not belittle the obvious merits of the novel. We are glad to have made the acquaintance of this writer and are ready to welcome new and significant works by him.

A few words concerning the Russian translation of the book. Having read *The Catcher in the Rye* in the original, I thought that the translator would be confronted with many difficulties. I considered it hardly possible to capture fully in Russian the peculiar colouring and expressiveness of Holden's slang language. Translator Rita Wright-Kovaleva, however, has coped admirably with the task. She succeeded in recreating in Russian a living portrait of Holden Caulfield with all his emotional experiences, individual intonation and specific words. One doesn't feel that it is a translation. /184/

XXIII

A Tight Three-Movement Structure*

BRIAN WAY

[Mr. Way's article was occasioned by the publication in England of *Franny and Zooey*. In the first two and and a half pages Mr. Way describes the book as "sickeningly inept" (p. 72), discussess the religious elements in some of the *Nine Stories,* and then proceeds to the most extended and detailed analysis of the form and structure of *The Catcher in the Rye* known to the editors.]

. . . After this [*Franny and Zooey*], it is not only a relief, but a necessity to return to *The Catcher in the Rye,* and remind oneself that Salinger is, after all, a great writer. *The Catcher* seems to me the best novel published since the war, one of those contemporary American novels that have recreated in twentieth century terms that simultaneous sense of character and society of the great nineteenth century realists. Salinger has fused a pessimistic portrait of his society with a classic dramatisation of adolescence.

His method is, of course, very unlike that of the great nineteenth century realists, more in the tradition of the American novels that create their sense of reality through a tone of voice. Holden Caulfield is the same kind of character-narrator as Huck Finn, Ishmael, the Lardner baseball players and small-town worthies, and Saul Bellow's Augie March and Henderson, with the resources of American popular speech behind him. One can

* Title supplied by the editors.
From " 'Franny and Zooey' and J. D. Salinger," by Brian Way, *New Left Review,* May-June 1962, pp. 72-82. Reprinted by permission of the author and *New Left Review.*

sense the concentration and comic vitality even in a short passage:

' "Oh, do you go to Pencey?" she said. She had a nice voice. A nice telephone voice, mostly. She should've carried a goddam telephone around with her.

"Yes, I do," I said.

"Oh, how lovely! Perhaps you know my son, then. Ernest Morrow? He goes to Pencey."

"Yes, I do. He's in my class." /74/

Her son was doubtless the biggest bastard that ever went to Pencey, in the whole crummy history of the school. He was always going down the corridor, after he had a shower, snapping his soggy old wet towel at people's asses. That's exactly the kind of a guy he was . . .

"Ernest's father and I sometimes worry about him," she said . . .

"He's a very sensitive boy. He's never been a terribly good mixer with other boys. Perhaps he takes things a little more seriously than he should at his age."

Sensitive. That killed me. That guy Morrow was about as sensitive as a goddam toilet seat.

I gave her a good look. She didn't look like any dope to me. She looked like she might have a pretty damn good idea what a bastard she was the mother of. But you can't always tell—with somebody's mother, I mean. Mothers are all slightly insane.'

Holden has the blend of penetration and immaturity in judgment which is the mark of the intelligent adolescent. The shrewd social observation of 'a nice telephone voice, mostly', and the recognition that mothers are not always very perceptive about their own children, are balanced by characteristically school-boyish crudities of overstatement: Morrow is not merely unpleasant, he is 'doubtless the biggest bastard . . .' and 'sensitive as a goddam toilet seat'; 'Mothers are all slightly insane'. In personal relations he shows a mixture of good-natured youthful spontaneity and innocently calculated mischief. His speech contains the mannerisms and stock reactions that help to create his tone of voice—naturally this is a quality that can only be fully sensed by reading the whole book. The mannerisms may be as simple as the familiar 'and all' and 'if you want to know the truth' tags; the reactions as elaborate as those channelled through the word 'phoney'. Their stock nature is perfectly valid, since it is usually in this way that we respond to life. It is an illusion of the Jamesian type of novel that our responses to situations are invariably unique and unrepeatable; there is always an element of routine in character. It is only when the author's own controlling sense of character becomes routinised that the life of the tale vanishes. Holden Caulfield's stock reaction to the movies can go with great achievement in the novel; P. G. Wodehouse's to Bertie Wooster cannot.

The Catcher is not only consistent in tone, but is an extremely well-constructed novel. Beneath its episodic brilliance is a tight three-movement structure. The first movement shows Holden Caulfield at school; the second, his escape to New York and search there for sexual adventure; the third, his collapse, at the conscious level, backward into childhood, at the unconscious forward into madness.

Holden at Pencey Prep can be taken as the young American in his natural setting, a character and a milieu which are strongly individualized and yet in an important sense representative. He is introduced as a complete misfit in the setting which his society considers appropriate for him. School is the agency by which America more than most countries consciously socializes the immature for entry /75/ into the approved adult activities: and so a boy's relation to his school becomes a microcosm of the individual's relation to his society. In this concentration upon a manageable network of representative relationships, we see at work the only method by which a novel can create with any living force the pressures of a society—as opposed to the cinemascope aspirations of a Dos Passos. Holden is hostile to the spirit of his school—

'Pencey Prep is this school that's in Agerstown, Pennsylvania. You probably heard of it. You've probably seen the ads, anyway.

—but also alienated from it: there is his impending expulsion; his losing the fencing foils; above all his relation to the football game—physically remote ('practically the whole school was there except me') and cynical in spirit ('you were supposed to commit suicide or something if old Pencey didn't win').

His detachment from the game is a key to his rejection of the ethos of his society. What depresses and infuriates him most about his headmaster and Spencer is their insistence that 'life is a game'—

'Game my ass. Some game. If you get on the side where all the hot-shots are, then it's a game, all right—I admit that. But if you get on the *other side,* where there aren't any hot-shots, then what's a game about? Nothing. No game.'

Games are a system devised for the benefit of the star-performer; the rules of the game enable him to shine, they are no protection for the weak—for those on the side where there aren't any hot-shots. The pretence of team-spirit is pure hypocrisy, and the cynicism of Holden's attitude the proper reaction to the assertion that the game is played for the common good. The game, as seen by Holden, is an image of the competitive society, in its glorification of success, callousness towards failure, and its most unpardonable assertion—that its hot-shots not only have the tangible benefits of success but the moral satisfaction of feeling that they are the finest flower of an incorruptible system. Old Ossenburger is the matured product—enormously rich from his cheap funeral parlours; treated with esteem by his society—his old school names a wing after him; and full of moral self-satisfaction:

'. . . the next morning, in chapel, he made a speech that lasted about ten hours. He started off with about 50 corny jokes, to show what a regular guy he was. Very big deal. Then he started telling us how he was never ashamed, when he was in some kind of trouble or something, to get right down on his knees to pray to God. He told us we should always pray to God—talk to Him and all—wherever we were. He told us we ought to think of Jesus as our buddy and all. He said *he* talked to Jesus all the time. Even when he was driving his car. That killed me. I can just see the big phoney bastard shifting into first gear and asking Jesus to send him a few more stiffs.' /76/

The only adequate reaction to him is Marsalla's brief pungent wordless comment. The influence of Ring Lardner is quite evident in this form of broad satiric comedy: Ossenburger is a bloated version of the man from Ogdensburg, New York State, who 'is a Rotarian and a very convincing speaker' (*The Golden Honeymoon*).

The other hot-shot at Pencey is Holden's room-mate Stradlater, an athlete and school hero, 'a very sexy bastard' who is outstandingly successful in the American form of adolescent sexuality—the infantile petting with automobile back-seat as indispensable locale. His fight with Holden over Jane Gallagher brings in the book's other area of concern, the agonies of adolescence. Structurally it is the event which projects Holden into his New York adventures.

This second phase is the best part of the book. It describes Holden's four successive attempts at sexual satisfaction: his telephone-call to the girl who is 'not quite a whore'; his evening in the Lavender Room with the three girls from Seattle, Washington; his encounter with the prostitute; and his proposal to Sally Hayes. Salinger captures with extraordinary power, as well as with comic verve, the euphoria of escape from the formal limits of school, and the excited sense of being on the town, with which Holden arrives in New York. Holden's excitement is the excitement of the fantasist: he is embarking on a dream which is both universally adolescent, and built into contemporary American mass-culture through Hollywood and television, advertising, pulp fiction and magazines, and social mores—the offer of unbelievable possibilities of sexual adventure and satisfaction. This erotic day-dream is confronted in each of the four incidents with harsh realities which the day-dream disqualifies the fantasist from handling, in a manner analogous to Gatsby's experience. Holden is caught in an ironic and painful dialectic: four times his participation in the communal day-dream propel him into real situations from which he recoils, even more incapacitated and humiliated, back into fantasy. The profound pessimism which grows steadily beneath the humour of this movement lies in the fact that the reassuring progressive nineteenth century conviction that one learns from experience is reversed. In a tale like *The Shadow-Line*, for instance, Conrad shows the young inexperienced commander taking his first ship through a series of difficult situations, and emerging at the end of the voyage matured, and accepted by his mentor, Captain Giles. In *The Catcher*, experience incapacitates and destroys, and after the failure of Holden's last attempt at satisfaction, he is moving towards mental collapse.

This nihilism is coloured and intensified by two atmospheric touches: a sense of New York as a nightmare—the theme of twentieth century urban despair rendered with a particularly intense local concentration:

'. . . it was so quiet and lonesome out, even though it was Saturday night. I didn't see hardly anybody on the street. Now and then you just saw a man and a girl crossing a street with their arms around each other's waists and all, or a bunch of hoodlumy-looking guys /77/ and their dates, all of them laughing like hyenas at something you could bet wasn't funny. New York's terrible when somebody laughs on the street very late at night.'

and an ironic compassion for the horrors of the human condition:

'The bellboy that showed me to the room was this very old guy around 65. He was even more depressing than the room was. He was one of those bald guys that comb all their hair over from the side to cover up their baldness. I'd rather be bald than do that. Anyway, what a gorgeous job for a guy around 65 years old. Carrying people's suitcases and waiting around for a tip. I suppose he wasn't too intelligent or anything, but it was terrible anyway.'

It is this compassionateness that distinguishes the social observation of *The Catcher* from that of *For Esmé* and *Franny and Zooey*.

I have said that *The Catcher* is the classic novel of adolescence—indeed the only great novel I know which handles this phase successfully. Others have tended either, like Gide in *Les Faux-Monnayeurs*, to dwell with obsessive intensity on the moments of horror and disgust, or, like Fitzgerald within the American novel itself, upon the romantic exaltation. The strength of Salinger's study of adolescence is that he does not stop with a succession of superficial manifestations as other novelists have done, but goes straight to the fundamental biological situation. He sees that all the contradictions, agonies, and exaltations of adolescence stem from the central fact: that the adolescent has newly gained the physical potentialities for sexual experience but has not learnt to integrate them either within himself or in any consistent relation to the demands of society. 'Sex', says Holden, 'is something I just don't understand'. From this flows everything—the confused idealism of his attitude to Jane Gallagher; the naively unscrupulous calculatingness of his adventures; the wish for experiment and the corresponding fear and revulsion; a general fascination and disgust with the physical— Ackley's pimples, Stradlater's toenails—a new horrified awareness of physical process.

The dialectic of Holden's sexual experiences is most fully and brilliantly exploded where he has a prostitute sent up to his hotel room. The expectations with which this adventure begins are suggested with superb comic skill—

'I read this book once, at the Whooton School, that had this very sophisticated suave, sexy guy in it, Monsieur Blanchard was his name . . . He said in this one part, that a woman's body is like a violin and all, and that it takes a terrific musician to play it right. It was a very corny book— I realise that—but I couldn't get that violin stuff out of my mind anyway. In a way, that's why I sort of wanted to get some practice in, in case I ever got married. Caulfield and his Magic Violin, boy. It's corny, I realise, but it isn't *too* corny. I wouldn't mind being pretty good at that stuff.' /78/

This is a penetrating and sympathetic view of the erotic fantasy of permanent sexual orgy—the adolescent's and the pornographer's view of sex as sensation and technique ('Caulfield and his Magic Violin'), immediately recalling, by contrast, the Lawrentian reality of sexual desire and fulfilment developed through relationship and tenderness.

When the prostitute arrives, Holden projects his fantasy into this real situation and begins rôle-playing, 'suave as hell, boy', like Monsieur Blanchard. He significantly introduces himself by the name Jim Steele, which suggests simultaneously a movie-star of the rugged type and a business tycoon. Immediately, however, this masquerade begins to break up under the stress of Holden's soon very-apparent sexual inexperience, and the drab reality of prostitution. Above all, the Monsieur Blanchard view of sex exists only in the head—its illusion of omnipotent control of sensation and perfection of technique postulates that only the fantasist actually exists. The partner is seen as a magic violin, passive and inanimate. Nothing breaks up this dream so quickly as discovering that the woman is a person with a very different approach of her own—here a nervous cold professionalism that knocks Holden's potency to pieces. The control of tone is remarkable—the way in which the farcical and the painful elements are brought out, and the dramatic impetus of Holden's rising panic as he begins to feel his dominance slipping—especially where the prostitute sits on his lap—physically pinning him down to the realities of the situation. She has now fully emerged as a person, and takes control: she has been insulted, and is not particularly pleasant or attractive anyhow. The dramatic reversal is complete—Holden is no longer Jim Steele-Blanchard, omnipotent sensualist in his Riviera château, but a frightened adolescent in the hands of a shrewdly calculating prostitute and her pimp. He goes through the humiliation of the prostitute's insults, and the pimp, Maurice's, brutal return. The reality is now intolerable, and the dialectic is completed by a return to fantasy—

'About halfway to the bathroom, I sort of started pretending I had a bullet in my guts. Old Maurice had plugged me. Now I was on the way to the bathroom to get a good shot of bourbon or something to steady my nerves and help me *really* go into action.'

With tight-lipped heroism he shoots Maurice, and then Jane Gallagher comes to nurse his wound. 'The goddam movies. They can ruin you. I'm not kidding.'

After this, his resilience begins to leak away and the fundamental despair of the book dominates the Sally Hayes passage, with its horrified vision of what the adult American world offers the young:

'. . . there wouldn't be marvellous places to go to after I went to college and all. Open your ears. It'd be entirely different. We'd have to go down stairs in elevators with suitcases and stuff. We'd have to phone up everybody and tell 'em goodbye and send 'em /79/ postcards from hotels and all. And I'd be working in some office, making a lot of dough, and riding to work in cabs and Madison Avenue buses, and reading newspapers, and playing bridge all the time, and going to the movies and seeing a lot of stupid shorts and coming attractions and newsreels.'

Holden feels almost with hysteria that he cannot escape, least of all into the earlier American log-cabin Thoreau-innocent existence he proposes to Sally Hayes.

After this, the novel's third phase, the account of Holden's collapse, begins. It takes place on two planes: a conscious groping back towards childhood represented most strongly by his clandestine visit to Phoebe. (The element of unconscious sexual symbolism is clear here—his creeping back into the dark room suggests the womb.) Irresistibly at the unconscious level, he is drifting toward mental breakdown. This part of the novel is much less successful than the two earlier, and contains many of the weaknesses of *For Esmé* and *Franny and Zooey*, both of which offer a number of useful clues to the understanding of the last part of *The Catcher*. Potentialities of mental collapse are suggested much more effectively in the fight with Stradlater, the laughter in New York passage, and the Sally Hayes incident, than anywhere in this last section. There is a general loss of narrative impetus and comic verve: Holden's visit to a movie, though funny, is only a repetition of effects already scored against the Lunts. Salinger's ironic compassion is replaced by a self-regarding, and slightly self-pitying whimsicality which recalls Truman Capote rather than any writer of importance.

His nihilism has a pattern as precise as an equation: conventional society is a nightmare too horrifying to contemplate—the expensive boarding school, the mockery of family-life, the executive's career, and the call-girl system in *The Catcher;* a respectable marriage in *Uncle Wiggily in Connecticut;* a businessman's adultery in *Pretty Mouth and Green my Eyes.* His despairing analysis does not permit even the stoical resistance of Camus, let alone the positive hope of Faulkner. The alternatives he presents—life-in-death conformity and mental collapse—eliminate all possibility of creative living.

In the two earlier phases of the novel, the tensions of this dilemma, fused as they are in a classic portrayal of the contradictions of adolescence, are inescapably challenging. In the last section, however, Salinger's moral analysis of the significance of neurosis is unsatisfying. He slips into the current American habit of equating mental disorder with innocence, recalling Benjy in *The Sound and the Fury;* Augie March's brother George; Dove Linkhorn—a commercialised version in Nelson Algren's *A Walk on the Wild Side;* and Dean Moriarty, the holy goof.

More important still is his failure with children, who are not seen with any of his insight into adolescence, but with all the sentimentalizing pre-Freudian unrestraint of a Victorian novelist—the cosiness of Holden's relationship with Phoebe, and his reminiscences of his own childhood visits to the Museum of Natural History. At the same /80/ time his children are miniature adults whose opinions gain the factitious piquancy of the pronouncements of Renaissance dwarfs. Esmé is odiously and precociously 'quaint'; Teddy a hateful little Christ disputing with the doctors; all the Glass children were star performers on a radio quiz 'It's a Wise Child'. Salinger's children are as detestable and unreal as Shakespeare's.

His failure here is curiously but closely linked to his success with adolescence: his understanding of adolescent sex is the strength of the earlier passages; his ignorance of the child's relation to sex ruins the close. In the scene where Holden delivers a note to the principal of Phoebe's school and suddenly sees the words '—— you' written on the wall, he reflects—

'It drove me damn near crazy. I thought how Phoebe and all the other little kids would see it, and how they'd wonder what the hell it meant,

and then some dirty kid would tell them—all cockeyed naturally—what it
meant, and how they'd all *think* about it and maybe even *worry* about it
for a couple of days. I kept wanting to kill whoever'd written it. I figured
it was some perverty bum that'd sneaked into the school late at night to
take a leak or something and then wrote it on the wall. I kept picturing
myself catching him at it, and how I'd smash his head on the stone steps
till he was good and goddam dead and bloody.'

Salinger is out of touch with the way children actually react
to obscenity; they accept it either with complete matter-of-fact-
ness, or with a delighted relish for the forbidden. The one thing
they don't do is worry about it. Salinger is not at all in control of
his material here, and although '—— you' is represented as being
a shock to the children, it is the shock to the rosy, sentimental,
backward view of childhood that is in fact resented. The hysterical violence of 'smash his head on the stone steps till he was good
and goddam dead and bloody' shows this, and so does the obsessive follow-up, where Holden finds '—— you' written up everywhere he goes, and is ultimately convinced that it will be inscribed on his gravestone.

The fable of the catcher in the rye itself belongs to the same
aberrant tendency. Holden wishes to protect children who are
playing happily in a field of rye from running over the edge of
the cliff that borders the field. Falling over a cliff is a classic unconscious sexual symbol, and here represents without any doubt
the dividing-line of puberty, separating the happy innocence of
childhood from the dangers and agonies of sexual capability.
This perpetuates the conventional view of the innocence of children, and shows an atavistic belief in the existence of a Fall from
grace. It may be objected here that Holden's sexual failures
could convincingly make him hanker for a return to a pre-sexual
state of existence. If one felt that Salinger were consciously planning this and directing one's responses this way, one would
agree, but my own feeling is that, by this point in the novel, he
is completely submerged in Holden Caulfield and no longer preserving that necessary detachment from his main character. Two
/81/ features of his writing support this view: first, his abrupt

abandonment of his sense of Holden's comic potentialities, expressed earlier in the novel through Holden's tone of voice as a note of ironically sympathetic self-mockery. It is this control of tone that gives the prostitute incident, without curbing the farce or minimising the pain, its essential sanity—a dimension which is obviously lacking in the '—— you' sequence. Secondly, to understand what is happening, one is forced to drag out unconscious sexual symbols and atavistic superstititons, evidence that the writer has failed to order his material, and has left in an unrealised form what he is really writing about—evidence not of profundity, but of a collapse of artistic control. Such examinations are always impertinent and usually irrelevant, but here the indications are so unmistakeable, and the connections with the artistic failure so clear, that one is forced to follow this line of analysis. In particular, there is the recurring unconscious symbol of a return to the womb—Phoebe's bedroom (which I have already mentioned); and the Pharaoh's tomb in the Museum, a peaceful and quiet place which Holden is hysterically enraged to find violated once again with the words '—— you'.

At the dénouement, Salinger sees Holden Caulfield's tragic predicament through the kind of closed system which nihilistic writers construct with diagrammatic clarity: childhood is the only state of existence which is innocent, unspoilt, uncorrupted; escape backwards into it is obviously impossible; the despair of knowing this inexorable situation is the tragedy. The effectiveness of the tragedy depends on our accepting the author's view of childhood—a view which is manifestly false. And so the novel's greatness is flawed by the dénouement and rests on those earlier scenes of adolescence where there is no falsity of observation, lapse of consciousness, or failure of control. /82/

XXIV

The Love Song of J. D. Salinger

ARTHUR MIZENER

A few months ago I gave a lecture in the Middle West, on Scott Fitzgerald, before about as intelligent an undergraduate audience as you are likely to find. When I finished, the first question from the floor was about J. D. Salinger. This humbling non-sequitur is too familiar to be any surprise, for Salinger is probably the most avidly read author of any serious pretensions in his generation. There are good reasons why he should be, for though his work has certain limitations—both of subject matter and of technique—it is, within these limitations, the most interesting fiction that has come along for some time.

Salinger has been writing since he was fifteen and is evidently a dedicated—not to say obsessed—writer, but the relatively small amount of work he has produced in a career of nearly twenty years suggests that he has a hard time writing. Moreover, there is in his work a very high incidence of emotional collapse and even violent death. One of the sharpest implications of his work, in short, is that perceptive people have difficulty remaining operative, or even surviving, in our world; a great deal of his most brilliant wit, like so much of James Thurber's, is close to desperation. There are good and even historical reasons in American culture for this state of mind, as I shall try to suggest, but they make the difficulty Salinger himself apparently faces no less disturbing to contemplate.

His immediate appeal is that he speaks our language, or, to be exact, makes a kind of poetry out of the raw materials of our speech. His ear picks up with stunning exactness the speech of

From *Harper's Magazine*, CCXVIII, February 1959, pp. 83-89. Reprinted by permission of the author.

many kinds of people: of the brutally conventional—"But my *gosh*. Honestly! I just can't stand to see somebody get away with absolute murder. It makes my blood boil"; of the earnestly ignorant—"They got their *pores* open the whole time. That's their *nature*, for Chrissake. See what I mean?"; of the army—"This here's officers' quarters, Mac." His people are wholly present, in devastating dramatic immediacy, in everything they say.

What is more, Salinger uses with great skill the very American device of conveying meaning by describing object, gesture, action. He can create this kind of poetry on the simplest occasion, as for instance when an ordinary girl is waiting for a long-distance telephone call:

> She read an article in a women's pocket-size magazine, called "Sex Is Fun—or Hell." She washed her comb and brush. She took the spot out of the skirt of her beige suit. She moved the button on her Saks blouse. She tweezed out two freshly surfaced hairs in her mole. When the operator finally rang her room, she was sitting on the window seat and had almost finished putting lacquer on the nails of her left hand.

But if Salinger is a poet in this sense, he is also a poet in the only sense that he himself would probably take seriously: he's a man with his own special insight into the meaning of experience. "A good horse," as his characters the Glass children learned from Li Po, "can be /83/ picked out by its general build and appearance. But the superlative horse—one that raises no dust and leaves no tracks—is something evanescent and fleeting, elusive as thin air."

An inescapable, intense awareness of this "poetry that flows through things, all things," marks every one of Salinger's significant characters. As Vincent Caulfield in "This Sandwich Has No Mayonnaise" (1945) remarks of his brother Holden, such people cannot "do anything but listen hectically to the maladjusted little apparatus [they wear] for a heart." That is what makes Holden worry all through *The Catcher in the Rye* about what the Central Park ducks do in the winter and constantly recall with delight that, when they played checkers, old Jane would never move her kings out of the back row.

Obviously Salinger did not burst on the world with these powers of observation and this sense of experience fully developed.
He had, in fact, rather more trouble than most writers in discovering his own way of feeling and the best mode of expression
for it. His first published stories, which appeared mainly in the
Saturday Evening Post and *Collier's* in the early forties, will
quickly destroy any romantic notions one may have had about
the value of the unpublished stories he wrote even earlier, by
flashlight under the bedclothes after "Lights," when he was a
student at Valley Forge Military Academy. The first published
stories deal, in a mechanical and overingenious way, with the
superficial interests of magazine readers of the time. In "The
Hang of It" (1941), for example, a father tells us about his com-
ically inept soldier son who keeps insisting that he will get the
hang of soldiering. At the end we find out that the speaker is also
the boy's commanding officer. This is intended to make what had
at first appeared the boy's stupidity seem pathetic anxiety, but
the events of the story are almost entirely farce and do not support the intention.

These trivial stories are nevertheless interesting. They show
us Salinger's preoccupation with close personal relations, particularly family relations. They make clear his marked preference
for first-person narration and interior monologue. And they show
the related difficulty he has in saying what he wants to and at the
same time constructing a "well-made" plot. In 1945 he was saying, "I am a dash man and not a miler, and it is probable that I
will never write a novel."

Perhaps that judgment was right, for *The Catcher in the Rye,*
despite its brilliance of observation and the virtuosity with which
Salinger keeps Holden Caulfield's monologue going for the
length of a novel, is primarily concerned neither with the working out of a plot nor the development of a character. It is a lyric
monologue in which the complex feelings of an essentially static
character are gradually revealed. For all Salinger's skill, *The
Catcher in the Rye* has a claustrophobic and, at the same time,
random quality.

The second stage of Salinger's career runs from 1943, when he published his first mature story, "The Varioni Brothers," in the *Post*, to about 1948. In this period his powers of observation became much sharper and he began to understand much better what he wanted to say. His plots, if they still cramped him, were not completely irrelevant, though it was still true—as it is today —that he was at his best in meditations like "Boy in France" (1945) and in the monologues of plotted stories like "Last Day of the Last Furlough" (1944). His material was still a little conventional—the vicissitudes of Gershwinlike song writers, cruiseship romances, soldiers going overseas. But his characteristic feelings about experience were beginning to come through. They are there in the beautifully revealed devotion of the letter from Babe Gladwaller's sister Mattie, age ten, that Babe reads in his foxhole in "Boy in France." They are there when Sonny Varioni, the talented, bored, ambitious song writer, realizes that he hears the music for the first time in his life when he reads his dead brother's book.

The best work of this second period is the group of independent but related stories about the Gladwaller and the Caulfield families, who are closely connected by the friendship of Babe Gladwaller and Vincent Caulfield. These stories appeared in four different magazines over a period of three years. The first four of them are mainly concerned with Babe and Vincent. Then, beginning in late 1945 with "I'm Crazy," Salinger began to focus on Holden Caulfield. Much of the family detail from the first four stories is kept in the two stories about Holden, but there are important changes, and, with only slight revisions, these two stories became chapters in *The Catcher in the Rye*. I think it is a fairly good guess that, after writing *The Catcher in the Rye*, which was published in 1951, Salinger decided that most of the things he had been working out in the Gladwaller- /84/ Caulfield stories could be more clearly realized if he started afresh without some of the awkward commitments of these stories.

In any event, in 1948 he began the third period of his career with the publication of "A Perfect Day for Bananafish" in *The New Yorker*. This is, in order of publication anyway, the first of his stories about the Glass family. It is anybody's guess, of course, whether Salinger had the whole, still unfinished history of the Glass family in mind when he wrote "A Perfect Day for Bananafish," but my guess is that, much as William Faulkner has apparently always had at least the main outlines of the McCaslin family history in mind, Salinger has known about all the Glasses from the beginning. For one thing, the order in which the stories have appeared (and probably were written) has little relation to the chronological order of events in the family history, yet all the minute particulars of the Glass family history are consistent. What we are told about Seymour Glass in 1948 in the first story fits precisely, both in fact and in implication, with what we have learned about him and the rest of the family since. Salinger's conception of the Glass children's situation has become richer during these nine years, but neither the facts nor the essential nature of that situation has changed.

Because the details about the Glass family are scattered and because a reasonable knowledge of them is necessary for an understanding of Salinger's best work, it may help to set down in outline what we so far know about them. The parents, Les Glass (Jewish) and Bessie Gallagher Glass (a fat Irish Rose, her youngest son lovingly calls her), were successful Pantages Circuit vaudevillians in the twenties. By the forties Les Glass was "hustling talent for a motion picture studio in Los Angeles." In the fifties they are living with their two youngest children in New York, in "an old but, categorically, not unfashionable apartment house in the East Seventies." They have had seven children.

The oldest, Seymour, was born in February, 1917, entered Columbia at the age of fifteen and took a Ph.D. in English. In 1940 he and his brother Buddy reluctantly gave up the room they had shared in the Glasses' apartment since 1929 and moved into an apartment of their own near Seventy-ninth and Madison. Seymour taught English for a year or two before entering the service. While he was stationed at Fort Monmouth, he met a girl named Muriel Fedder, whom he married on June 4, 1942. When he returned from the service, he was—as he had promised Muriel and her mother he would be—psychoanalyzed, presumably by what Buddy calls one of those *"summa-cum-laude* Thinker[s] and intellectual men's-room attendant[s]" so greatly admired by people like Muriel's mother. Possibly as a result, Seymour one day deliberately drove the Fedder's car into a tree, and it was decided that he and Muriel should take a vacation in Florida, at the place where they had spent their honeymoon. There, in Room 507 of a fashionable beach hotel, on the afternoon of March 18, 1948, Seymour made his second, successful attempt to commit suicide, by putting a bullet from an Ortgies caliber 7.65 through his right temple.

The second child, Buddy (whose given name is, I think, Webb), was born in 1919, as was Jerome David Salinger. Buddy is the writer of the family, and it is sometimes difficult to distinguish his voice from Salinger's. *"The Great Gatsby,"* he says, ". . . was my "Tom Sawyer' /85/ when I was twelve." Buddy never finished college (nor did Salinger, who tried three). He entered the service early in 1942 and, when he got out, became "a writer in residence." In 1955 he was teaching "at a girl's junior college in upper New York state, where he lived alone, in a small, unwinterized, unelectrified house about a quarter of a mile away from a rather popular ski run."

The next child and first girl in the family is Boo Boo Glass. "Her joke of a name aside, her general unprettiness aside, she is—in terms of permanently memorable, immoderately perceptive, small-area faces—a stunning and final girl." She appears to be—we do not know a great deal about her yet—more successfully reconciled to the world than the rest of the Glass children. Boo Boo was a Wave, stationed in Brooklyn. During the war she met "a very resolute-looking young man" named Tannenbaum, whom she later married. The Tannenbaums live in Tuckahoe and have a summer place in New England. By 1955 they had three children, the oldest of whom is Lionel, the central character in "Down at the Dinghy," which was published in *Harper's* in 1949.

Boo Boo was followed by twins, Waker and Walt. Waker spent the war in a conscientious objector's camp in Maryland and by 1955 had become a Catholic priest: "If you tell Waker it looks like *rain,* his eyes all fill up." Walt entered the service in the spring of 1941 and by May of 1942 was in the Pacific. In Japan, late in the autumn of 1945, a Japanese stove he was packing as a souvenir for his commanding officer exploded and killed him.

The sixth child, Zachary Martin Glass, known in the family as Zooey, was born in 1929. Zooey's face is close to being "a wholly beautiful face" or, as Boo Boo says, he looks like "the blue-eyed Jewish-Irish Mohican scout who died in your arms at the roulette table at Monte Carlo." After college he became a television actor, though his mother very much wanted him to take his Ph.D. in Mathematics or Greek, as he easily could have. By 1952 he was playing leads.

The youngest child is a girl named Frances, born in 1934. Like Zooey she is extraordinarily beautiful. In the summer of 1954, between her junior and senior years in college, she played summer stock. Zooey, an enthusiastically unrelenting critic, says she was very good, and Franny clearly loves the theater. In her junior year she became interested in a boy named Lane Coutell—interested enough to sleep with him. But in November of 1955 she was plunged into a spiritual crisis—"I'm sick of ego, ego, ego. My own and everybody else's. I'm sick of everybody that wants to get somewhere, do something distinguished and all, be somebody interesting. It's disgusting—it is, it *is*. I don't care what anybody says." After three difficult days at home, she is saved from collapse by her brother Zooey, who possibly saves himself at the same time.

Over a period of nearly eighteen years, beginning in 1927, one or more of the Glass children were performing, under the name of Black, on a famous radio quiz show known—"with perhaps typical Coast-to-Coast irony"—as "It's a Wise Child." Their educations were paid for by these performances.

This is the barest outline of what we know about the Glass family. Even so, the fullness of these details and their exactness are striking evidence of the imaginative intensity with which they have been conceived. They also make it possible for Salinger, for the first time, to use consistently the technique he is most happy with and to convey directly the feelings he cares most about.

For example, they provide the fullest opportunity for the kind of surprise an author can get from delayed or implied explanation, which writers of monologues like Salinger and Faulkner usually substitute for narrative suspense—an awkward and artificial device in a monologue. In Faulkner, one has to reconstruct the genealogy of the McCaslin family from dozens of scattered allusions before one fully understands any particular McCaslin story. In the same way one has to reconstruct the history of the Glass family.

Salinger uses suspended explanation much less extravagantly than Faulkner, but he has nonetheless confused some readers. Some of them, for instance, seem to have thought (until the matter was fully explained in "Zooey" in 1957) that the heroine of "Franny" (1955) was so badly upset during her football weekend with Lane Coutell not because she was in a spiritual crisis but because she was pregnant. There is no real reason for a careful reader to make this mistake about "Franny." In that story, Franny describes at length the idea of prayer in *The Way of a Pilgrim,* the little book she carries with her everywhere; and at the end of the story her lips are moving in the Jesus Prayer the Pilgrim recommends. Nevertheless, a good many readers apparently did misunderstand "Franny." Some even seem to have doubts about who pushed /86/ whom into the empty swimming pool at the end of "Teddy," where, for much the same dramatic reasons that are at work in "Franny," Salinger depends on our understanding of Teddy's attitude to make us understand that it is Teddy who dies.

This kind of surprise is one of the most effective devices available to a writer like Salinger, and he uses it with great skill. He always plays fair; any careful reader knows what is going on. But we are frequently astonished and delighted when we catch our first glimpse of the precise connections between what had before seemed unconnected events. It must be some time, for instance, before a reader discovers that the Walt whom the drunken Eloise is talking about in "Uncle Wiggily in Connecticut" (1948) is Walt Glass, whose family connections did not begin to emerge in any detail until "Raise High the Roof Beam, Carpenters" (1955). But when the reader makes this discovery, a fascinating and important aspect of the Glass family falls into place for him. Walt was Bessie Glass's "only truly lighthearted son"; as such he shows us an important aspect of Salinger's sense of human possibilities.

The fact that the Glass family is large and closely knit is also important to the feelings Salinger cares most about. The essential reality for him subsists in personal relations, when people, however agonizingly, love one another. "I say," remarks Buddy Glass as he begins to tell us the story "Zooey," "that my current offering isn't a mystical story, or a religiously mystifying story, at all. *I* say it is a compound, or multiple, love story, pure and complicated."

This is true of all Salinger's mature stories. Their subject is the power to love, pure and—in children and the childlike—simple, but in aware people, pure and complicated. Salinger's constant allusions to the Bhagavad-Gita, Sri Ramakrishna, Chuang-tzu, and the rest are only efforts to find alternate ways of expressing what his stories are about. This power to love can be realized —and represented—most fully in complicated personal relations like those of the Glasses.

Salinger's conception of these relations is an impressive—and certainly unconscious—evidence of the way he fits into a major tradition of American literature, what might be called the effort to define the Good American. For this tradition, American experience creates a dilemma by encouraging the individual man to cultivate his perception to the limit according to his own lights and at the same time committing him to a society on which the majority has firmly imposed a well-meaning but imperceptive and uniform attitude. People in this tradition of our cultural history have a highly developed, personal sense of their experience. At the same time, they have a strong conviction—even if a bitter conviction like Henry Adams'—that no man can survive in isolation and that the only community they have to love is the American community to which they have been committed by a lifetime's involvement. Such people cannot /87/ escape knowing that the Good American must be a member of a particularly demanding and not very perceptive community and simultaneously a supremely aware man, because they themselves live partly in the world of ordinary American experience and partly in what may perhaps fairly be called the transcendental world of extraordinary American experience.

The Glass children stand in this way at the center of our dilemma as, with less clarity of perception and less intensity of feeling, large numbers of Americans do. Like Thoreau and Henry Adams, Huck Finn and Ike McCaslin, Ishmael and Jay Gatsby, the Glass children are well aware of where they stand—committed, involved, torn.

"I'd enjoy [doing a movie in France], yes," says Zooey. "God, yes. But I'd hate like hell to leave New York. If you must know, I hate any kind of so-called creative type who gets on any kind of ship. I don't give a goddam what his reasons are. I was *born* here. I went to *school* here. I've been *run over* here—*twice*, and on the same damn *street*. I have no business acting in Europe, for God's sake."

This sounds like the speaker in Allen Tate's "Ode to the Confederate Dead," except that the voice is wholly Northern and urban and is—for all its desperateness—less despairing.

It is the effort to convey their full sense of this situation that leads the Glass children to talk the way they do. For this extra dimension of understanding they use the everyday urban speech Salinger has been listening to all his life. The Glass children must speak the language of the place where they were born, went to school, were run over; it is their native language, the only one wholly theirs, just as the place itself is. But they need to express in this language an understanding of their experience which, if possessed to some degree by many Americans, is wholly clear to only a few of them.

An effort to resolve a similar conflict of feelings affects most of the writers of this tradition, with the result that they too develop odd, brilliant styles. Salinger's style most obviously resembles that of Mark Twain, Lardner and Hemingway, who prided themselves on using homely American speech with great accuracy, but were saying things with it that few homely Americans are wholly conscious of.

Like Twain and Lardner, Salinger depends more than most

prose writers on the fine shading of his style to convey his meaning. That is why he is at his best when one of his characters is speaking. When Buddy Glass writes his brother Zooey about Zooey's unprofitable love of Greek, he says, "Of course, you can go to Athens. Sunny *old* Athens." When Zooey wants to get out of the bathtub, he says to his mother, "I'm getting out of here in about three seconds, Bessie! I'm giving you fair warning. Let's not wear out our welcome, buddy." Each of these clichés is made absurd by the special quality of the Glass child's feeling, but it is at the same time what holds him, for all his special insight, in contact with the perception of ordinary people.

This perception is at its purest in children, whose wonderful directness fascinates Salinger. But he respects it wherever he finds it, whether in "the very corny boy" who gave Franny the gold swizzle stick she cannot bear to throw away, or in Zooey's producer LeSage, who delights in scripts that are down-to-earth, simple and untrue, but believes with beautiful innocence that his "tired, bosomy, Persian-looking blonde [wife is] a dead ringer [for] the late Carole Lombard, in the movies." As Bill Gorton in *The Sun Also Rises* says of Cohn, "The funny thing is, he's nice, too. I like him. But he's just so awful."

The Glass family's most treasured jokes hover close to this reluctant sympathy with people like LeSage. For instance, at the end of Buddy's trip to Florida after Seymour's suicide, when he had wept nearly all the way, he heard a woman back of him in the plane saying, "with all of Back Bay Boston and most of Harvard Square in her voice, '. . . and the *next morning,* mind you, they took a pint of pus out of that lovely young body of hers.'" As a result, when he got off the plane and Muriel "the Bereaved Widow came toward me all in Bergdorf Goodman black, I had the Wrong Expression on my face. I was grinning." It is this delicately balanced perception that gives the Glass children their special quality.

But if it makes them remarkable, it is also a quite terrible burden. "Smart men," as Dick Diver said a long time ago about Abe North in *Tender Is the Night,* "play close to the line because they have to—some of them can't stand it, so they quit." Like Abe

North, Seymour, the most gifted of the Glass children, kills himself. He knows that, in spite of—because of—the unusual depth and intensity of his perception of experience, he needs to be a part of the daily life of the ordinary world. He tries, by psycho- /88/ analysis and marriage, to become part of Muriel Fedder's world. This commitment is not merely an intellectual need; it is a desperate emotional necessity for him: "How I love and need her undiscriminating heart," he says of Muriel. But Seymour finds it impossible to love simultaneously the life of his own discriminating heart and Muriel's life, with its "primal urge to play house permanently . . . to go up to the desk clerk in some very posh hotel and ask if her Husband has picked up the mail yet . . . to shop for maternity clothes . . . [to have] her own Christmas-tree ornaments to unbox annually." He is torn apart by two incompatible worlds of feeling.

This, then, is the hard thing—not to find out "what it [is] all about," which the Glass children have known from very early, but "how to live it." Knowing what it is all about, in fact, is the burden.

"Those two bastards," says Zooey of Seymour and Buddy, who had taught Franny and him what wisdom is, "got us nice and early and made us into freaks with freakish standards, that's all. We're the Tattooed Lady, and we're never going to have a minute's peace, the rest of our lives, till everybody else is tattooed, too. . . . The minute I'm in a room with somebody who has the usual number of ears, I either turn into a goddam *seer* or a human hatpin. The Prince of Bores."

This, Zooey knows, is not a failure of love— /89/ he would not be concerned with his own freakishness if love failed—but a distortion of it. As his mother says to him:

"If you [take to somebody] then you do all the talking and nobody can even get a word in edgewise. If you *don't* like somebody—which is most of the time—then you just sit around like death it*self* and let the person talk themself into a hole. I've seen you do it. . . . You do," she said, without accusation in her voice. "Neither you nor Buddy knows how to talk to people you don't like." She thought it over. "Don't love, really," she amended.

"Which is most of the time" because, apart from children and the occasionally simple adult, the world is made up of people who are innocently imperceptive and emotionally dead.

Of the drastic limitations of such people, Salinger has a terrifyingly lucid perception. His stories are filled with undergraduates "giving the impression of having at least three lighted cigarettes in each hand"; young teachers "who come . . . in, in [their] little button-down-collar shirt[s] and striped tie[s], and start . . . knocking Turgenev for about half an hour . . . [and] if you get into an argument with them, all they do is get this terribly *benign* expression"; parents who say, "I'll exquisite day *you*, buddy, if you don't get down off that bag this minute. And I mean it." Such people, as Teddy, in the story which bears his name, says of his parents, "love their reasons for loving us almost as much as they love us, and most of the time more."

Nevertheless the power to love can exist in unimaginative people, and when it does, as the Glass children know they ought to know, nothing else really counts. Bessie Glass "often seem[s] to be an impenetrable mass of prejudices, clichés, and bromides"; these are a continual irritation to her children: Franny is driven nearly frantic by Bessie's insistence on nice cups of chicken soup when Franny is suffering something like a crisis of the soul. But Zooey is right when he points out to her that she is "missing out on every single goddam religious action that's going on around this house. You don't even have sense enough to *drink* when somebody brings you a cup of consecrated chicken soup—which is the only kind of chicken soup Bessie ever brings anybody around this madhouse."

Even if the acts of such people are not consecrated by love, they must not be hated. "What I don't like," Zooey says to Franny, ". . . is the way you talk about all these people. I mean you don't just despise what they represent—you despise them. It's too damned personal, Franny."

What Zooey knows he must learn to do in order to survive is to love even what he calls the "fishy" people—because they are all the Fat Lady for whom Seymour told him to shine his shoes

before going on the air, even though the audience could not see
his feet.

"This terribly clear, clear picture of the Fat Lady formed in
my mind," he tells Franny. "I had her sitting on this porch all
day, swatting flies, with her radio going full-blast from morning
till night. I figured the heat was terrible, and she probably had
cancer and—I don't know. Anyway, it seemed goddam clear why
Seymour wanted me to shine my shoes when I went on the air.
It made *sense*."

It makes sense because the highest standard of performance a
man's own understanding can set for him must ultimately be embodied—however mystically—in the ordinary, suffering members
of the community of his fellows. Otherwise there can be no solution to the dilemma the Glass children are caught in. Zooey puts
this conviction in the highest possible terms:

> "But I'll tell you a terrible secret [he says to Franny]—Are you listening
> to me? *There isn't anyone out there who isn't Seymour's Fat Lady.* . . .
> Don't you know that? Don't you know that goddam secret yet? And don't
> you know—*listen* to me, now—*don't you know who that Fat Lady really
> is?* . . . Ah, buddy. Ah, buddy. It's Christ Himself. Christ Himself, buddy."

What Salinger has seen in American life is the extraordinary
tension it sets up between our passion to understand and evaluate
our experience for ourselves, and our need to belong to a community that is unusually energetic in imposing its understanding
and values on its individual members. Whatever one may think
of Salinger's answer to the problem, this view of American life
is important; it has a long and distinguished history. But Salinger's achievement is not that he has grasped an abstract idea of
American experience, important as that idea may be in itself; it
is that he has seen this idea working in the actual life of our
times, in our habitual activities, in the very turns of our speech,
and has found a way to make us see it there, too. /90/

XXV

J. D. Salinger: "Everybody's Favorite"

ALFRED KAZIN

The publication of his two well-known stories from the *New Yorker* in book form, *Franny and Zooey* (Little, Brown), brings home the fact that, for one reason or another, J. D. Salinger now figures in American writing as a special case. After all, there are not many writers who could bring out a book composed of two stories—both of which have already been read and argued over and analyzed to death by that enormous public of sophisticated people which radiates from the *New Yorker* to every English Department in the land. Yet Salinger's fascination for this public is so great that, although he has refused this book to every book club, it may yet sell as if it were being pushed by book clubs. Since 1953, when *The Catcher in the Rye* was reprinted as a paperback, it has become the favorite American novel on the required or suggested reading lists of American colleges and secondary schools, and it has sold well over a million and a half copies. No less unusual is the fact that the *New Yorker*—which, if it did not originate, certainly brought to perfection the kind of tight, allusive, ironic story with which Salinger's earlier stories (reprinted in *Nine Stories,* 1953) felt so much at home—published in "Zooey" (41,130 words) the longest story it had ever published, and a story for which the *New Yorker* obviously felt personal affection and some particular intellectual sympathy.

In one form or another, as a fellow novelist commented unlovingly, Salinger is "everybody's favorite." He is certainly a favorite of the *New Yorker,* which in 1959 published another long

From *The Atlantic Monthly,* CCVIII, August 1961. Copyright © 1961 by Atlantic Monthly Company. Reprinted by permission of the author.

story around the Glass family called "Seymour: An Introduction" (almost 30,000 words), and thus gave the impression of stretching and remaking itself to Salinger's latest stories, which have been appearing, like visits from outer space, at two-year intervals. But above all, he is a favorite with that audience of students, student intellectuals, instructors, and generally literary, sensitive, and sophisticated young people who respond to him with a consciousness that he speaks for them and virtually *to* them, in a language that is peculiarly honest and their own, with a vision of things that captures their most secret judgments of the world. The only thing that Salinger does not do for this audience is to meet with them. Holden Caulfield said in *The Catcher in the Rye* that "What really knocks me out is a book that, when you're all done reading it, you wish the author that wrote it was a terrific friend of yours and you could call him up on the phone whenever you felt like it." It is well for him that all the people in this country who now regard J. D. Salinger as a "terrific friend" do not call him up and reach him.

A fundamental reason for Salinger's appeal (like that of Hemingway in the short stories that made *him* famous) is that he has exciting professional mastery of a peculiarly charged and dramatic /27/ medium, the American short story. At a time when so much American fiction has been discursive in tone, careless in language, lacking in edge and force—when else would it have been possible for crudities like the Beat novelists to be taken seriously?—Salinger has done an honest and stimulating professional job in a medium which, when it is expertly handled, projects emotion like a cry from the stage and in form can be as intense as a lyric poem. A short story which is not handled with necessary concentration and wit is like a play which does not engage its audience; a story does not exist unless it hits its mark with terrific impact. It is a constant projection of meanings at an audience, and it is a performance minutely made up of the only possible language, as a poem is. In America, at least, where, on the whole, the best stories are the most professional stories and so are published in the most famous magazines, second-rate stories belong in the same limbo with unsuccessful musical comedies; unless you hit the bull's-eye, you don't score.

This does not mean that the best-known stories are first-rate pieces of literature any more than that so many triumphant musical comedies are additions to the world's drama; it means only that a story has communicated itself with entire vividness to its editor and its audience. The profundity that may exist in a short story by Chekhov or Tolstoy also depends upon the author's immediate success in conveying his purpose. Even in the medieval tale, which Tolstoy in his greatest stories seems to recapture in tone and spirit, the final comment on human existence follows from the deliberate artlessness of tone that the author has managed to capture like a speech in a play.

What makes Salinger's stories particularly exciting is his intense, his almost compulsive need to fill in each inch of his canvas, each moment of his scene. Many great novels owe their grandeur to a leisurely sense of suggestion, to the imitation of life as a boundless road or flowing river, to the very relaxation of that intensity which Poe thought was the aesthetic perfection of a poem or a story. But whatever the professional superficiality of the short story in American hands, which have molded and polished it so as to reach, dazzle, and on occasion deceive the reader, a writer like Salinger, by working so hard to keep his tiny scene alive, keeps everything humming.

Someday there will be learned theses on *The Use of the Ash Tray in J. D. Salinger's Stories;* no other writer has made so much of Americans lighting up, reaching for the ash tray, setting up the ash tray with one hand while with the other they reach for a ringing telephone. Ours is a society complicated with many appliances, and Salinger always tells you what his characters are doing with each of their hands. In one long stretch of "Zooey," he describes that young man sitting in a bathtub, reading a long letter from his brother, and smoking; he manages to describe every exertion made and every sensation felt in that bathtub by the young man whose knees made "dry islands." Then the young man's mother comes into the bathroom; he draws the shower curtains around the tub, she rearranges the medicine cabinet, and while they talk (in full), everything they do is described.

Everything, that is, within Salinger's purpose in getting at such detail, which is not the loose, shuffling catalogue of the old-fashioned naturalists, who had the illusion of reproducing the whole world, but the tension of a dramatist or theater director making a fuss about a character's walking just so.

For Salinger, the expert performer and director (brother Buddy Glass, who is supposed to be narrating "Zooey," speaks of "directing" it and calls the story itself a "prose home movie"), gesture is the essence of the medium. A short story does not offer room enough for the development of character; it can present only character itself, by gesture. And Salinger is remarkable, I would say he is almost frenetically proficient, in getting us, at the opening of "Franny," to *see* college boys waiting on a train platform to greet their dates arriving for a big football weekend. They rush out to the train, "most of them giving the impression of having at least three lighted cigarettes in each hand." He knows exactly how Franny Glass would be greeted by Lane Coutell: "It was a station-platform kiss—spontaneous enough to begin with, but rather inhibited in the follow-through, and with something of a forehead-bumping aspect."

And even better is his description of the boy at a good restaurant, taking a first sip of his Martini and then looking "around the room with an almost palpable sense of well-being at finding himself (he must have been sure no one could dispute) in the right place with an unimpeachably right-looking girl." Salinger knows how to prepare us with this gesture for the later insensitivity of a boy who is exactly one of those elaborately up-to-date and anxiously sophisticated people whom Franny Glass, pure in heart, must learn to tolerate, and even to love, in what she regards as an unbearably shallow culture.

But apart from this, which is the theme of *Franny and Zooey,* the gesture itself is recognized by the reader not only as a compliment to himself but as a sign that Salinger is working all the time, not merely working to get the reader to see, but /28/ working to make his scene itself hum with life and creative observation. I don't know how much this appearance of intensity on the part of Salinger, of constant as well as full coverage, is due to *New*

Yorker editorial nudging, since its famous alertness to repetitions of words and vagueness of diction tends to give an external look of freshness and movement to prose. Salinger not only works very hard indeed over each story, but he obviously writes to and for some particular editorial mind he identifies with the *New Yorker;* look up the stories he used to write for the *Saturday Evening Post* and *Cosmopolitan,* and you will see that just as married people get to look alike by reproducing each other's facial expressions, so a story by Salinger and a passage of commentary in the *New Yorker* now tend to resemble each other.

But whatever the enormous influence of any magazine on those who write regularly for it, Salinger's emphasis of certain words and syllables in American speech and his own compulsiveness in bearing down hard on certain details (almost as if he wanted to make the furniture, like the gestures of certain people, tell *everything* about the people who use them) do give his stories the intensity of observation that is fundamental to his success. Lane Coutell, sitting in that restaurant with Franny and talking about a college paper on Flaubert he is horribly well satisfied with, says, "I think the emphasis I put on *why* he was so neurotically attached to the *mot juste* wasn't too bad. I mean in the light of what we know today. Not just psychoanalysis and all that crap, but certainly to a certain extent. You know what I mean. I'm no Freudian man or anything like that, but certain things you can't just pass over as capital F Freudian and let them go at that. I mean to a certain extent I think I was perfectly justified to point out that none of the really good boys—Tolstoy, Dostoevski, *Shake*speare, for Chrissake—were such goddam word-squeezers. They just wrote. Know what I mean?" What strikes me about this mimicry is not merely that it is so clever, but that it is also so relentless. In everything that this sophisticated ass, Lane Coutell, says, one recognizes that he is and will be wrong. Salinger disapproves of him in the deepest possible way; he is a spiritual enemy.

Of course, it is a vision of things that lies behind Salinger's expert manner. There is always one behind every manner. The language of fiction, whatever it may accomplish as representation, ultimately conveys an author's intimation of things; makes us hear, not in a statement, but in the ensemble of his realized efforts, his quintessential commentary on the nature of existence. However, the more deliberate the language of the writer, as it must be in a short story, the more the writer must convey his judgment of things in one highlighted dramatic action, as is done on the stage.

At the end of "Franny," the young girl collapses in the ladies' room of the restaurant where she has been lunching with her cool boy friend. This conveys her spiritual desperation in his company, for Lane typifies a society where "Everything everybody does is so—I don't know—not *wrong,* or even mean, or even stupid necessarily. But just so tiny and meaningless and—sad-making." Her brother Zooey (Zachary Glass), at the end of the long second story, calls her up from another telephone number in the same apartment and somehow reaches to the heart of her problem and gives her peace by reminding her that the "Fat Lady" they used to picture somnolently listening to them when they were quiz kids on the radio—the ugly, lazy, even disgusting-looking Fat Lady, who more and more typifies unattractive and selfish humanity in our day—can be loved after all, for she, too, is Jesus Christ.

In each story, the climax bears a burden of meaning that it would not have to bear in a novel; besides being stagy, the stories are related in a way that connects both of them into a single chronicle. This, to quote the title of a little religious pamphlet often mentioned in it, might be called "The Way of a Pilgrim." Both Franny and Zooey Glass are, indeed, pilgrims seeking their way in a society typified by the Fat Lady, and even by Lane Coutell's meaningless patter of sophistication. No wonder Franny cries out to her unhearing escort: "I'm sick of just liking people. I wish to God I could meet somebody I could respect." The Glasses (mother Irish, father Jewish) are ex-vaudevillians whose children were all, as infant prodigies, performers on a radio quiz program called *It's a Wise Child.* Now, though engaged in normally sophisticated enterprises (Franny goes to a fashionable women's college, Zooey is a television actor, Buddy a college instructor), they have retained their intellectual precocity—and, indeed, their precocious charm—and have translated, as it were, their awareness of themselves as special beings into a conviction that they alone can do justice to their search for the true way.

The eldest and most brilliant of the children, Seymour, shot himself in 1948 while on his honeymoon in Florida; this was the climax of Salinger's perhaps most famous story, "A Perfect Day For Banana Fish." And it is from Seymour's old room in the Glass apartment that Zooey calls up his sister, Franny, on a phone that is normally never used, that is still listed in the name of Seymour /29/ Glass, and that has been kept up by Buddy (who does not want a phone in his own country retreat) and by Zooey in order to perpetuate Seymour's name and to symbolize his continuing influence on them as a teacher and guide. It is from reading over again, in Seymour's old room, various religious sayings from the world's literature that Seymour had copied out on a piece of beaverboard nailed to the back of a door that Zooey is inspired to make the phone call to Franny that ends with the revelation that the horrible Fat Lady is really Jesus Christ.

This final episode, both in the cuteness of its invention and in the cuteness of speech so often attributed to Seymour, who is regarded in his own family as a kind of guru, or sage, helps us to understand Salinger's wide popularity. I am sorry to have to use the word "cute" in respect to Salinger, but there is absolutely no other word that for me so accurately typifies the self-conscious charm and prankishness of his own writing and his extraordinary cherishing of his favorite Glass characters.

Holden Caulfield is also cute in *The Catcher in the Rye*, cute in his little-boy suffering for his dead brother, Allie, and cute in his tenderness for his sister, "Old Phoebe." But we expect that boys of that age may be cute—that is, consciously appealing and consciously clever. To be these things is almost their only resource in a world where parents and schoolmasters have all the power and the experience. Cuteness, for an adolescent, is to turn the normal self-pity of children, which arises from their relative weakness, into a relative advantage vis-à-vis the adult world. It

becomes a role boys can play in the absence of other advantages,
and *The Catcher in the Rye* is so full of Holden's cute speech
and cute innocence and cute lovingness for his own family that
one must be an absolute monster not to like it.

And on a higher level, but with the same conscious winsome-
ness, the same conscious mournfulness and intellectual loneliness
and lovingness (though not for his wife), Seymour Glass is cute
when he sits on the beach with a little girl telling her a parable
of "banana fish"—ordinary-looking fish when "they swim into a
hole where there's a lot of bananas," but "after that they're so
fat they can't get out of the hole again. . . . They die." His wife,
meanwhile busy in their room on the long-distance phone to her
mother in New York, makes it abundantly clear in the hilariously
accurate cadences and substance of her conversation, why her
husband finds it more natural to talk to a four-year-old girl on
the beach than to her. Among other things, Seymour expects not
to be understood outside the Glass family. But agonizing as this
situation is, the brilliantly entertaining texture of "A Perfect Day
For Banana Fish" depends on Seymour Glass's conscious cleverness as well as on his conscious suffering—even his conscious
cleverness *about* the suffering of "ordinary-looking" fish who get
so bloated eating too many bananas in a "hole" they shouldn't
have been attracted to in the first place.

In the same way, not only does the entertaining surface of
Franny and Zooey depend on the conscious appealingness and
youthfulness and generosity and sensitivity of Seymour's brother
and sister, but Salinger himself, in describing these two, so obviously feels such boundless affection for them that you finally get
the sense of all these child prodigies and child entertainers being
tied round and round with veils of self-love in a culture which
they—and Salinger—just despise. Despise, above all, for its intellectual pretentiousness. Yet this is the society, typified by the Fat
Lady (symbolically, they pictured her as their audience), whom
they must now force themselves to think of as Jesus Christ, and
whom, as Christ Himself, they can now at last learn to love.

For myself, I must confess that the spiritual transformation
that so many people associate with the very sight of the word

"love" on the printed page does not move me as it should. In what has been considered Salinger's best story, "For Esmé—with Love and Squalor," Sergeant X in the American Army of Occupation in Germany is saved from a hopeless breakdown by the beautiful magnanimity and remembrance of an aristocratic young English girl. We are prepared for this climax or visitation by an earlier scene in which the sergeant comes upon a book by Goebbels in which a Nazi woman had written, "Dear God, life is hell." Under this, persuaded at last of his common suffering even with a Nazi, X writes down, from *The Brothers Karamazov:* "Fathers and teachers, I ponder 'What is hell?' I maintain that it is the suffering of being unable to love."

But the love that Father Zossima in Dostoevsky's novel speaks for is surely love for the world, for God's creation itself, for all that precedes us and supports us, that will outlast us and that alone helps us to explain ourselves to ourselves. It is the love that D. H. Lawrence, another religious novelist, spoke of as "the sympathetic bond" and that in one form or another lies behind all the great novels as a primary interest in everyone and everything alive with us on this common earth. The love that Salinger's horribly precocious Glass characters speak of is love for certain people only—forgiveness is for the rest; finally, through Seymour Glass's indoctrination of his brothers and sister in so many different (and pretentiously assembled) religious teachings, it is love of certain ideas. So what is ultimate in their love is the love of their own moral and intellectual excellence, of /30/ their chastity and purity in a world full of banana fish swollen with too much food. It is the love that they have for themselves as an idea.

The worst they can say about our society is that they are too sensitive to live in it. They are the special case in whose name society is condemned. And what makes them so is that they are young, precocious, sensitive, different. In Salinger's work, the two estates—the world and the cutely sensitive young—never really touch at all. Holden Caulfield condemns parents and schools because he knows that they are incapable of understanding him; Zooey and Franny and Buddy (like Seymour before them) know that the great mass of prosperous spiritual savages in our society will never understand them.

This may be true, but to think so can lead to a violation of art. Huckleberry Finn, so often cited as a parallel to the hero of *The Catcher in the Rye,* was two years younger than Holden, but the reason he was not afraid of an adult's world is that he had respect for it. He had never even seen very much of it until he got on that raft with a runaway Negro slave he came to love and was able to save. It was still all God's creation, and inspired him with wonder. But Holden and, even more, the Glass children are beaten before they start; beaten in order not to start. They do not trust anything or anyone but themselves and their great idea. And what troubles me about this is not what it reflects of their theology but what it does to Salinger's art.

Frank O'Connor once said of this special métier, the short story, that it is "the art form that deals with the individual when there is no longer a society to absorb him, and when he is compelled to exist, as it were, by his own inner light." This is the condition on which Salinger's work rests, and I should be sorry to seem unsympathetic toward it. It is an American fact, as one can see from the relative lack in our literature of the ripe and fully developed social novel in which the individual and society are in concrete and constant relationship with each other. But whatever this lack, which in one sense is as marked in the novels of Scott Fitzgerald as it is in Salinger's emphasis upon the short story, it is a fact that when Fitzgerald describes a character's voice, it is because he really loves—in the creative sense, is fully interested in—this character. When Salinger describes a character's voice, it is to tell us that the man is a phony. He has, to borrow a phrase from his own work, a "categorical aversion" to whole classes and types of our society. The "sympathetic bond" that Lawrence spoke of has been broken. People stink in our nostrils. We are mad with captious observation of one another. As a friend of mine once said about the novels of Mary McCarthy, trying to say with absolute justice what it was that shocked her so much in them, "The heroine is always right and everyone else is wrong." Salinger is a far more accomplished and objective writer of fiction than Mary McCarthy, but I would say that in his work the Glass children alone are right and everyone else is wrong.

And it is finally this condition, not just the famous alienation of Americans from a society like our own, that explains the popularity of Salinger's work. Salinger's vast public, I am convinced, is based not merely on the vast number of young people who recognize their emotional problems in his fiction and their frustrated rebellions in the sophisticated language he manipulates so skillfully. It is based perhaps even more on the vast numbers who have been released by our society to think of themselves as endlessly sensitive, spiritually alone, gifted, and whose suffering lies in the narrowing of their consciousness to themselves, in the withdrawal of their curiosity from a society which they think they understand all too well, in the drying up of their hope, their trust, and their wonder at the great world itself. The worst of American sophistication today is that it is so bored, so full of categorical aversion to things that writers should never take for granted and never close their eyes to.

The fact that Salinger's work is particularly directed against the "well fed sun-burned" people at the summer theater, at the "section men" in colleges parroting the latest fashionable literary formulas, at the "three-martini" men—this, indeed, is what is wrong. He hates them. They are no longer people, but symbols, like the Fat Lady. No wonder that Zooey tells his sister: Love them, love them all, love them anyway. But the problem is not one of spiritual pride or of guilt; it is that in the tearing of the "sympathetic bond" it is not love that goes, but the deepest possibilities of literary art. /31/

XXVI

Franny and Zooey

JOHN UPDIKE

Quite suddenly, as things go in the middle period of J. D. Salinger, his later, longer stories are descending from the clouds of old *New Yorkers* and assuming incarnations between hard covers. "Raise High the Roof Beam, Carpenters," became available last year in *Stories from the New Yorker 1950-1960,* and now "Franny" and "Zooey" have a book to themselves. These two stories—the first medium-short, the second novella-length—are contiguous in time, and have as their common subject Franny's spiritual crisis.

In the first story, she arrives by train from a Smith-like college to spend the week-end of the Yale game at what must be Princeton. She and her date, Lane Coutell, go to a restaurant where it develops that she is not only unenthusiastic but downright ill. She attempts to explain herself while her friend brags about a superbly obnoxious term paper and eats frogs' legs. Finally, she faints, and is last seen lying in the manager's office silently praying at the ceiling.

In the second story, Franny has returned to her home, a large apartment in the East Seventies. It is the Monday following her unhappy Saturday. Only Franny's mother, Bessie, and her youngest brother, Zooey, are home. While Franny lies sleeplessly on the living-room sofa, her mother communicates, in an interminably rendered conversation, her concern and affection to Zooey, who then, after an even longer conversation with Franny, manages to gather from the haunted atmosphere of the apartment the

From *The New York Times Book Review,* September 17, 1961, pp. 1, 52. Copyright 1961 by the New York *Times.* Reprinted by permission of the New York *Times* and the author. [Several emendations of the text originally published by the *Times* have been made at Mr. Updike's request.—Eds.]

crucial word of consolation. Franny, "as if all of what little or much wisdom there is in the world were suddenly hers," smiles at the ceiling and falls asleep.

Few writers since Joyce would risk such a wealth of words upon events that are purely internal and deeds that are purely talk. We live in a world, however, where the decisive deed may invite the holocaust, and Salinger's conviction that our inner lives greatly matter peculiarly qualifies him to sing of an America where, for most of us, there seems little to do but to feel. Introversion, perhaps, has been forced upon history; an age of nuance, of ambiguous gestures and psychological jockeying on a national and private scale, is upon us, and Salinger's intense attention to gesture and intonation help make him, among his contemporaries, a uniquely relevant literary artist. As Hemingway sought the words for things in motion, Salinger seeks the words for things transmuted into human subjectivity. His fiction, in its rather grim bravado, its humor, its morbidity, its wry but persistent hopefulness, matches the shape and tint of present American life. It pays the price, however, of becoming dangerously convoluted and static. A sense of composition is not among Salinger's strengths, and even these two stories, so apparently complementary, distinctly jangle as components of one book.

The Franny of "Franny" and the Franny of "Zooey" are not the same person. The heroine of "Franny" is a pretty college girl passing through a plausible moment of disgust. She has discovered—one feels rather recently—a certain ugliness in the hungry human ego and a certain fatuity in her college environment. She is attempting to find her way out with the help of a religious book, The Way of a Pilgrim, which was mentioned by a professor. She got the book out of the college library. Her family, glimpsed briefly in the P.S. of a letter she has written, appear to be standard upper-middle gentry. Their name is nowhere given as Glass, though some "brothers" are mentioned—once—in passing. Her boy friend is crass and self-centered but not entirely unsympathetic; he clumsily does try to "get through" to Franny, with a love whose physical bias has become painfully inappropriate. Finally, there is a suggestion—perhaps inadvertent—that the girl may be pregnant.

The Franny of "Zooey," on the other hand, is Franny Glass, the youngest of the seven famous Glass children, all of whom have been in turn wondrously brilliant performers on a radio quiz program, "It's a Wise Child." Their parents, a distinctly unstandard combination of Jewish and Irish, are an old vaudeville team. From infancy on, Franny has been saturated by her two oldest brothers, Seymour and Buddy, in the religious wisdom of the East. *The Way of a Pilgrim,* far from being newly encountered at college, comes from Seymour's desk, where it has been for years.

One wonders how a girl raised in a home where Buddhism and crisis theology were table talk could have postponed her own crisis so long and, when it came, be so disarmed by it. At any rate, there is no question of her being pregnant; the very idea seems a violation of the awesome Glass ethereality. Lane Coutell, who for all his faults was at least a considerable man in the first Franny's universe, is now just one of the remote millions coarse and foolish enough to be born outside the Glass family.

The more Salinger writes about them, the more the seven Glass children melt indistinguishably together in an impossible radiance of personal beauty and intelligence. Franny is described thus: "Her skin was lovely, and her features were delicate and most distinctive. Her eyes were very nearly the same quite astonishing shade of blue as Zooey's but were set farther apart, as a sister's eyes no doubt should be. . . ." Of Zooey, we are assured he has a "somewhat preposterous ability to quote, instantaneously and, usually, verbatim, almost anything he had ever read, or even listened to, with genuine interest." The /1/ purpose of such sentences is surely not to particularize imaginary people but to instill in the reader a mood of blind worship, tinged with an understandable envy.

In "Raise High the Roof Beam, Carpenters" (the best of the Glass pieces: a magic and hilarious prose-poem with an enchanting end effect of mysterious clarity), Seymour defines sentimental-

ity as giving "to a thing more tenderness than God gives to it."
This seems to me the nub of the trouble: Salinger loves the
Glasses more than God loves them. He loves them too exclusively. Their invention has become a hermitage for him. He loves
them to the detriment of artistic moderation. "Zooey" is just too
long; there are too many cigarettes, too many goddams, too much
verbal ado about not quite enough.

The author never rests from circling his creations, patting
them fondly, slyly applauding. He robs the reader of the initiative upon which love must be given. Even in "Franny," which is,
strictly, pre-Glass, the writer seems less an unimpassioned observer than a spying beau vindictively feasting upon every detail
of poor Lane Coutell's gaucherie. Indeed, this impression of a
second male being present is so strong that it amounts to a social
shock when the author accompanies Franny into the ladies' room
of the restaurant.

"Franny," nevertheless, takes place in what is recognizably our
world; in "Zooey" we move into a dreamworld whose zealously
animated details only emphasize an essential unreality. When
Zooey says to Franny, "*Yes,* I have an ulcer, for Chrissake. This
is Kaliyuga, buddy, the Iron Age," disbelief falls on the "buddy"
as much as on "Kaliyuga," and the explanatory "the Iron Age"
clinches our suspicion that a lecturer has usurped the writing
stand. Not the least dismaying development of the Glass stories
is the vehement editorializing on the obvious—television scripts
are not generally good, not all section men are geniuses. Of
course, the Glasses condemn the world only to condescend to it,
to forgive it, in the end. Yet the pettishness of the condemnation
diminishes the gallantry of the condescension.

Perhaps these are hard words; they are made hard to write by
the extravagant self-consciousness of Salinger's later prose, where-
in most of the objections one might raise are already raised. On
the flap of this book jacket, he confesses, ". . . there is a real-
enough danger, I suppose, that sooner or later I'll bog down,
perhaps disappear entirely, in my own methods, locutions, and
mannerisms. On the whole, though, I'm very hopeful." Let me
say, I am glad he is hopeful. I am one of those—to do some con-

fessing of my own—for whom Salinger's work dawned as something of a revelation. I expect that further revelations are to come.

The Glass saga, as he has sketched it out, potentially contains great fiction. When all reservations have been entered, in the correctly unctuous and apprehensive tone, about the direction he has taken, it remains to acknowledge that it *is* a direction, and that the refusal to rest content, the willingness to risk excess on behalf of one's obsessions, is what distinguishes artists from entertainers, and what makes some artists adventurers on behalf of us all. /52/

XXVII

Finally (Fashionably) Spurious

JOAN DIDION

When I first came to New York during the fall of 1956, I went to a party on Bank Street which I remember with particular clarity for a number of reasons, not the least of them my surprise that no one present wished William Knowland were running for President. (I had only been in New York a few days, and the notion that Democrats might be people one met at parties had not yet violated what must have been, in retrospect, my almost impenetrable western innocence.) There were a couple of girls who "did something interesting" for *Mademoiselle* and there were several rather tweedy graduate students from Princeton, one of whom intimated that he had a direct wire to the *PMLA*, baby; there was, as well, a stunningly predictable Sarah Lawrence girl who tried to engage me in a discussion of J. D. Salinger's relationship to Zen. When I seemed unresponsive, she lapsed into language she thought I might comprehend: Salinger was, she declared, the single person in the world capable of *understanding her*.

Five years work certain subtle changes. I have become downright blasé about Democrats at parties; that particular Sarah Lawrence girl found that she could, after all, be understood well enough for everyday purposes by someone else, an electronics engineer; and nobody, not even on Bank Street, thinks much any more about Adlai Stevenson for President.

The idea that J. D. Salinger is a kind of middle-class American guru, however, has somehow resisted those gently abrasive

From *National Review*, XI (November 18, 1961), 341-42. Reprinted by permission.

sands. Among the reasonably literate young and young in heart, he is surely the most read and reread writer in America today, exerting a power over his readers which is in some ways extra-literary. Those readers expect him to teach them something, something that has nothing at all to do with fiction. Not only have his vague metaphysical hints been committed to rote by *New Yorker* readers from here to Dubuque, but his imaginary playmates, the Glass family, have achieved a kind of independent existence; I rather imagine that Salinger readers wish secretly that they could write letters to Franny and Zooey and their brother Buddy, and maybe even to Waker (who is a Jesuit and apparently less disturbed than his kin), much as people of less invincible urbanity write letters to the characters in *As the World Turns* and *The Brighter Day.*

What actually happens in *Franny and Zooey,* the two Glass family novelettes published this fall, is really nothing much. In "Franny," Franny Glass arrives at Princeton for a football weekend and is met by her date, strictly another of those boys with a direct wire to the *PMLA,* baby. He has frogs' legs for lunch and talks about Flaubert, all of which gets on Franny's nerves, especially because all she wants to do at the moment is say something called "The Jesus Prayer." ("The thing is," she explains, "the marvellous thing is, when you first start doing it, you don't even have to have *faith* in what you're doing . . . then eventually what happens, the prayer becomes self-active. Something *happens* after a while.")

When her date somehow fails to get the point about the Jesus Prayer, Franny faints. In "Zooey," which picks up the action the next morning, we find Franny laid up at home on East 79th Street with what her brother, a television actor named Zooey, calls "a tenth-rate nervous breakdown." She is tired of everybody's ego, not excepting her own. ("Just because I'm choosy about what I want—in this case, en*light*enment, or peace, instead of money or pres*tige* or *fame* or any of those things—doesn't mean I'm not as egotistical and self-seeking as everybody else.") Zooey eventually effects a cure of sorts by convincing Franny that

everybody out there—no matter how given to /341/ ego, to eating
frogs' legs and "*name*-dropping in a terribly quiet, *casual* voice"
and wanting "to *get* somewhere"—is "Christ himself. Christ himself, buddy." ("Don't you know that? Don't you know that goddam secret yet?")

To anyone who has ever felt over-exposed to the world, to
anyone who has ever harbored hatred in his or her heart toward
droppers of names, writers of papers on Flaubert, toward eaters
of frogs' legs, all of this has a certain seductive lure; there is a
kind of lulling charm in being assured in that dazzling Salinger
prose, that one's raw nerves, one's urban hangover, one's very
horridness, is really not horridness at all but instead a kind of
dark night of the soul; there is something very attractive about
being told that one finds en*light*enment or *peace* by something
as eminently within the realm of the possible as tolerance toward
television writers and section men, that one can find the peace
which passeth understanding simply by looking for Christ in one's
date for the Yale game.

However brilliantly rendered (and it is), however hauntingly
right in the rhythm of its dialogue (and it is), *Franny and
Zooey* is finally spurious, and what makes it spurious is Salinger's
tendency to flatter the essential triviality within each of his readers, his predilection for giving instructions for living. What gives
the book its extremely potent appeal is precisely that it is self-
help copy: it emerges finally as *Positive Thinking* for the upper
middle classes, as *Double Your Energy and Live Without Fatigue*
for Sarah Lawrence girls. /342/

XXVIII

Up from Adolescence

LESLIE FIEDLER

I am not sure why I have liked so much less this time through a story which moved me so deeply when I first read it in *The New Yorker* four or five years ago. I mean, of course, "Zooey," to which "Franny" is finally an appendage, like the long explanatory footnote on pages 52 and 53, the author's apologetic statement on the jacket, the pretentiously modest dedication: all the gimmicks, in short, which conceal neither from him nor from us the fact that he has not yet made of essentially novelistic material the novel it wants to become.

It was, I guess, the novel which "Zooey," along with a handful of earlier stories, seemed to promise to which I responded with initial enthusiasm: the fat chronicle of the Glass family which might have caught once and for all the pathos and silliness of middle-class, middle-brow intellectual aspiration—the sad and foolish dream that certain families, largely Jewish, dreamed for their children listening to the Quiz Kids perform on the radio two long decades ago. For the sake of that novel, Salinger seemed at the point of making a new start, of breaking through certain bad habits picked up along the way from *Good Housekeeping* to *The New Yorker*. Certainly in "Zooey" Salinger had begun untypically to specify the times and circumstances of his characters; to furnish patiently the rooms through which they moved; to eschew slickness and sentimentality and easy jokes in favor of a style almost inept enough to guarantee honesty; to venture beyond an evocation of adolescent self-pity and adolescent concern with sex titillating chiefly to adolescents themselves.

From *Partisan Review*, XXIX (Winter 1962), 127-131. Reprinted by permission of the author.

But there is, as yet, no novel—only "Zooey," well-leaded and in hard-covers, flanked by apologies and new promises, but still un-fulfilled: and it is this, I suppose, which has left me baffled and a little disappointed. In a magazine, Salinger's documentation seemed not quite so irrelevant, his furnishings not quite so dis-proportionate to the events they frame, the awkwardness of his writing not quite so much a tic of embarrassment or a posture of false modesty. /127/

"Franny" itself, which I had not read before, seems to me an eminently satisfactory piece of reportage, turned in as evidence (at the demonstration trial of the generations, in which it is not clear who is the plaintiff, who the defendant) by a middle-aged eavesdropper on station-platforms and at restaurants where the Ivy League young ritually prepare for watching games and get-ting laid. It is, at least, scarcely ever cute, like much of "Zooey" and all of the mere apparatus which with it ekes out a book; and it ends ambiguously before its author, whose resolutions are often disasters, can manage to be either sentimental or sage. In "Franny" for once Salinger demonstrates that he can write of adolescence without disappearing into it; but "Franny," alas, is completed by "Zooey," which itself completes nothing.

We have been, I begin slowly to understand, living through a revolution in taste, a radical transformation of the widest Ameri-can literary audience from one in which women predominate to one in which adolescents make up the majority. Controlling the market (it is, for instance, largely to reach them that the more expensive paperbacks were invented and marketed in new ways by new generations of editors scarcely older than themselves), they control also the mode. And the mode demands, in lieu of the teen-age novelists who somehow refuse to appear, Teen-age Impersonators, among whom one might list, say, Norman Mailer, Jack Kerouac, even William Burroughs—certainly the Salinger who wrote *Catcher in the Rye* and invented Holden Caulfield, a figure emulated by the young themselves, though not by all the young.

Each of the Impersonators I have mentioned speaks only for a portion of our youth: hip or beat or square, straight or queer or undecided. No one writes for all, but inevitably takes his stand:

with those who "turn on" or those who do not, with those who write papers on Kierkegaard and Flaubert or those who scrawl on the walls of saloons "Ez for Pres." Salinger, of course, speaks for the cleanest, politest, best-dressed, best-fed and best-read among the disaffected (and who is not disaffected?) young; not junkies or faggots, not even upper-bohemians, his protagonists travel a road bounded on one end by school and on the other by home. They have families and teachers rather than lovers or friends; and their crises are likely to be defined in terms of whether or not to go back for the second semester to Vassar or Princeton, to Dana Hall or St. Mark's. Their *angst* is improbably cued by such questions as: "Does my date for the Harvard Weekend *really* understand what poetry is?" or "Is it possible that my English instructor hates literature after all?"

I do not mean by reduction to mock the concerns of Salinger's /128/ characters; they cannot, in any case, be reduced, and I should mock myself making fun of them. For better or for worse, a significant number of sensitive young Americans live in a world in which the classroom and the football game provide customary arenas for anguish and joy, love and death; and to that world, Salinger has been more faithful than it perhaps deserves. Which is why in the end he is a comic novelist or nothing. If the Temple Drake of Faulkner's *Sanctuary* stands as the classic portrait of a co-ed in the 'twenties, the Franny of Salinger's Glass stories bids to become her equivalent for the 'fifties, and the decline in terror and intensity from one to the other, the descent toward middlebrow bathos is the fault not of Salinger but of the times. Temple's revolt was against vestigial Puritanism and obsolescent chivalry and her weapons were booze and sex; Franny's is against literature and the New Criticism and her weapon is the "Jesus Prayer."

Certainly, this is fair enough; for, in the thirty years that separate the two refugees from college, the Culture Religion of Western Europe has replaced Christianity as the orthodox faith for middle-class urban Americans; and the Pastors to whom our hungry sheep look up in vain are Ph.D.'s in Literature and the "section men" who are their acolytes. In a society presided over by this new clergy, to play with Vedanta or Buddhism or even

Catholicism, except as these are represented in certain recent poetic texts, i.e., to seek a salvation beyond the reach of art, is considered heresy or madness or some blasphemous compound of both. Franny, at any rate, who will not write the proper papers or go out for the next college play, seems, not only to her elders and her peers, but to herself as well a heretic guilty as charged and therefore self-condemned to what her world calls a "nervous breakdown."

I am less sure this time though than I was the first that Salinger really understands just how splendid and horrifying a joke this all is, but begin to suspect that he has only stumbled on the comic possibilities of his subject in pursuit of a more pathetic theme which has obsessed him ever since the writing of his popular little tear-jerker, "To Esmé with Love and Squalor." It is this theme which lies at the center of *Catcher in the Rye* and which becomes the main interest if not of "Franny," certainly of the much longer "Zooey." I am referring, of course, to Salinger's presentation of madness as the chief temptation of modern life, especially for the intelligent young: and his conviction that, consequently, the chief heroism possible to us now is the rejection of madness, the decision to be sane. What suicide was for the young Werther or running away from home for Huck Finn, the "nervous breakdown," Salinger urges us to believe, is for the sensitive adolescent of our time. /129/ Having been taught, chiefly by the psychoanalysts (who haunt Salinger's books, ambiguous and omnipresent almost as his teachers), that insanity itself lies within the scope of choice, we have been able to make of it a theme for debate, our own to-be-or-not-to-be.

Before the present volume, Salinger had always presented madness as a special temptation of males; perhaps because, in the myth he was elaborating, it is a female image of innocence that, at the last moment, lures his almost-lost protagonists back from the brink of insanity: a little girl typically, pre-pubescent and therefore immune to the world's evil, which, in his work, fully nubile women tend to embody. The series which begins with "Esmé" goes on through "A Perfect Day for Bananafish," where the girl-savior appears too late to save Seymour, oldest of the Glass family; and reaches an appropriate climax in *Catcher in the Rye,* where the savior is the little sister and the myth achieves its final form. It is the Orestes-Iphigenia story, we see there, that Salinger all along had been trying to rewrite, the account of a Fury-haunted brother redeemed by his priestess-sister; though Salinger demotes that sister in age, thus downgrading the tone of the legend from tragic to merely pathetic.

In "Zooey," where the brother saves, the sister is redeemed and neither is a child, the myth struggles back toward the tragic dimension; and it is for this, too, perhaps, that I responded so strongly at first to the story, to its implicit declaration of Salinger's resolve to escape what had become for him a trap. Yet though the girl-savior does not operate in "Zooey" to produce the pat Happy Ending of *Catcher in the Rye,* she floats disconcertingly in and out of its action, a not-quite-irrelevant ghost. It is, for instance, the chance meeting with a four year old girl at the meat counter of a Supermarket that prompts the long letter from his oldest surviving brother, Buddy, which Zooey is reading as his story opens; and in that letter, we are permitted to see at last the *haiku* found in Seymour's hotel room after his suicide: "The little girl on the plane/Who turned her doll's head around/To look at me."

Buddy, however, released from long silence by his little girl and the memory of Seymour's, has tried to save Zooey, through the mails, by advising him to "act" (Buddy is a teacher of writing, Zooey a T.V. star); and Zooey, trying in turn to save Franny, can only repeat in Buddy's voice and over Seymour's still-listed telephone the same advice. Behind it all, at any rate, is the inevitable little girl, her message echoed and re-echoed through the linked ventriloquist's dummies of the three brothers, who seem sometimes only three versions of the single author, listening faithfully to Esmé down the years. /130/

But "Zooey" is, at last, a fable of reconciliation as well as of salvation; for the saved Franny, we are left to believe, will return perhaps to school, certainly to "acting," as her brothers recommend, not so much for her own sake as for the sake of what Seymour had been accustomed to call, in their Quiz Kid days, the Fat Lady, i.e., the audience out front. But the Fat Lady, Zooey announces as his story ends, is Christ; the mass audience is

Christ. It is an appropriate enough theophany for a popular entertainer, for Salinger as well as Zooey, and the cue for a truce with all the world, with bad teachers, mad television producers, bad psychoanalysts, bad everyone.

Finally, like his characters, Salinger is reconciled with everything but sex. The single voice in his novella which advocates marriage is the voice of Bessie Glass, a stage-Irish comic mother married to an off-stage comic Jew; but she raises it in vain in a fictional world where apparently only women marry and where certainly no father appears on the scene. It is to Zooey she speaks, the one son of hers not already killed by marriage like Seymour, or safe in monastic retirement, secular like Buddy's or ecclesiastical like his Jesuit brother Waker's. Zooey, who fears his own body and his mother's touch on it, turns her aside with a quip; though he might well have repeated what he had cried earlier in deep contempt, "That's just sex talking, buddy . . . I know that voice." These words, too, he had addressed to her; since for him men and women alike are "buddy," as if unlike the actual Buddy, he needed no little girl to remind him of what Seymour had once tried to teach them all: that "all legitimate religious study *must* lead to unlearning . . . the illusory differences between boys and girls . . ."

To unlearn the illusory differences: this is what for Salinger it means *to be as a child*. And the Glasses, we remember, are in this sense children, holy innocents still at twenty or thirty or forty, Quiz Kids who never made the mistake of growing up, and whose most glorious hours were spent before the microphones on a nation-wide radio program called "It's a Wise Child." The notion of the Quiz Kids, with their forced precocity, their meaningless answers to pointless questions faked by station employes as heroes, sages, secret saints of our time is palpably absurd. But Salinger himself ironically qualifies what he seems naively to offer by the unfinished quotation he uses to give his only half-mythical program its name. It is with his collaboration, we remind ourselves, that we are able to say of his hidden saints, when they become insufferably cute or clever or smug, "The little bastards!" Surely, this is Salinger's joke, not just one on him and on his world. /131/

XXIX

Salinger's Oasis of Innocence

ANNE MARPLE

Salinger's first full length novel, *The Catcher in the Rye,* emerged after scattered fragments concerning his characters appeared during a seven year span. For some time now, it has been evident that Salinger's second novel may be developing in the same way. Salinger writes of *Franny and Zooey:* "Both stories are early, critical entries in a narrative series I am doing about a family of settlers in 20th Century New York, the Glasses."

Franny is a beautifully balanced short story. Franny, at twenty, is on the edge of "a tenth-rate nervous breakdown." There is a certain resemblance to the emotional crisis faced by Holden Caulfield in *The Catcher in the Rye.* But Franny is not to be saved by a contact with innocence. Instead, she begins a weekend with her pseudo-intellectual lover, Lane Coutell.

In a brilliant scene between the two at lunch, Franny speaks of the writings of a holy man. She tries to explain the Jesus Prayer:

". . . if you keep saying that prayer over and over and over again—you only have to do it with your *lips* at first—then eventually what happens, the prayer becomes self-active . . . you do it to purify your whole outlook and get an absolutely new conception of what everything's about."

Lane's preoccupation with the mechanics of eating afford a subtle contrast of spirit versus flesh. Failing to communicate her feelings to Lane, Franny flees his belated declaration of love and col-

From *New Republic,* CXLV, September 18, 1961, pp. 22-23. Copyright 1961 by *New Republic.* Reprinted by permission.

lapses. Her lips "began to move, forming soundless words" repeating the Jesus Prayer, "Lord Jesus Christ, have mercy on me."

Zooey continues the story of Franny's emotional crisis three days later. This "prose home movie" is unwieldy as a short story. Its possible future incorporation into a novel may justify its present form, but at present we must judge it as a short story.

The first person introduction by Buddy Glass seems unnecessary. Buddy is surely the least lovable and most self-conscious of the Glass children to date. Salinger seems not entirely unaware of this. (Seymour has said of his brother, that cleverness is his "permanent affliction.") Great demands are made on the reader's credulity by Buddy's insistence that he was able to reconstruct the action of *Zooey* second hand.

The puzzling intrusion of the Buddy Glass introduction also serves as an apologia for Salinger. Buddy warns, "The plot line itself, to finish up, is largely the result of a rather unholy collaborative effort." The frequent inclusion of diaries and letters in the Glass Saga indicate that Salinger is having additional mechanical difficulties with his embarrassing wealth of Glassiana. He has become so enmeshed in his material that his artistic judgment is clouded. Sections of *Zooey* are bearable only if one has a prior affection for the Glass family.

The first half of *Zooey* (sans introduction), is a momentarily interrupted scene between Zooey and his mother. In this Salingeresque masterpiece of characterization and dialogue, Zooey comes off second best to Salinger's loving treatment of Mrs. Glass. The conversation between the two reflects Salinger's early interest in playwriting.

The rest of *Zooey* records his several attempts to pry Franny loose from her frantic grasp on the Jesus Prayer. He is well qualified for the task, for as he tells her, ". . . you've been funnel *fed* on just about the same amount of religious phi*lo*sophy that I have. . . ." Zooey's success is not immediate. Franny is suffering the hell "of being unable to love." Only when Zooey convinces Franny that "anyone *any*where" is "Seymour's Fat Lady" is "Christ Himself" does Franny find release.

Buddy Glass has described *Zooey* as "a compound, or multiple, love story, pure and complicated." The use of the word *pure* is echoed in Franny's explanation of the goal of the Jesus Prayer, "you do it to purify your whole outlook." Franny's quest for purity ties *Franny and Zooey* to a subterranean theme that underlies most of the work Salinger has published during the last twenty-one years.

There is evident, throughout Salinger's writing, a consistent preoccupation with innocence, a preference for the chaste, complemented by the inability of his adult characters to reconcile physical and spiritual love. It is obvious on a re-examination of Salinger's work that his characters are extremely limited in their choice of sexual expression.

Salinger's first novel, *The Catcher in the Rye,* is his most eloquent defense of innocence in conflict with an amoral world. There is a certain logic in Salinger's choice of an adolescent protagonist. The chastity of adolescence needs little explanation—idealism will suffice. It is to children and to nuns that Holden turns briefly as outposts of the innocence he desires. Holden places women on a comfortably distant pedestal, divorced from sex. Although he loved Jane, he never puts the purity of his love to any test of physical expression. He avoids contacting her. What is suggested or hinted at in Salinger's earlier work is full grown in his novel /22/ —the idealization of the celibate, the chaste, and the innocent.

Salinger's adult characters cannot integrate physical and spiritual love. Even the reconciliation of both in marriage is denied them. Married couples are invariably mismated and miserable—marriage itself a badly bungled affair. The insensitive girl friend runs a close second to the shallow wife. In the Salinger world, woman plays her ancient role of Eve, Pandora, or Lorelei. She can exist beloved or uncriticized only as an asexual saint or mother. When she expresses herself as a sexual creature, Salinger sees her as witch or vampire. As William Wiegand has said, "Where object of delight is found in women, these women are often little girls or nuns, and what is admired is sexless in essence."

If the Glass family are to form the basis for Salinger's second novel, it is clear that his unremitting emphasis on sexual innocence or abstinence will be reinforced. Boo Boo alone seems to be happily married, but we have seen her only in the role of a mother. As a wife, she may well share the inability of Salinger's other characters to find love and sex anything but antagonistic to her happiness.

Walt Glass is killed before his romance can consummate in marriage; his twin Waker is a Jesuit priest. Seymour's repeated concern for his bride's chastity precedes his temporary flight from the wedding ceremony. He later kills himself while on a second honeymoon. Buddy is maladjusted and unmarried at 38. Zooey, a bachelor in his late twenties, suffers from ulcers and has an abnormal fear of his own beauty. Franny evades the physical demands of her lover by a "tenth-rate nervous breakdown" and temporarily embraces the esoteric philosophy of a holy man.

It is not likely that a pattern so firmly rooted in Salinger's earliest work and so consistently developed, is likely to change—nor is this particularly desirable. Lesser talents have wallowed in the sexual without a fraction of the illumination of character Salinger is able to give us. But admittedly, it is difficult to see how the avoidance of so obvious a part of human life cannot impede the free flow of Salinger's creative life. /23/

XXX

J. D. Salinger's Closed Circuit

MARY MCCARTHY

Who is to inherit the mantle of Papa Hemingway? Who if not J. D. Salinger? Holden Caulfield in *The Catcher in the Rye* has a brother in Hollywood who thinks *A Farewell to Arms* is terrific. Holden does not see how his brother, who is *his* favorite writer, can like a phony book like that. But the very image of the hero as pitiless phony-detector comes from Hemingway. In *Across the River and Into the Trees,* the colonel gets a message on his private radar that a pock-marked writer he darkly spies across the room at Harry's Bar in Venice has "outlived his talents"—apparently some sort of crime. "I think he has the same pits on his heart and in his soul," confides the heroine, in her careful foreign English. That was Sinclair Lewis.

Like Hemingway, Salinger sees the world in terms of allies and enemies. He has a good deal of natural style, a cruel ear, a dislike of ideas (the enemy's intelligence system), a toilsome simplicity, and a ventriloquist's knack of disguising his voice. The artless dialect written by Holden is an artful ventriloquial trick of Salinger's, like the deliberate, halting English of Hemingway's waiters, fishermen, and peasants—anyone who speaks it is a good guy, a friend of the author's, to be trusted.

The Catcher in the Rye, like Hemingway's books, is based on a scheme of exclusiveness. The characters are divided into those who belong to the club and those who don't—the clean marlin, on the one hand, and the scavenger sharks on the other. Those who don't belong are "born that way"—headmasters, philanthropists, roommates, teachers of history and English, football

From *Harper's Magazine,* CCXXV, October 1962, pp. 46-48. Reprinted by permission of the author.

coaches, girls who like the Lunts. They cannot help the way they are, the way they talk; they are obeying a law of species—even the pimping elevator operator, the greedy prostitute, the bisexual teacher of English who makes an approach to Holden in the dark.

It is not anybody's fault if just about everybody is excluded from the club in the long run—everybody but Ring Lardner, Thomas Hardy, Gatsby, Isak Dinesen, and Holden's little sister Phoebe. In fact it is a pretty sad situation, and there is a real adolescent sadness and lonely desperation in *The Catcher in the Rye;* the passages where Holden, drunk and wild with grief, wanders like an errant pinball through New York at night are very good.

But did Salinger sympathize with Holden or vice versa? That remained dubious. Stephen Dedalus in a similar situation met Mr. Bloom, but the only "good" person Holden meets is his little sister—himself in miniature or in apotheosis, riding a big brown horse on a carrousel and reaching for the gold ring. There is something false and sentimental here. Holden is supposed to be an outsider in his school, in the middle-class world, but he is really an insider with the track all to himself.

And now, ten years after *The Catcher in the Rye* we have *Franny and Zooey.* The event was commemorated by a cover story in *Time;* the book has been a best-seller since *before* publication.

Again the theme is the good people against the stupid phonies, and the good is still all in the family, like a family-owned "closed" corporation. The heroes are or were seven children (two are dead), the wonderful Glass kids of a radio quiz show called "It's a Wise Child," half-Jewish, half-Irish, the progeny of a team of vaudevillians. These prodigies, nationally known and the subjects of many psychological studies, are now grown up: one is a writer-in-residence in a girls' junior college; one is a Jesuit priest; one is a /46/ housewife; one is a television actor (Zooey); and one is a student (Franny). They are all geniuses, but the greatest genius of them all was Seymour, who committed suicide on vacation in an early story of Salinger's called "A Perfect Day for Bananafish." Unlike the average genius, the Glass kids are good guys; they love each other and their parents and their cat and their goldfish, and they are expert phony-detectors. The dead sage Seymour has initiated them into Zen and other mystical cults.

During the course of the story, Franny has a little nervous breakdown, brought on by reading a small green religious book titled *The Way of a Pilgrim,* relating the quest for prayer of a simple Russian peasant. She is cured by her brother Zooey in two short séances between his professional television appointments; he recognizes the book (it was in Seymour's library, of course) and, on his own inspiration, without help from their older brother Buddy or from the Jesuit, teaches her that Jesus, whom she has been sweating to find via the Jesus Prayer, is not some fishy *guru* but just the Fat Lady in the audience, the average ordinary humanity with varicose veins, the you and me the performer has to reach if the show is going to click.

This democratic commercial is "sincere" in the style of an advertising man's necktie. The Jesus Zooey sells his sister is the old Bruce Barton Jesus—the word made flesh, Madison Avenue's motto. The Fat Lady is not quite everybody, despite Zooey's fast sales patter. She is the kind of everybody the wonderful Glass kids tolerantly approve of. Jesus may be a television sponsor or a housewife or a television playwright or your Mother and Dad, but He (he?) cannot be an intellectual like Franny's horrible boyfriend, Lane, who has written a paper on Flaubert and talks about Flaubert's "testicularity," or like his friend Wally, who, as Franny says plaintively, "looks like somebody who spent the summer in Italy or someplace."

These fakes and phonies are the outsiders who ruin everything. Zooey feels the same way. "I hate any kind of so-called creative type who gets on any kind of ship. I don't give a goddam what his reasons are." Zooey likes it here. He likes people, as he says, who wear horrible neckties and funny, padded suits, but he does not mind a man who dresses well and owns a two-cabin cruiser so long as he belongs to the real, native, video-viewing America. The wonderful Glass family have three radios, four portable phonographs, and a TV in their wonderful living-room, and their wonderful, awesome medicine cabinet in the bathroom is full of sponsored products all of which have been loved by someone in the family.

The world of insiders, it would appear, has grown infinitely larger and more accommodating as Salinger has "matured." Where Holden Caulfield's club excluded just about everybody but his kid sister, Zooey's and Franny's secret society includes just about everybody but creative types and students and professors. Here exception is made, obviously, for the Glass family: Seymour, the poet and thinker, Buddy, the writer, and so on. They all have college degrees; the family bookshelves indicate a wide, democratic culture:

> *Dracula* now stood next to *Elementary Pali, The Boy Allies at the Somme* stood next to *Bolts of Melody, The Scarab Murder Case* and *The Idiot* were together, *Nancy Drew and the Hidden Staircase* lay on top of *Fear and Trembling.*

The Glass family librarian does not discriminate, in keeping with the times, and books are encouraged to "mix." In Seymour's old bedroom, however, which is kept as a sort of temple to his memory, quotations, hand-lettered, from a select group of authors are displayed on the door: Marcus Aurelius, Issa, Tolstoy, Ring Lardner, Kafka, St. Francis de Sales, Mu Mon Kwan, etc. This honor roll is extremely institutional.

The broadening of the admissions policy—which is the text of Zooey's sermon—is more a propaganda aim, though, than an accomplishment. No doubt the author and his mouthpiece (who is smoking a panatela) would like to spread a message of charity. "Indiscrimination," as Seymour says in another Salinger story, ". . . leads to health and a kind of very real, enviable happiness." But this remark itself exhales an ineffable breath of gentle superiority. The club, for all its pep talks, remains a closed corporation, since the function of the Fat Lady, when you come down to it, is to be what?—an audience for the Glass kids, while the function of the Great /47/ Teachers is to act as their coaches and prompters. And who are these wonder kids but Salinger himself, splitting and multiplying like the original amoeba?

In Hemingway's work there was never anybody but Hemingway in a series of disguises, but at least there was only one Papa per book. To be confronted with the seven faces of Salinger, all wise and lovable and simple, is to gaze into a terrifying narcissus pool. Salinger's world contains nothing but Salinger, his teachers, and his tolerantly cherished audience—humanity; outside are the phonies, vainly signaling to be let in, like the kids' Irish mother, Bessie, a home version of the Fat Lady, who keeps invading the bathroom while her handsome son Zooey is in the tub or shaving.

The use of the bathroom as stage set—sixty-eight pages of "Zooey" are laid there—is all too revealing as a metaphor. The bathroom is the holy-of-holies of family life, the seat of privacy, the center of the cult of self-worship. What methodical attention Salinger pays to Zooey's routines of shaving and bathing and nail cleaning, as though these were rituals performed by a god on himself, priest and deity at the same time! The scene in the bathroom, with the mother seated on the toilet, smoking and talking, while her son behind the figured shower curtain reads, smokes, bathes, answers, is of a peculiar snickering indecency; it is worth noting, too, that this scene matches a shorter one in a public toilet in the story "Franny," a scene that by its strange suggestiveness misled many *New Yorker* readers into thinking that Franny was pregnant—that was why, they presumed, such significance was attached to her shutting herself up in a toilet in the ladies' room, hanging her head and feeling sick.

These readers were not "in" on the fact that Franny was having a mystical experience. Sex is unimportant for Salinger; not the bed but the bathroom is the erotic center of the narcissus ego, and Zooey behind the shower curtain is taboo, even to the mother who bore him—behind the veil. The reader, however, is allowed an extended look.

A great deal of attention is paid, too, to the rituals of cigarette lighting and to the rites of drinking from a glass, as though these oral acts were sacred—epiphanies. In the same way, the family writings are treated by Salinger as sacred scriptures or the droppings of holy birds, to be studied with care by the augurs: letters from Seymour, citations from his diary, a letter from Buddy, a

letter from Franny, a letter from Boo Boo, a note written by Boo
Boo in soap on a bathroom mirror (the last two are from another
story, "Raise High the Roof Beam, Carpenters").

These imprints of the Glass collective personality are preserved as though they were Veronica's veil in a relic case of well-
wrought prose. And the eerie thing is, speaking of Veronica's veil,
a popular subject for those paintings in which Christ's eyes are
supposed to follow the spectator with a doubtless reproachful
gaze, the reader has the sensation in this latest work of Salinger
that the author is sadly watching him or listening to him read.
That is, the ordinary relation is reversed, and instead of the
reader reading Salinger, Salinger, that Man of Sorrows, is reading the reader.

At the same time, this quasi-religious volume is full of a kind
of Broadway humor. The Glass family is like a Jewish family in
a radio serial. Everyone is a "character." Mr. Glass with his tan-
gerine is a character; Mrs. Glass in her hair-net and commodious
wrapper with her cups of chicken broth is a character. The
shower curtain, scarlet nylon with a design of canary-yellow
sharps, clefs, and flats, is a character; the teeming medicine cabinet is a character. Every phonograph, every chair is a character.
The family relationship, rough, genial, insulting, is a character.

In short, every single object possessed by the Glass communal
ego is bent on lovably expressing the Glass personality—eccentric,
homey, good-hearted. Not unlike "Abie's Irish Rose." And the
family is its own best audience. Like Hemingway stooges, they
have the disturbing faculty of laughing delightedly or smiling
discreetly at each other's jokes. Again a closed circuit: the Glass
family is the Fat Lady, who is Jesus. The Glass medicine cabinet
is Jesus, and Seymour is his prophet.

Yet below this self-loving barbershop harmony a chord of terror is struck from time to time, like a judgment. Seymour's suicide
suggests that Salinger guesses intermittently or fears intermittently that there may be something wrong somewhere. Why did
he kill himself? Because he had married a phony, whom he wor-
shiped for her "simplicity, her terrible honesty"? Or because he
was so happy and the Fat Lady's world was so wonderful?

Or because he had been lying, his author had been lying, and
it was all terrible, and he was a fake? /48/

Appendix A

FOUR EXPLICATIONS OF
"FOR ESMÉ—WITH LOVE AND SQUALOR"

1

The High Point of Salinger's Art:
"For Esmé—with Love and Squalor"

FREDERICK L. GWYNN AND JOSEPH L. BLOTNER

At the outset, it might be well to consider Salinger's major fictional victory—the victories being the only reason for considering any of the failures that punctuate his unique career. The high point of his art, the moment at which particular narrative and general truth are identified most successfully with one another, comes in his most famous story, "For Esmé—with Love and Squalor," when Sergeant X, stationed in Bavaria after V-E Day, reads a German inscription in a German book and caps it with a Russian quotation written in English. The four agents in this process are perfectly chosen, and three of them are presented simply and at top speed. The reader is told that the book is *Die Zeit ohne Beispiel* by /4/ Joseph Goebbels, that one inscription is by a 38-year-old unmarried woman, "a low official in the Nazi Party," and that the other inscription is from Dostoevsky. The fourth agent, Sergeant X, whose gesture of quotation sounds the

From *The Fiction of J. D. Salinger* by Frederick L. Gwynn and Joseph L. Blotner. Copyright © 1958 by University of Pittsburgh Press. Reprinted by permission.

depths of the human condition, thereby prepares himself and the reader for the salvation he receives from someone else's gesture later in the story.

What Goebbels represents should be obvious to anyone over thirty, but surely the range of this evil can not be fully registered on the generation that adores Salinger, and it may even have dimmed in the more timeworn mind. To make any kind of contact with Joseph Goebbels is to be overwhelmed by the very type of psychotic hatred for everything weaker or more human than itself. His diaries show him to be "the unflagging motive force behind the vicious anti-Semitism of the Nazi regime," as Hugh Gibson says, whose "aim was the extermination of all Jews"; an ex-Catholic, he planned to "deal with the churches after the war and reduce them to impotence." It was this man, the holder of a *bona fide* doctorate, who in 1933 personally selected and had burned thousands of printed pages in which man had communicated with man. Less known than the genocide and the book-burning is Goebbels's hatred for humanity itself. In 1925 he wrote in his diary: "I have learned to despise the human being from the bottom of my soul. He makes me sick in my stomach." A year later he concluded that "The human being is a *canaille*."

But as Louis Lochner says, "Nobody who has not lived under Nazism can grasp how absolute was Goebbels's control of the German mind." It is this irresistible influence that (we may guess) had stimulated the second agent in the Salinger situa-/5/tion first to her Nazi Party activities and later to the revulsion that she expressed by penning in the Goebbels book that X finds: " 'Dear God, life is hell.' " To X, "the words appeared to have the stature of an uncontestable, even classic indictment," and he impulsively writes a comment underneath, one of Father Zossima's exhortations in *The Brothers Karamazov:* " 'Fathers and teachers, I ponder 'What is hell?' I maintain that it is the suffering of being unable to love.' "

The woman's substitution of the Christian God for Hitler and Goebbels is paralleled by the Sergeant's reference to Russian Christianity, and her implicit recognition of *Die Zeit ohne Beispiel*—The Unprecedented Era—as unprecedented hell is paralleled by Zossima's and X's awareness of the non-love that brings about disintegration and war; together these form not only a "classic indictment" but a profound objective correlative for the love and "squalor" experienced by Sergeant X—and the reader— in the rest of the story. (It is the young girl Esmé who asks Sergeant X to write her an "extremely squalid and moving" story, adding the question, " 'Are you at all acquainted with squalor?' " The Sergeant's answer is typically ironic but correct: "I said not exactly but that I was getting better acquainted with it, in one form or another, all the time. . . .") We may now see exactly what is correlated.

The conflict of "Esmé" places the protagonist, Sergeant X, against four "squalid" forces in the four chronological sections of the story. (1) In 1950, the present, he is set off against his wife, "a breathtakingly levelheaded girl," and his mother-in-law. (2) Back in April 1944, he is set off against the dullness of pre-Invasion training and the in-/6/communicativeness of his sixty male mates, as well as against his wife and his mother-in-law, the women who write selfish civilian letters to this soldier about to be landed in France. (3) In the long year from D-Day in 1944 to V-E-Day in 1945 (referred to only briefly in the story), the protagonist is set off against war itself (which has resulted in his nervous breakdown) as well as against his jeep-mate, Corporal Clay. (4) In May 1945, Sergeant X's combat fatigue is set off against the insensitivity of the loutish Clay, as well as against the selfish civilian triviality of his brother (who writes asking for souvenirs) and Clay's girl Loretta (who sits at home callously and amateurishly derogating X's psyche).

To balance these "squalid" antagonists there are four demonstrations of "love." (1) In 1950, exactly six years after X met Esmé, and apparently without any communication between them during this period, he receives an invitation to her wedding that makes him want to fly to it, "expenses be hanged." (2) In 1944, he has met Esmé, a brave English orphan of thirteen, who, nervous like X ("her nails were bitten down to the quick," "her hand, as I'd suspected, was a nervous hand, damp at the palm"), is also precociously sensitive to artistic, intellectual, and emotional values. (3) Set opposite X's shattering experience in the war against Germany is the simple inscription in the book that communicates to him the shattering experience of a German in the war against the Allies. In answering the *cri de coeur* of an enemy whom he has actually just arrested as a criminal, Sergeant X equates himself with her simply as human beings against the total war they have suffered in—"a method of existence that is ridiculous to say the least," as Esmé naively but perceptively describes /7/ World War II. (4) Finally, in 1945, X receives the wrist watch which Esmé mailed to him the day after D-Day, almost a year before. It is a stunning gesture for a titled gentlewoman who is "Usually not terribly gregarious" thus to give her father's watch to a G.I., a foreigner casually and briefly met, a man who had countered almost every one of her statements with an ironic answer. The gift, which belonged to a British nobleman "s-l-a-i-n" in war (in her younger brother's hearing she spells out crucial words), helps restore the possibility of life ("f-a-c-u-l-t-i-e-s") for the American Staff Sergeant X. /8/

————————2————————

J. D. Salinger: Hello Hello Hello

JOHN HERMANN

Salinger's story, "For Esmé—with Love and Squalor," has been anthologized, selected as his best story,[1] and in general accorded the high point of his as yet beginning career. And the attention that has been given to Esmé is warranted, for it juxtaposes in one story two of Salinger's major theses, love and squalor, in one of

From *College English*, XXII (January 1961), 262-64. Reprinted by permission of the author and the National Council of Teachers of English.
[1] Frederick L. Gwynn and Joseph L. Blotner, *The Fiction of J. D. Salinger* (Pittsburgh, 1958), p. 4. /262/

his favorite subjects, children: Esmé, the distillation of squalor, of people who are, according to the choir director in the story, "silly-billy parrots" if they sing without knowing the meaning of the words; and Charles, Esmé's five year old brother, the epitome of love. Not all critics agree, but I should like to suggest, contrary to some recent interpretations, that it is Charles, rather than Esmé, who is the key to the story. It is his riddle of what one wall says to another: "Meetcha at the corner," which is the nexus between Sergeant X and the world, and it is Charles's final, spontaneous, and insistent Hello, Hello, Hello, Hello, Hello, affixed to the end of Esmé's letter, that brings Sergeant X's F-A-C-U-L-T-I-E-S back together.

The contrast between Charles and Esmé /262/ is the burden of the first half of the story. The second half, in which the *I* point-of-view is shifted to Sergeant X "so cunningly that even the cleverest reader will fail to recognize me," is "the squalid or moving part of the story," and shows a projection of Esmé's squalor (lack of compassion, of affection) in Corporal Clay, his girl friend, Loretta in the States, her psychology professor, Sergeant X's older brother—the same squalor, magnified further, which war itself shows in the punishment of a German girl who has been a minor Nazi official. It is the extension of this squalor, that war engenders, that has driven Sergeant X to the brink of disintegration, of faculties shattered. Esmé's letter, with Charles's P.S. at the end, brings the worlds of *I* and Sergeant X together at the conclusion of the story.

In the first half, the character of the narrator has been well established by the time he meets Esmé, Charles, and their governess, Miss Megley, in a tea-room in England during the war. From an introductory two paragraphs, we know that it is six years after the end of the war, that the narrator is married to "a breath-takingly levelheaded girl" in the States, that he has been invited to Esmé's wedding, that with the help of his mother-in-law they have decided he is not going, and that instead he is jotting down a few notes for Esmé's groom: "And if they give him an uneasy moment or two, all the better. Nobody's aiming to please here. More really, to edify, to instruct." The notes that

give not only Esmé's groom but everyone an uneasy moment or
two follow, based on experiences during the war.

The narrator has been undergoing commando training at a
small town in England in preparation for D-day. Finished with
the training, waiting for orders and the chance to liberate Europe,
he looks out the window of his quonset hut, "his trigger finger
itching imperceptibly, if at all." It is our first indication of what
he thinks training to kill other people is worth—nothing. We
know that he also synchronizes his over-the-top watch by the
clock in the latrine (what he thinks of their regulations), and
wears his overseas cap (Two fingers above the left eye, soldier)
jammed straight down over both ears. His gas mask long ago has
been chucked out the window of the ship coming overseas and its
case used as a convenient knapsack. The *esprit de corps* of his
outfit manifests itself in isolated heads bent over V-mail letters
home, in the thoughtless whack-whack of a ping-pong ball back
and forth across the net "an axe length away" from where he sits.
Except for the two introductory paragraphs, the tone has been
wry, jocular—a man making fun not only of the army but of himself.

Later, wandering the streets in the rain, he hears children singing in church and enters. They are practicing. One of the singers
is a young girl "whose eyes seemed to be counting the house."
Even in a church. It is the first intimation we have of Esmé's character, and it is given by the narrator half in admiration, half in
amazement.

After the practice, they meet by accident again at a nearby tea-
room, where Esmé comes with Charles and their governess. Before the narrator quite realizes how, Esmé is standing with "enviable poise" beside his table. Invited, she sits down, a "truth
lover or a statistics lover" of thirteen. He is the eleventh American
she has met. She sits beautifully straight on her chair so that he
too must come out of his army slouch. Her conversation with the
narrator is that of a census taker—"Are you deeply in love with
your wife?" "How were you employed before entering the army?"
—or has the tone of an almanac dispensing facts—"To be quite
candid Father really needed more of an intellectual companion
than Mother was" (her parents become case histories in psychol-

ogy); her wet hair, now straight, is when dry "not actually curly
but quite wavy" (she is meticulously exact even in a situation in
which a young girl might normally be tempted to alter truth a
trifle, claiming curls rather than waves).

She finally asks the narrator, even though she is somewhat disappointed that he is not a published writer, to write her a story
about squalor. "About what?" he says, incredulous, for he is confronted with a girl who believes everything can be learned by
statistics, by so many notes taken, by so /263/ many Americans
kept count of, by so many figures put together. "Silly-billy parrots" the choir director had said of those who mouth words without knowing their meanings. She is talking about Esmés.

In contrast is Charles, disdainful of appearances like wet hair,
of the facts that his sister cherishes ("He certainly has green eyes.
Haven't you, Charles?" the narrator asks him. "They're orange,"
Charles says); enjoying his game of riddles; arching his back
across the chair in contrast to Esmé's perfectly achieved poise;
covering up his face with his napkin; giving a Bronx cheer at one
point of the conversation between his sister and the narrator; en-
gulfed with laughter at his own jokes; and furiously disappointed
when the Sergeant tells him the answer to the riddle when asked
the second time. He is everything his sister is not (She takes his
wet cap from his head when they enter the tea-room "by lifting
it off his head with two fingers, as if it were a laboratory specimen"). The last image that we have of the two of them in this
part of the story is the picture that remains: Charles, blushing
but determined, comes back to kiss the Sergeant good-bye. Asked
the answer to the riddle, his face lights up. He shrieks: "Meet
you at the corner," (and he does at the end of the story, saying
at the corner of sanity and insanity to the Sergeant, Hello, Hello,
Hello) and races out of the room "possibly in hysterics." Esmé
leaves too, "slowly, reflectively, testing the ends of her hair for
dryness"; one risking embarrassment to show his friendship; the
other, worried about her own appearance.

The second, or squalid part of the story, extends Esmé's attitude to other people, etching the dilettantism into callousness,
into stupidity, into destruction. For what does it mean to know
squalor without love? It means a Corporal Clay who uses Sergeant

X to write letters home to impress his girl, Loretta. It means a Loretta who uses the war experiences of men overseas as case histories in her psychology class (Esmé's treatment of her father and mother's relationship). It means a psychology professor explaining what war is about to soldiers who have suffered in it and have made other people suffer.It means an older brother, stateside, who writes: "Now that the g.d. war is over, how about sending the kids a couple of bayonets or swastikas." It means Goebbels's book, *Die Zeit Ohne Beispiel,* and on the fly-leaf the words of the thirty-eight year old, unmarried German daughter of the household where Sergeant X is staying and whom he has had to arrest: "Dear God, life is hell." It means finally the last protest of Sergeant X, scribbled almost illegibly underneath: "Fathers and teachers, I ponder 'What is hell?' I maintain it is the suffering of being unable to love," which are the words of Father Zossima in *The Brothers Karamozov.* (Esmé: "My Aunt says that I'm a terribly cold person." "I am training myself to be more compassionate.") And Sergeant X's faculties under these pressures begin to disintegrate.

On his desk is a pile of packages, letters, books, that he has left unopened for days. He pushes them aside to use his typewriter to write a letter connecting him to someone, somewhere. But he cannot. He collapses on the typewriter. When he opens his eyes again, he sees a green package ("He certainly has green eyes, haven't you, Charles?" "They're orange," Charles says). Unconsciously Sergeant X moves to open the package.

It is a present and a note from Esmé—her father's watch (broken), and the notation that it was an extremely pleasant afternoon that they had spent "in each other's company on April 30, 1944, between 3:45 and 4:15 P.M. in case it slipped your mind."

But appended to the note is a message from Charles, of one wall saying to another, without thought, without knowledge, without statistics, but with compassion and affection: Hello Hello Hello Hello Hello. And Sergeant X's F-A-C-U-L-T-I-E-S disintegrating under squalor gradually come back together again. Much as we like Esmé's intelligence, poise, and breath-taking levelheadedness, it is her brother Charles, with the orange eyes and the arching back and the smacking kiss, who knows without counting the house, without 3:45 and 4:15 P.M.'s, the riddles of the heart. /264/

————————————3————————————

Rebuttal: In Defense of Esmé

ROBERT M. BROWNE

I'm for critical ingenuity and latitude of interpretation and all, but there is some stuff up with which I will not put. Like Mr. John Hermann's view of Salinger's Esmé (January 1961) as a symbol of squalor, of lack of compassion and affection. Mr. Hermann gets facts wrong, as when he says that Charles, "blushing but determined . . . risking embarrassment to show his friendship," comes back into the tearoom to kiss Sergeant X good-bye. In context it is obvious that Esmé has to "drag" and "push" Charles to get him to kiss the sergeant.

But more important, Mr. Hermann has committed two basic errors. One is to read the story in the light of a rather romantic preconception, the other is to neglect the role of the narrator. The romantic preconception is that love of truth, including statistics, makes one unable to love people. Since Esmé is a statistic-lover, she must be unable to love people; Charles, not a truth-lover, is the real people-lover in the story. (In passing, I wonder how Mr. Hermann gets around Charles's scientific curiosity about kissing in the movies.) But Esmé's love of truth is simply part of her admirable integrity. She is still child enough not to have lost wonder and curiosity; her intelligence has not been corrupted

From *College English*, XXII (May 1961), 584-85. Reprinted by permission of the author and the National Council of Teachers of English.

by wishful thinking (her cool appraisal of her mother, her refusal, which Mr. Hermann thinks abnormal, to pretend that her hair is curly when it's only wavy). True enough, her literalness is a trifle comic, but it is not morally disabling, as it might be in an adult.

In the tearoom Esmé approaches X in part because her aunt had told her she was "terribly cold," and she was "training herself to be more compassionate." Despite Mr. Hermann, this passage does not put her in Dostoevsky's hell of being unable to love; on the contrary, her willingness to try is enough to save her. Esmé's fidelity to truth and her acute though unseasoned intelligence do not prevent her from loving people; on the contrary they cause her to bestow her love fully on adults who, she perceives, have somehow escaped the general corruption: her father and X, whose "extremely sensitive face" attracted her in church. Though Mr. Hermann found her inattention in church objectionable, she wasn't simply counting the house, she was making an acute judgment of X, and ultimately the right response to him. For aren't we too meant to like him, and to think him worthy of love? If Esmé doesn't love him, why in the world does she write him and send him her dearest possession, the watch?

Of course her love of people, like her love of truth, has its comic side. The nervous concern about her hair, the question about X's love for his wife, the fear of seeming either too childish or too forward, these all indicate a schoolgirl's crush on a soldier. But it seems unfortunately necessary to insist on the obvious: Esmé is comic as well as admirable. Her slips when she tries to be grown-up in speech and manners, like her ignorance of Ohio and of physical squalor, are both funny and charming in X's eyes. He never tries to squelch her; he is amused, and he is also aware that her effort to act grown-up is a tribute of love to the adults she admires. Thus, after one of her polysyllabic speeches, "I said I imagined her father had had quite an extraordinary vocabulary." Throughout the story there is nothing in X's tone, explicit or implicit, which modifies the admiration for Esmé he so frequently exhibits: for her forehead, voice, smile, dress, posture, feet and ankles.

And how authoritative a narrator is X? By Mr. Hermann's own account of the preliminary section, he is wry and jocular. This sophisticated, ironic person is the most intelligent and mature observer in the story. Without discussing X's views, Mr. Hermann accepts the position of the aunt and of the choir coach with the dissonant voice, who sees Esmé and her choirmates as "silly-billy /584/ parrots." (The choir coach gets the treatment she deserves from the children, "a steady, opaque look.") When Esmé asks X if he, like her aunt, finds her terribly cold, the reply of this ordinarily reserved man is, "absolutely not—very much to the contrary, in fact." I will back him against the aunt, the choir coach, and Mr. Hermann. /585/

———————————4————————————

J. D. Salinger: The Identity of Sergeant X

TOM DAVIS

On the book jacket of *Franny and Zooey* J. D. Salinger writes:

. . . I'm doing [a narrative series] about a family of settlers in twentieth-century New York, the Glasses. . . . A couple of stories in the series besides "Franny" and "Zooey" have already been published in *The New Yorker,* and some new material is scheduled to appear there soon or Soon.

Apparently the stories he refers to are actually the three (not two) already published dealing with the history of Seymour, the oldest of the Glass children. Seymour is the suicide in "A Perfect

From *Western Humanities Review,* XVI (Spring 1962), 181-83. Reprinted by permission.

Day for Bananafish" (January 31, 1948); his wedding day is described, by Buddy Glass the narrator, in "Raise High the Roof
Beam, Carpenters" (November 19, 1955), and parts of his early
life in "Seymour, An Introduction" (June 6, 1959). These three
stories are apparently the only ones yet published dealing with
Seymour, except for minor references elsewhere, particularly in
Franny and Zooey. But there are persuasive reasons for thinking
that Salinger's most famous *New Yorker* story, "For Esmé—with
Love and Squalor" (April 8, 1950), is also a part of the Seymour
saga—and that Sergeant X is Seymour Glass.

There are certain thematic parallels between "For Esmé" and
the Seymour stories which help to establish the identity of Sergeant X as Seymour Glass. In "For Esmé" the breaking point for
Sergeant X came when his crude and insensitive companion,
Corporal Clay, killed a cat that had jumped on the hood of a
jeep during a shelling at Valognes. X doesn't want to talk about
the incident; Clay, oblivious to Sergeant X's feelings, rambles on
until X vomits into a waste-basket. Some critics have suggested
that this episode is technically weak, that Sergeant X's reaction
is too extreme. But if Sergeant X is Seymour Glass, then there are
parallels in other stories which place the reaction in a different
light.

In "Raise High the Roof Beam, Carpenters," for example,
Charlotte Mayhew, a fellow quiz kid panelist, visits the Glasses
at a lake cottage. One morning, while Charlotte is petting Boo
Boo's cat, Seymour throws a stone at her, cutting the corner of
her mouth. Though she never did understand the incident, explains Buddy Glass the narrator, Seymour "threw it at her because she looked so beautiful sitting there in the middle of the
driveway with Boo Boo's cat." And in the same story when Seymour's future mother-in-law asks him what he plans to do after
the war, he replies that he wants to be a "dead cat." Though
Mrs. Fedder is, understandably, confused by the answer, Seymour
later explains to Muriel that when a Zen Buddhist master "was
once asked what was the most valuable thing in the world . . . the
master answered that a dead cat was, because no one could put
a price on it." To Sergeant X then (as Seymour Glass) Clay's act

embodies the destruction of the Buddhist concept of sentient love, symbolized by the master's koan-like answer, and the childhood innocence of Charlotte Mayhew and Boo Boo's cat. /181/

Furthermore, the pattern of character development that Salinger employs in creating Seymour Glass, his second major protagonist, parallels the development he used in creating Holden Caulfield, the major figure of *The Catcher in the Rye*—a kind of biography in reverse. There are three stories dealing with Holden that precede the novel. In the first, an *Esquire* story called "This Sandwich Has No Mayonnaise" (October, 1945), nineteen-year-old Holden has been reported missing in action in the South Pacific. In the second story in the series, a *Collier's* piece, "I'm Crazy" (December 22, 1945), the substance of Holden's revolt is presented. And finally, in a *New Yorker* story, "Slight Rebellion Off Madison" (December 21, 1946), Salinger develops a single incident which later becomes Chapter XVII of *The Catcher.* The same pattern is repeated in the development of Seymour Glass's character: his death in "A Perfect Day," his conflict in a world without love in "For Esmé," and extended incidents in Seymour's life in two further stories. Apparently the pattern will end in the long-awaited next novel.

And finally, Salinger's characterization of Sergeant X and Seymour Glass reveals too many parallels to be accidental. Both have been in the army in Germany, both have been treated for mental disorders in army hospitals, both treat children as equals, and, significantly, both are married—a fact which several critics have ignored. In his essay in *Harper's*, "The Love Song of J. D. Salinger" (February, 1959), Arthur Mizener suggests that Salinger "has known all about the Glasses from the beginning." And further, that "what we are told about Seymour Glass in 1948 in the first story fits precisely, both in fact and in implication with what we have learned about . . . him since." Mizener feels that most of the stories since "A Perfect Day" are related to the Glass family chronicle, and though he does not explicitly identify the "writer" in "For Esmé" with Buddy Glass, the identification is implied. Another critic, Dan Wakefield, in a *New World Writing* essay called "Salinger and the Search for Love" (December,

1958), states that Buddy Glass is "the writer who appeared as 'Sergeant X.'" But if Sergeant X is a member of the Glass family, as there are many reasons for believing, then he could not be Buddy Glass. For there is an obvious fact which does not jibe with such an identification—Buddy is single. The only member of the Glass family who is married (except for Boo Boo) is Seymour. Sergeant X is Seymour Glass, and the "breathtakingly level-headed" wife and self-centered mother-in-law in "For Esmé" are Muriel Fedder Glass and her mother. Before D-Day in Normandy, for example, the mother-in-law writes to ask for some cashmere yarn; when Esmé asks Sergeant X if he loves his wife and then wonders if she is being too personal, he says he'll tell her when she becomes too personal—but he does not answer her first question. And his reply, in indirect discourse, ironically underlines the lack of love in Sergeant X's—and Seymour's—life.

If the identification of Sergeant X as Seymour Glass is correct, then one may note several things. Seymour's suicide, as seen in the light of Sergeant X's experience, is an exercise of will, and not an act of desperation. Zooey, for example, tells Franny that the first thing one must learn about the religious life is "detachment." But Seymour knows that detachment is simply another name for the "suffering of being unable to love," and that without involvement, the religious /182/ life is impossible. His marriage to Muriel was Seymour's attempt to escape the hell of detachment. Further, if the identification is correct, then Salinger's vision of Seymour is not based primarily on the Eastern concept of the oneness of things, but upon the basic dichotomies of Western fiction—right and wrong, good and evil, and, the conflict between "love and squalor." And without love, it is "a perfect day for bananafish." /183/

————————Appendix B————————

A CHECKLIST OF J. D. SALINGER'S WORK

"The Young Folks," *Story,* XVI (March-April 1940), 26-30.

"The Hang of It," *Collier's,* CVIII (July 12, 1941), 22.

"The Heart of a Broken Story," *Esquire,* XVI (Sept. 1941), 32+.

"The Long Debut of Lois Taggett," *Story,* XXI (Sept.-Oct. 1942), 28-34.

"Personal Notes on an Infantryman," *Collier's,* CX (Dec. 12, 1942), 96.

"The Varioni Brothers," *Saturday Evening Post,* CCXVI (July 17, 1943), 12-13+.

"Both Parties Concerned," *Saturday Evening Post,* CCXVI (Feb. 26, 1944), 14+.

"Soft-Boiled Sergeant," *Saturday Evening Post,* CCXVI (April 15, 1944), 18+.

"Last Day of the Last Furlough," *Saturday Evening Post,* CCXVII (July 15, 1944), 26-27+.

"Once a Week Won't Kill You," *Story,* XXV (Nov.-Dec. 1944), 23-27.

"A Boy in France," *Saturday Evening Post,* CCXVII (March 31, 1945), 21+.

"Elaine," *Story,* XXVI (March-April 1945), 38-47.

"This Sandwich Has No Mayonnaise," *Esquire,* XXIV (Oct. 1945), 54-56+.

"The Stranger," *Collier's,* CXVI (Dec. 1, 1945), 18+.

"I'm Crazy," *Collier's,* CXVI (Dec. 22, 1945), 36+.

"Slight Rebellion Off Madison," *New Yorker,* XXII (Dec. 21, 1946), 82-86.

"A Young Girl in 1941 with No Waist at All," *Mademoiselle,* XXV (May 1947), 222-223+.

"The Inverted Forest," *Cosmopolitan,* CXXIII (Dec. 1947), 73-109.

"A Perfect Day for Bananafish," *New Yorker,* XXIII (Jan. 31, 1948), 21-25.

"A Girl I Knew," *Good Housekeeping,* CXXVI (Feb. 1948), 36-37+.

"Uncle Wiggily in Connecticut," *New Yorker,* XXIV (March 20, 1948), 30-36.

"Just before the War with the Eskimos," *New Yorker,* XXIV (June 5, 1948), 37-40.

"Blue Melody," *Cosmopolitan,* CXXV (Sept. 1948), 50-51+.

"The Laughing Man," *New Yorker*, XXV (March 19, 1949), 27-32.

"Down at the Dinghy," *Harper's*, CXCVIII (April 1949), 87-91.

"For Esmé—with Love and Squalor," *New Yorker*, XXVI (April 8, 1950), 28-36.

The Catcher in the Rye. Boston: Little, Brown and Co., 1951.

"Pretty Mouth and Green My Eyes," *New Yorker*, XXVII (July 14, 1951), 20-24.

"Teddy," *New Yorker*, XXVIII (Jan. 31, 1953), 26-34.

Nine Stories. Boston: Little, Brown and Co., 1953. [Reprints "A Perfect Day for Bananafish," "Uncle Wiggily in Connecticut," "Just before the War with the Eskimos," "The Laughing Man," "Down at the Dinghy," "For Esmé—with Love and Squalor," "Pretty Mouth and Green My Eyes," and "Teddy." Also includes "De Daumier-Smith's Blue Period," not previously published.]

"Franny," *New Yorker*, XXX (Jan. 29, 1955), 24-43.

"Raise High the Roof Beam, Carpenters," *New Yorker*, XXXI (Nov. 19, 1955), 51-116.

"Zooey," *New Yorker*, XXXIII (May 4, 1957), 32-139.

"Seymour: An Introduction," *New Yorker*, XXXV (June 6, 1959), 42-119.

Franny and Zooey. Boston: Little, Brown and Co., 1961. [Reprints two stories of the Glass family, first published in the *New Yorker*.]

Raise High the Roof Beam, Carpenters, and Seymour: An Introduction. Boston: Little, Brown and Co., 1963. [Reprints two more stories of the Glass family from the *New Yorker*.]

Appendix C

SUGGESTED TOPICS FOR WRITING

A. Short papers

[Topics within this group can be handled almost entirely by reference to the articles in this book along with *The Catcher in the Rye* and *Nine Stories.*]

1. Some examples of symbolism in *The Catcher in the Rye.*
2. Salinger's audience.
3. Is Mr. Antolini a "phoney"?
4. Holden's family.
5. Holden's sister Phoebe: her function in the novel.
6. Holden's views on sex.
7. Holden as narrator.
8. The "phonies" at Pencey Prep.
9. The significance of the museum scene in *The Catcher in the Rye.*
10. The New York background in *The Catcher in the Rye.*
11. The significance of the movies for Holden.
12. Holden's knowledge of literature.
13. Is Holden Caulfield a typical adolescent?
14. Aldridge says, "Mr. Salinger's Holden Caulfield . . . is a compound of urban intelligence, juvenile contempt, and *New Yorker* sentimentalism." Which other critics agree with this judgment? Which disagree?
15. Kaplan and Branch: comparisons and contrasts.
16. Kegel and Bungert: comparisons and contrasts.
17. Myth criticism of *The Catcher in the Rye.*
18. "*The Catcher in the Rye* protests, to be sure, against both the academic and social conformity of its period. But what does it argue *for?*"—Maxwell Geismar. Give reasons for agreeing or disagreeing with Geismar's criticism.
19. Three hostile critics: Geismar, Aldridge, Kermode.
20. Wakefield, Hicks, and Wiegand: what they admire in Salinger.
21. "But Holden is not merely a rebel. . . . What is strongest in him is compassion."—Granville Hicks. How do other critics discuss Holden's rebelliousness?
22. Is "incommunicability" a proper term to apply to Holden?

23. What brings Holden to the sanitarium? Should he, in your view, be there?
24. We know that Holden is fleeing from mediocrity and conformity, but is he fleeing *toward* anything?
25. Is Salinger "sentimental" about children?
26. Harvey Breit has said that the "decisive failure" of *The Catcher in the Rye* is that "whatever is serious and implicit in the novel is overwhelmed by the more powerful comic element." Assess this critical judgment. What other critics agree with Breit?
27. Gwynn and Blotner assert that "For Esmé—with Love and Squalor" is "the high point of Salinger's art." How do other critics evaluate this story?
28. The structure of "Teddy" (or one of the other *Nine Stories*).

B. Long papers

[Some of the topics within this group may require additional investigation beyond the selections included in this book.]

1. Salinger's early stories, 1940-1951.
2. The critical reception of *Franny and Zooey*.
3. Steiner's "The Salinger Industry": a refutation.
4. Salinger and the censors.
5. Salinger and American society: the views of European critics.
6. Children and adults in Salinger's fiction.
7. Symbolism in Salinger's fiction.
8. Salinger's Sergeant X (see the article by Tom Davis, pp. 261-264, and also the replies by Tosta and Slabey in *Western Humanities Review*, Autumn 1962).
9. Salinger and Zen.
10. Salinger as a social critic.
11. Academic critics of J. D. Salinger.
12. Spiritual illness in Salinger characters.
13. The critical reception of *Raise High the Roofbeam, Carpenters and Seymour: An Introduction*.
14. Hostile critics: their objections to Salinger.
15. *The Catcher in the Rye* and Golding's *Lord of the Flies*: a comparative study.
16. Salinger and F. Scott Fitzgerald: a comparison of their reputations.
17. Salinger's influence on other writers today.
18. Is there a *New Yorker* school of fiction? A study of short stories by Salinger and other *New Yorker* writers.
19. A portrait of the Glass family.
20. Granville Hicks has said that Salinger is trying to create a "contemporary saint." Trace the development of the character of Seymour, in this respect, in the stories dealing with the Glass family.

21. Is the "Fat Lady" an adequate symbol for either Jesus or humanity?
22. A critic has said that in Salinger's work "anything is possible" for the child, but that for the adult the choice is only "conformity or death." Support or attack this view with reference to *The Catcher in the Rye*.
23. George Steiner says that "Salinger flatters the very ignorance and moral shallowness of his young readers." Defend or attack this view.
24. Several critics have charged that Salinger cherishes his fictional creations excessively. John Updike complains that Salinger "loves them more than God does." What do you perceive as Salinger's own attitude toward his characters?
25. Is there a development in Salinger's thought from the early stories to *Franny and Zooey?*
26. A common criticism of Salinger is that his heroes seem always to be right and everyone else wrong. Evaluate this charge with respect to Holden, Seymour, and Franny.
27. A comparative study of critical approaches: Heiserman and Miller, Strauch, and Mizener.
28. The meanings of "love" in Salinger's fiction.
29. Is the "Salinger vogue" declining?

Notes on the Critics

JOHN W. ALDRIDGE is author of a provocative study of post World War II novelists, *After the Lost Generation,* and of a study of later literary trends, *In Search of Heresy.* He is also editor of *Essays and Critiques in Modern Fiction.* Mr. Aldridge has been a professor of English at several colleges.

JOSEPH L. BLOTNER teaches American Literature at the University of Virginia.

EDGAR M. BRANCH is author of *The Literary Apprenticeship of Mark Twain* and compiler of *A Bibliography of James T. Farrell's Writings, 1921-1957.* He is Chairman of the Department of English at Miami University (Ohio).

ROBERT M. BROWNE teaches English at Notre Dame University.

HANS BUNGERT, a German scholar who specializes in American Literature, is currently (1963) at Harvard.

FREDERIC I. CARPENTER is Research Fellow in Engish, University of California (Berkeley). He is author of *American Literature and the Dream* and other studies.

KONSTANTIN CHUGUNOV is an editor of *Soviet Literature,* a journal published in several languages for international distribution. Primarily an official organ for publication of new work by Soviet writers, each issue of the journal also includes some reviews of literature originating outside the Soviet Union.

EDWARD P. J. CORBETT teaches English at Creighton University and is a frequent contributor of articles on literary topics to *America.*

DONALD P. COSTELLO was formerly on the faculty of Roosevelt University in Chicago and now teaches English at the University of Notre Dame.

TOM DAVIS, who teaches English at the University of Missouri, is compiler of a Salinger bibliography published in the journal of the Bibliographical Society of America.

JOAN DIDION is a feature editor of *Vogue* and also does occasional book reviews for *National Review,* a conservative journal of opinion.

LESLIE FIEDLER, Professor of English and Chairman of the English Department at Montana State University, is known for his iconoclastic criticism of literature. Among his books are *An End to Innocence, Love and Death in the American Novel, No in Thunder!* and a recent collection of short stories, *Nude Croquet.*

MAXWELL GEISMAR is editor, critic, and essayist. He is author of a multi-volume critical history of the American novel since 1890, including *Rebels and Ancestors, The Last of the Provincials, Writers in Crisis,* and *American Moderns: From Rebellion to Conformity.*

ROBERT GUTWILLIG is novelist, critic, and an editor at the McGraw-Hill Publishing Company. His articles on the contemporary literary scene appear frequently in the New York *Times.*

FREDERICK L. GWYNN, formerly editor of *College English,* is on the faculty at Trinity College, Connecticut. Mr. Gwynn is co-author with Joseph L. Blotner *(q.v.)* of *The Fiction of J. D. Salinger* (1958), the first extended critical study of the entire body of Salinger's work.

IHAB HASSAN teaches English at Wesleyan University. He is author of *Radical Innocence: Studies in the Contemporary American Novel* and of the forthcoming *Aspects du Héros Americain.* His reviews and critical articles appear frequently in major newspapers and magazines.

JOHN HERMANN is the author of numerous short stories. He is Associate Professor of English at Long Beach State College.

ARTHUR HEISERMAN has published short stories, critical articles, and a scholarly study entitled *Skelton and Satire.* He is a member of the English Department at the University of Chicago.

GRANVILLE HICKS is the author of many books including *The Great Tradition, Figures of Transition,* and *Small Town.* He writes a weekly page for *Saturday Review* under the heading "Literary Horizons."

CHARLES KAPLAN is Professor of English and Chairman, Division of Language and Literature, San Fernando Valley State College. He has published a number of critical articles on American fiction, is the author of several short stories, and is co-editor of a textbook for composition courses.

ALFRED KAZIN is author, editor, and critic. Among his books are *On Native Grounds, A Walker in the City, F. Scott Fitzerald: The Man and His Work,* and *Contemporaries.* His essays and critical reviews appear regularly in such magazines as *Atlantic Monthly, Partisan Review,* and *Commentary.* He also teaches at the New School in New York City.

CHARLES H. KEGEL heads the Division of Language, Literature, and Philosophy at Idaho State College. He is co-author of a freshman text for English composition.

FRANK KERMODE, a British critic, is a regular contributor of reviews, essays, and critical studies to both British and American periodicals. Among his books is *Puzzles and Epiphanies.*

ANNE MARPLE contributes occasional reviews to *New Republic.*

MARY McCARTHY, who now lives in Paris, has long been known as one of the most independent minded of American writers and critics. She is author of two widely read satirical novels, *The Groves of Academe* and *The Company She Keeps.* On the occasion of publication in Britain of *Franny and Zooey* in June 1962 her dissenting review appeared in *The Observer,* a distinguished

Sunday newspaper; later in that year the review was reprinted as a featured essay in *Harper's Magazine*.

JAMES E. MILLER, JR., formerly Professor of English at the University of Nebraska, is now at the University of Chicago. He is editor of *College English* and is author of *A Critical Guide to Leaves of Grass* and *The Fictional Techniques of F. Scott Fitzgerald*. He is also editor of *Myth and Method: Modern Theories of Fiction* and of *Walt Whitman: Complete Poetry and Selected Prose*.

ARTHUR MIZENER, Professor of English at Cornell University, has published many critical essays on contemporary American writers. His biography of F. Scott Fitzgerald, *The Far Side of Paradise*, was an important contribution to the recent reappraisal of Fitzgerald's life and work.

EVERETT T. MOORE contributes a regular column entitled "Intellectual Freedom" to the *ALA Bulletin*, the official journal of the American Library Association.

GEORGE STEINER, now a Fellow at Churchill College, Cambridge, was formerly at Princeton University. His books include *Tolstoy or Dostoevsky* and *The Death of Tragedy*. Reviews by Mr. Steiner appear frequently in *Saturday Review*, New York *Times Book Review*, and other publications.

CARL F. STRAUCH is Professor of English at Lehigh University and is the author of numerous studies of American writers.

HARVEY SWADOS is novelist, short story writer, and literary critic. He is author of *Out Went the Candle, Nights in the Gardens of Brooklyn, False Coin, A Radical's America*, and other books. He has taught courses in writing at several colleges.

JOHN UPDIKE (born 1932) is rapidly acquiring a reputation as a leading writer of the new generation. His several books of fiction include *Poorhouse Fair; Rabbit, Run; Pigeon Feathers and Other Stories;* and *The Centaur*. He is a frequent contributor of short stories, poems, and satirical sketches to the *New Yorker*.

DAN WAKEFIELD, a former reporter and news editor, is now a free lance writer. He is author of *Island in the City* and has published articles in *The Nation, Harper's,* and *Commentary*.

BRIAN WAY has been Staff Tutor in English, Department of Extra-Mural Studies, University College of Swansea, Wales. In 1962-63 he was a visiting lecturer in English at Elmira College, New York. Mr. Way is at work on a book dealing with the American novel since 1920, in which his essay on Salinger will appear.

WILLIAM WIEGAND is a faculty member in the Department of English at Harvard University. He has published two novels and several critical studies. Another of his studies of Salinger, "J. D. Salinger: Seventy-Eight Bananas," appeared in *Chicago Review*, Winter 1958.